Energy Law in Uganda

Energy Law in Uganda

Emmanuel B. Kasimbazi

This book was originally published as a monograph in the International Encyclopaedia of Laws/Energy Law.

Founding Editor: Roger Blanpain
General Editor: Frank Hendrickx
Volume Editors: Kurt Deketelaere & Bram Delvaux

Wolters Kluwer

Published by:
Kluwer Law International B.V.
PO Box 316
2400 AH Alphen aan den Rijn
The Netherlands
E-mail: lrs-sales@wolterskluwer.com
Website: www.wolterskluwer.com/en/solutions/kluwerlawinternational

Sold and distributed by:
Wolters Kluwer Legal & Regulatory U.S.
920 Links Avenue
Landisville, PA 17538
United States of America
E-mail: customer.service@wolterskluwer.com

ISBN 978-94-035-3466-4

e-Book: ISBN 978-94-035-3886-0
web-PDF: ISBN 978-94-035-3896-9

The Author

Professor Emmanuel B. Kasimbazi, a Ugandan, is a Professor of Law at the School of Law, Makerere University.

Emmanuel's areas of expertise include Environmental Law, International Environmental Law, Natural Resources Law and Criminal Law. He is also a policy, legal and institutional expert and has worked as a consultant on a number of projects on Environmental Law and Policy related projects in Uganda and other countries.

He is an advocate of the High Court of Uganda and the Managing Partner of Kasimbazi and Company Advocates. He has a PhD in Law from the University of KwaZulu-Natal, South Africa; a Master of Laws (LLM) from the University of Calgary, Canada; a Bachelor of Laws (LLB) from the University of Dar es Salaam and a Diploma in Legal Practice from the Law Development Centre. He is the Environmental Law Expert of the Agreement on the Conservation of African-Eurasian Migratory Water birds.

He has been a visiting scholar at various institutions across the globe; these include the University of Reading as a British Academy Scholar, United Kingdom (UK); the University of Maryland, United States (US) as a Fulbright Scholar; the University of Bergen, Norway as a visiting scholar; the University of Warwick, UK as a visiting lecturer and Centre for International Environmental Law, US as American Bar Association visiting fellow.

He is a member of different networks such as the International Union for Conservation of Nature (IUCN) Academy on Environmental Law and a member of the IUCN Commission on Environmental Law, the Allard Law Agenda 2063 Project UBC and a Fellow of the Uganda National Academy of Sciences, the African Academy of Sciences and the World Academy of Sciences. He has over fifty publications in different legal aspects relating to the environment, water, soils, mining, climate change, oil and gas, energy, wildlife, crimes, human rights, forests and health. He routinely presents his works at domestic and international conferences.

His unequivocal leadership qualities are demonstrated through his leadership at Makerere University, where he has served as Acting Dean, Deputy Dean, Head of Public and Comparative Law, and the Chair of the Environmental Law Centre and Coordinator of Intergovernmental Authority on Development. Currently, he is the Chair of the Biodiversity Law Specialist Group, World Commission on Environmental

The Author

Law, the Vice President of the Association for Environmental Law, a Lecturer in African Universities, and the President of the East African Association for Impact Assessment.

Table of Contents

List of Tables

List of Tables

List of Figures

List of Figures

List of Abbreviations

ADB	African Development Bank
BCF	Billion Cubic Feet
BECS	Bundibugyo Electricity Cooperative Society
BFP	Budget Framework Papers
BGR	German Federal Institute for Geosciences and Natural Resources
BOPD	barrels of oil per day
BoU	Bank of Uganda
BST	bulk supply tariff
CAO	Chief Administrative Officer
CDO	Community Development Officer
CEO	Chief Executive Officer
CIF	Cost, Insurance, and Freight
CNG	Compressed Natural Gas
CNOOC	China National Offshore Oil Corporation
CPR	Central Petroleum Registry
DC	District Council
DEAP	District Environment Action Plan
DEC	District Environment Committee
DEO	District Environment Officers
DLB	District Land Boards
DRC	Democratic Republic of the Congo
DWD	Department of Water Development
DWRM	Directorate of Water Resources Management
EACOP	East African Crude Oil Pipeline
EDT	Electricity Disputes Tribunal
EHS	Environment, Health & Safety
EIR	Environmental Impact Review
EIS	Environmental Impact Study
EITI	Extractives Industries Transparency Initiative

List of Abbreviations

EPCC	Engineering, Procurement, Construction, and Commissioning
ERA	Electricity Regulatory Authority
ESIA	Environmental and Social Impact Assessment
ESIP	Education Sector Investment Plan
FDP	Field Development Plan
FEED	AU: Query raised in the text.
FID	Final Investment Decision
GDP	Gross Domestic Product
GHG	greenhouse gas
GIIP	Gas Initially in Place
GIZ	German Agency for International Cooperation
GoU	Government of Uganda
GSMD	Geological Survey and Mines Department
HDI	Human Development Index
HSE	Health, Safety and Environment
HSIP	Health Sector Investment Plan
HVTG	High-Voltage Transmission Grid
IAEA	International Atomic Energy Agency
ICT	information and communications technology
IEEE	Institute of Electrical and Electronics Engineers
IGA	Inter-Governmental Agreement
INIR	Integrated Nuclear Infrastructure Review
ITCZ	Inter-Tropical Convergence Zone
IUCN	International Union for Conservation of Nature
KCC	Kampala City Council
KIL	Kilembe Investments Limited
KIS	Kalangala Infrastructure Services Limited
KPC	Kenya Pipeline Company
KRECS	Kyegegwa Rural Energy Cooperative Society
KSW	Kakira Sugar Works
LAA	Lease and Assignment Agreement
LC	Local Council
LGA	Local Government Act
LGBFP	Local Government Budget Framework Papers
LNG	Liquefied Natural Gas
LPG	Liquefied Petroleum Gas
MEMD	Ministry of Energy and Mineral Development
MoFPED	Ministry of Finance, Planning and Economic Development
MTEF	Medium-Term Expenditure Framework

NBES	National Biomass Energy Strategy
NDP	National Development Plan
NEA	National Environment Act
NEAP	National Environment Action Plan
NEMA	National Environment Management Authority
NEPIO	Nuclear Energy Programme Implementing Organisation
NFA	National Forestry Authority
NGOs	Non-Governmental Organizations
NPIS	National Petroleum Information System
NRM	National Resistance Movement
NSE	Nairobi Stock Exchange
NSSF	National Social Security Fund
PACMECS	Pader-Abim Community Multi-Purpose Electric Cooperative Society
PAP	Project Affected Persons
PAU	Petroleum Authority of Uganda
PEAP	Poverty Eradication Action Plan
PEDP	Petroleum (Exploration, Development and Production)
PEPD	Petroleum Exploration and Production Department
PEWG	Poverty Eradication Working Group
PFA	Project Framework Agreement
PFE	Permanent Forest Estate
PIP	Public Investment Programme
PLC	Parish Land Committees
PRR	Petroleum Reservoir Report
PSA	Production Sharing Agreement
PSRPS	Power Sector Restructuring and Privatization Strategy
PV	Photovoltaic
RAP	Resettlement Action Plan
RCTMS	Refining, Conversion, Transmission and Midstream Storage
RDC	Resident District Commissioner
RDP	Rehabilitation and Development Programme
RE	Rural Electrification
REA	Rural Electrification Agency
REB	Rural Electrification Board
REDD+	Reduced Emissions from Deforestation and Forest Degradation+
REP	Renewable Energy Policy
RETs	Renewable Energy Technologies

List of Abbreviations

RSIP	Road Sector Investment Plan
SAFE	Safety Analysis Function Evaluation
SAIL	Sugar and Allied Industries Limited
SCADA	Supervisory Control and Data Acquisition
SSA	Sub-Saharan Africa
STOIIP	Stock Tank Oil Initially in Place
TOE	Tons of Oil Equivalent
ToR	Terms of Reference
TPDC	Tanzania Petroleum Development Corporation
UEB	Uganda Electricity Board
UEDCL	Uganda Electricity Distribution Company Limited
UEGCL	Uganda Electricity Generation Company Limited
UETCL	Uganda Electricity Transmission Company Limited
UIA	Uganda Investment Authority
ULC	Uganda Land Commission
UN	United Nations
UNBS	Uganda National Bureau of Standards
UPE	Universal Primary Education
USE	Uganda Securities Exchange
USE	Universal Secondary Education
VAT	value added tax
VAR	Volt-Ampere Reactive
WENRECO	West Nile Rural Electrification Company
WHO	World Health Organization
WSIP	Water Sector Development Plan
WWF	World Wide Fund for Nature

General Introduction

§1. General Background

1. Uganda has abundant energy resources, especially hydrological and other renewable resources. However, there is widespread energy poverty throughout the country.[1] The country's energy sector still faces considerable challenges like acute power shortages, increased energy demand, and a lack of new power generation projects. Climate change has had an impact on hydropower generation.[2] Investment in other forms of renewable energy is hampered by the high upfront cost of installing technologies such as solar.[3]

2. Following the liberalization of Uganda's economy in 1987, the energy sector has played a key role.[4] On one side, the sector provides a major contribution to treasury resources. This is through fuel taxes, value added tax (VAT) on electricity, a levy on transmission of bulk purchases of electricity, licence fees and royalties.[5] On the other side, significant public investment has been made in the sector, particularly in the area of electricity supply. Uganda has achieved strong economic growth, averaging about 6% per annum. There has also been macroeconomic stability over the last decade. This stability is due to the implementation of an ambitious programme of macroeconomic adjustment and structural reforms.[6]

3. Energy development in Uganda and environmental damage are intricately related. The energy sector has bigger environmental impacts than most other economic sectors.[7] Hence, energy investments in Uganda are subject to greater environmental scrutiny.[8] The energy sector in Uganda is directly linked to the other

1. R. Tumwesigye, et al. (2011), Pro-Biodiversity Conservationists in Uganda (2011), Key Issues in Uganda's Energy Sector, International Institute for Environment and Development. https://pubs.iied.org/sites/default/files/pdfs/migrate/16030IIED.pdf (accessed 10 Jan. 2022).
2. V. Sridharan (and others) (2018), *Vulnerability of Uganda's Electricity Sector to Climate Change: An Integrated Systems Analysis* in Handbook of Climate Change Resilience. https://link.springer.com/10.1007/978-3-319-71025-9_45-1 (accessed 10 Jan. 2022).
3. Tumwesigye, *supra* n. 1.
4. *Ibid.*
5. *Ibid.*
6. *Ibid.*
7. World Wide Fund for Nature (WWF) – Uganda Country Office (2015), *Energy Report for Uganda: A 100% Renewable Energy Future by 2050.* https://d2ouvy59p0dg6k.cloudfront.net/downloads/energy_report_for_uganda_2015_1.pdf (accessed 11 Jan. 2022).
8. *Ibid.*

sectors of the economy and is a vital input for many. It is a major contributor to government revenues. Moreover, decisions taken in the sector have a direct bearing on the performance of the other sectors. There are institutional and legal weaknesses, especially in the areas of the downstream petroleum industry, renewable energy, energy conservation, efficiency and atomic energy applications.

4. Rising international oil prices also make thermal power generation very expensive. Additionally, fuel-supply constraints inhibit thermal power generation. Moreover, protracted procurement processes delay the implementation of energy projects. In 1997, the Ugandan government formulated a Strategic Plan to reform the energy industry. This was led by the Ministry of Energy and Mineral Development (MEMD). The main objectives of the plan were to:

- increase the sector's efficiency;
- meet the growing demands for electricity and increasing area coverage;
- improve the reliability and quality of electricity supply;
- attract private capital and entrepreneurs to improve the sector's commercial performance;
- take advantage of export opportunities.

5. The energy sector in Uganda is predominantly dependent on wood fuel, which accounts for up to 93% of the country's total energy needs.[9] The main other sources of energy are petroleum products (5%) and hydroelectricity (1.5%).[10] Wood fuel is the main source of heating and cooking in rural and urban areas. The high demand for fuel wood has resulted in the depletion of forests and exacerbates land degradation. Uganda has considerable renewable energy resources, including biomass supplies and hydropower potential (of over 2000 MW).[11] It also has solar and biomass residues from agricultural production. However, renewable resources are not fully exploited, and this further increases the high demand for wood fuel.

6. The transport sector is the major consumer of fossil fuels and accounts for about 75% of the fossil-fuel import bill.[12] Previous energy planning in Uganda has emphasized supply-side challenges such as increasing generation and attracting more private investors. Demand-side issues, such as subsidies to counteract the very high end-user power tariffs and meeting energy demand by increasing area coverage, have received less attention. This approach has tended to favour the urban population, which is the major user of commercial fuels, while marginalizing the energy needs of the majority of the population in rural areas, which mainly depends on biomass. The rural areas also contain the largest proportion of the poor

9. D. Bamwesigye (2020), *Charcoal and Wood Biomass Utilization in Uganda: The Socioeconomic and Environmental Dynamics and Implications.* https://www.mdpi.com/2071-1050/12/20/8337/pdf (accessed 11 Jan. 2022).
10. Tumwesigye, *supra* n. 1.
11. *Ibid.*
12. *Ibid.*

population. Despite the good national economic performance, about 21.4% of Uganda's population still lives below the poverty line.[13]

The government of Uganda's (GoU's) strategy on the energy sector has been to:

- promote legal, regulatory and structural sector reforms, including leveraging private sector investment;
- provide adequate, reliable and low-cost power generation. This is with the goal of meeting urban and industrial demand and increasing access;
- scale up rural access to underpin broad-based development.

I. Geography

7. Uganda is a landlocked country located in the Eastern region of Africa. It lies between latitudes 1°30' South and 4° North and longitude 29°30' East and 35° East.[14] It occupies an area of about 241,500 square kilometres, of which 15.3% is open water, 3.0% permanent wetlands, 9.4% seasonal wetlands, 6.5% game reserves and national parks and 6.3% forest reserves. Uganda borders the Republic of Kenya in the East, Tanzania and Rwanda in the South, the Democratic Republic of Congo (former Zaire) in the West, and South Sudan in the North.[15]

8. A number of natural resources in Uganda, like lakes, rivers, forests, and mountains, are transboundary. Therefore, their management requires close cooperation with the riparian and neighbouring states, respectively.

9. Uganda is characterized by flat-topped hills in the Central, Western and Eastern parts of the country. The country has spectacular mountainous topography along the borders, such as the Rwenzori Mountains and Mufumbira volcanoes in the West. It also has Mount Elgon, Mount Moroto, Mount Morungole and Mount Timu in the East. On a straight-line alignment, Mount Otce in Moyo District is the highest point between the Ugandan border and Kenya.[16]

10. Uganda is the home of both the second largest freshwater lake, Lake Victoria, and the River Nile, the longest river in the world. The waters of Lake Victoria drain through the Owen Falls dam, traversing Victoria Nile and Lake Kyoga into Lake Albert, the Albert Nile and White Nile in Sudan and down to the Mediterranean Sea through Egypt. Lakes cover almost one-fifth of the total area of the country. Lake Victoria, shared with Kenya and Tanzania, is the most dominant water

13. World Bank (2016), *Poverty Assessment for Uganda – Farms, Cities and Good Fortune: Assessing Poverty Reduction in Uganda from 2006 to 2013*. Washington, DC: The World Bank.
14. R. Wangalwa (2021), Occurrence of Citropsis articulata in Tropical Forests in Uganda: Implication for Ex Situ Conservation, International Journal of Forestry Research. https://www.hindawi.com/journals/ijfr/2021/5582461/ (accessed 11 Jan. 2022).
15. World Population Review, Where Is Uganda in the World? https://worldpopulationreview.com/country-locations/where-is-uganda (accessed 11 Jan. 2022).
16. Country Studies – Uganda, Mountains – Country Studies. http://countrystudies.us/uganda/17.htm (accessed 11 Jan. 2022).

body and has spectacular scenic contrasts. Associated with the Western Rift Valley are the crater lakes in the western part of the country.[17]

11. The geological formations of Uganda reveal rocks formed between 3,000 and 6,000 million years ago (pre-Cambrian era).[18] The younger rocks are either of sedimentary or of volcanic origin, formed from about 135 million years ago (Cretaceous period) to the present.[19] Thus, there is a gap in the geological history of Uganda of about 460 million years.[20] The soils of Uganda are defined by many parameters, which include parent rock, age of soil and climate.[21]

12. The most dominant soil type is ferralitic soil, which accounts for about two-thirds of the soils found in the country. Uganda's soils are divided into six categories according to productivity as follows:

(1) very high-to-high productivity;
(2) moderate productivity;
(3) fair productivity;
(4) low productivity;
(5) negligible productivity; and
(6) nil productivity.[22]

The high-productivity soils cover 8% of the area of Uganda.[23]

13. The Inter-Tropical Convergence Zone (ITCZ) and the southeast and northeast monsoons (air currents) influence the Ugandan climate. In most parts of the country, the seasons are fairly well marked as rainy and dry seasons. The mean temperatures over the country show great variation depending on elevation and landscape. For areas next to water bodies, such as Lake Victoria, maritime conditions tend to change the temperatures. The variation in monthly mean and annual evaporation rates is much smaller than corresponding variations in rainfall (10%–20% in the southern and 20%–40% in the northern parts of Uganda). Uganda has five climatic zones, with rainfall received in a given area as the dependent variable.

The zones are:

(a) zone I, the Lake Victoria Zone;

---

17. Country Studies – Uganda, Lakes and Rivers. http://countrystudies.us/uganda/18.htm (accessed 11 Jan. 2022).
18. National Environment Management Authority (2017), State of the Environment Report for Uganda 2006/2007. https://wedocs.unep.org/bitstream/handle/20.500.11822/9237/-State%20of%20the%20Environment%20Report%20-%20Uganda-2007soer_2007.pdf?sequence=3&isAllowed=y (accessed 11 Jan. 2022).
19. *Ibid.*
20. *Ibid.*
21. *Ibid.*
22. M. Kamanyire (2000), Natural Resource Management and Policy in Uganda: Overview Paper, Economic Policy Research Centre. https://assets.publishing.service.gov.uk/media/57a08d70e5274a27b200184f/3Kamanyire.pdf (accessed 11 Jan. 2022).
23. *Ibid.*

(b) zone II, the Karamoja region;
(c) zone III, Western Uganda;
(d) zone IV, the Acholi-Kyoga region; and
(e) zone V, Ankole-Southern Zone.

II. Population

14. At the turn of the 20th century, there were only about two million Ugandans, but the population now stands at over 42 million people.[24] Between July 1960 and September 2016, the population of Uganda rapidly grew over time from 6.8 million in 1960 to 41.5 million in 2016. The population is unevenly distributed among regions and districts of Uganda. The Central region had 27% of the population in 2002, followed by the Western region (26%) and Eastern region (25%).[25]

15. The Northern region is the least populated, with 22%. This distribution pattern of the population among the regions has remained the same since 1991. The Eastern region had the highest population density of 226 persons per square kilometre, while the Northern region had the lowest population density of sixty-five persons per square kilometre. The population densities for the Central and Western regions were 176 and 126 persons per square kilometre, respectively.[26] Population density by district varied between twenty-two persons per square kilometre for Moroto district and 7,259 persons per square kilometre for Kampala district.[27]

16. The majority of the population of Uganda lives in rural areas. The population living in urban areas was 635,000 in 1969, 938,000 in 1980, 1.9 million in 1991 and nearly 3 million in 2002. Thus, only 12% of the population in 2002 was living in urban areas. Kampala is the prime urban Centre. However, the proportion of the population of Kampala city to the total urban population declined from 54% in 1969 to 40% in 2002. This is because of the fixed geographical boundaries of Kampala city, as well as the growth of many urban centres, especially with the creation of new districts. More than half of the urban population lived in the central region (54%), while the other regions had almost equal proportions of the urban population (northern 17%, western 14% and eastern 13%). The high proportion of the urban population in the central region is attributed to Kampala City, which had 40% of the total urban population in 2002. If Kampala is excluded from the central region, the proportion of the urban population for this region drops to 15%, which compares well with the other regions.[28]

---

24. Uganda Bureau of Statistics (2020), Statistical Abstract. https://www.ubos.org/wp-content/uploads/publications/11_2020STATISTICAL__ABSTRACT_2020.pdf (accessed 11 Jan. 2022).
25. *Ibid.*
26. UNICEF (2020), 'Economic Policy Research Institute, Harnessing the Demographic Dividend in Uganda: An Assessment of the Impact of Multisectoral Approaches' https://www.unicef.org/uganda/media/5996/file/UNICEFUgandaDemDivReport_final-LORES.pdf (accessed 11 Jan. 2022).
27. *Ibid.*
28. *Ibid.*

17. The higher urban population in the northern region compared to the other regions is partly due to insecurity. This has resulted in the population moving to towns. For example, Gulu and Lira municipalities are shown to have been the second and third largest urban centres in Uganda, but this is mainly due to the influx of people to these urban centres. Uganda's population may influence the environment and, consequently, its development. This is seen through the characteristics of the country by structure, fertility and mortality rate.[29]

18. Women constitute 51% of the population and men 49%. Women are the most affected by the scarcity of natural resources and by environmental hazards. In addition, at least 52% of the population of Uganda is under 15 years of age. When this high population proportion of the young reaches reproductive age, the result will be a high population growth rate. This may also mean increased pressure on the country's natural resources and higher levels of environmental pollution. Conversely, a youthful population offers opportunities for the creation of increased environmental awareness. This could be through education within the Universal Primary Education (UPE) system, Universal Secondary Education (USE) and the higher institutions learning systems.[30]

§2. Legal and Political Structure

19. Uganda has undergone one of the most turbulent political changes since its independence in 1962.[31] The political terrain has switched from multiparty elections (1962–1971) to dictatorship (1971–1979) and back to multiparty democracy (1980–1985).[32] The main characteristics of these changes have been wars, civil strife and economic mismanagement. These violent, frequent changes of governments, together with political processes, undermined all attempts to create national management institutions, especially for the environment. Uganda was a fast-growing country until the early 1970s. Growth of gross domestic product (GDP) in the country averaged 5.1% between 1961 and 1970. During that period, productivity of the country's natural resources was high since degradation was still negligible.

20. During the reign of Idi Amin in 1971, the economy and infrastructure started to crumble. Environment degradation grew rapidly as a result of the political instability that ensued and the dictatorial, undemocratic systems of government that followed.

21. Human rights violations became the norm rather than the exception.[33] Civil society organizations that existed before 1971 were weakened or disappeared, and

29. *Ibid.*
30. Uganda Bureau of Statistics, *supra* n. 24.
31. J.F. Wapakhabulo (2001), *Uganda's Experience in Constitution Making*, Common LII. http://www.commonlii.org/ke/other/KECKRC/2001/33.html (accessed 12 Jan. 2022).
32. *Ibid.*
33. *Ibid.*

citizens could not participate in political, social and economic affairs. During this period, many Ugandans are said to have died for expressing views that differed from those of dictatorial rulers. Attention was not given to the natural resources and the environment of the country in general, and moreover, the government investment in this area was practically zero.

22. Between 1974 and 1986, Uganda's socioeconomic development was set back by civil wars, human rights violations, economic chaos and a drastic decline in GDP.[34] In 1986, the growth rate of GDP was only around 2%, less than the rate of population growth, and by 1995 inflation had reached 127%.[35] Between 1983 and 1986, the decline in industrial production reached 17%. There was also serious deterioration in the energy supply, water supply, and transport, health, education services, among others.

23. Soon after, the National Resistance Movement (NRM) took power in 1986. Then it launched various political and socioeconomic changes that resulted in various policies and programmes.[36] These changes included the rehabilitation and development programme (RDP).[37] It was later designated as the public investment programme (PIP). The unique political reform that the NRM carried out had far-reaching consequences in bringing about a democratic and participatory form of governance which freed Uganda.

24. The NRM instituted a broad-based political arrangement with a participatory system of local government. Unlike the conventional multiparty parliamentary system, where those opposing the government can form a party to participate in elections. Also, participation in politics is based on personal merit. Political candidates run for elections in their personal capacity and not as representatives of political parties. Participation in the process is not precluded as a result of the religious, social or political views held by a candidate.[38]

25. Uganda, which was under the movement or no party system, held a referendum in 2005, through which the people opted for multiparty democracy. The local government system of administration obtained in Uganda is based on decentralization. Local authority is based at the district level, but residual authority is further decentralized to lower structures known as LCs. This ensures people's participation and democratic control in decision-making.

---

34. F. Golooba-Mutebi, *Collapse, War and Reconstruction in Uganda: An Analytical Narrative on State-Making, Makerere Institute of Social Research, Makerere University* (Crisis States Research Centre, January 2008). https://www.lse.ac.uk/international-development/Assets/Documents/PDFs/csrc-working-papers-phase-two/wp27.2-collapse-war-and-reconstruction-in-uganda.pdf (accessed 12 Jan. 2022).
35. F. Byarugaba, 'Transition to Democracy in Africa; Government in Transition to Democracy in Uganda', paper at a Workshop on Transition to Democracy in East Africa (Novotel Mount Meru, Arusha, Tanzania, 2–6 Apr. 1997).
36. Ministry of Natural Resources (1995), The Draft National Environment Action Plan for Uganda, pg. xiii. https://pdf.usaid.gov/pdf_docs/PNABW415.pdf (accessed 12 Jan. 2022).
37. *Ibid.*
38. *Ibid.*

26. Decentralization in Uganda stems from Article 176(b) of the Constitution, where it is stated that decentralization should apply to all levels of local government. This is legally guided by the Local Government Act (LGA).[39] The Act's objectives are to give full effect to the decentralization of functions, powers, responsibilities and services at all levels of local governments. This ensures democratic participation in and control of decision-making by the people concerned. Furthermore, the Act is to establish a democratic, political and gender-sensitive administrative setup in local governments. Additionally, it establishes revenue sources and financial accountability and also provides for the election of LCs.

27. The long-term goal of decentralization is to allow district-level local managers to develop organizational structures. These are tailored to local circumstances so as to improve financial accountability and responsibility. This is done by establishing a clear link between the payment of taxes and provision of services. It is also to improve the capacity of LCs to plan, finance and manage the delivery of services to constituents.

28. The system of local government is based on the district as a unit rather than a part of a political movement. There are no intermediate levels between the national and local governments. Under the district are lower local governments and administrative units. Every local government council is a body corporate. In the case of urban councils, the city is equivalent to a district, while municipal councils and town councils are equivalent to the sub-county as lower local governments.

29. According to the LGA, councils and committees are constituted by elected representatives. The LCs' hierarchy is from LC 1 to LC 5, which is the highest local government in the district, with representatives at all levels through councillors. These are elected by universal adult suffrage on the basis of a ward system, representing sub-counties and parishes, respectively. Women, as well as youth and people with disability, representation is under the Act through separate elections in the respective Electoral Colleges.

30. The district, the highest tier, is governed by a District Council (DC), which is, in turn, presided over by a (full-time) Executive Committee. This committee consists of the district chairperson, elected as a political head by adult suffrage. A speaker and deputy, who are elected from among the members of the DC, as well as the vice chairperson and secretaries, are nominated by the chair and approved by the council. Councils at the sub-county level are constituted by the chairperson,

39. Described in its preamble as an Act to amend, consolidate and streamline the existing law on local governments in line with the Constitution, to give effect to the decentralization and devolution of functions, powers and services; and to provide for decentralization at all levels of local governments to ensure good governance and democratic participation in, and control of decision-making by the people; and to provide for revenue and the political administrative set-up of local governments; and to provide for election of local councils and any other matters connected to the above.

elected by universal suffrage, and councillors elected according to their constituencies. The administrative units, namely, the county, parish and village levels, are governed by committees and are mainly to assist in implementation of district programmes.

31. Translated and detailed by the LGA, the above powers mean that local governments are thus legally vested with planning and legislative functions. The DC, as the supreme organ in local government, has the power to enact district laws as long as they are not inconsistent with the Constitution or any other law made by the national legislature. The LGA permits local governments to budget and make development plans and allows local government to levy charges and collect fees and taxes, including rates, royalties, stamp duties, and registration and licensing fees.[40]

32. The various functions of local government are exercised through a number of structures. DCs are mandated to appoint standing committees (not exceeding five) for the efficient performance of their functions.[41] Standing committees are constituted by councillors, and the chairperson of each committee is elected by a simple majority from members of the council who are not members of the Executive Committee.

33. Standing Committees, also referred to as sectoral committees, are supposed to be key arenas for planning and monitoring where councillors deliberate on budget estimates and reports from relevant sectors. The decentralized NRM system has gone a long way towards ensuring the devolution of functions and powers from the centre to all levels of local government. The direct people's participation in political, economic and social affairs has improved the competence of officials who hold office. This is because people have the right to question government officials or elected politicians if the actions and measures they take are indifferent to what is going on within their communities. This has strengthened accountability.

§3. Economic Characteristics

34. Uganda is still undergoing a political metamorphosis, which is greatly affecting its economy. The economy is predominantly agricultural, with the majority depending entirely on land and a very underdeveloped agro-based industry. Although the country has a very rich potential for minerals, political instability and lack of capital have always militated against any meaningful development of mineral-based manufacturing industries. With the return of political stability since 1986, considerable success has been scored in rejuvenating the tourism industry, contributing more than 24% in foreign exchange earnings. In 1992, the fisheries

40. Section 80(1) of the Local Government Act, Chapter 243 of the Laws of Uganda.
41. Section 22(1) Local Government Act.

sector started to earn more than USD 100 million from exports.[42] The country has generally gone through a period of macro and microeconomic instability as a result of gross mismanagement coupled with political turmoil. This led to an unprecedented decline in all productive sectors of the economy, worsening terms of trade and a chronic balance of payment problem. The period between the 1970s and 1986 was characterized by rampant corruption, high inflation rates, speculation and the general impoverishment of socioeconomic and political infrastructure. A combination of political instability and economic mismanagement inhibited any possibility of investing in mineral and energy development.

35. Since 1987, Uganda's economy has registered steady trends of growth, stabilizing at an average of 5% annually. International Monetary Fund statistics of 2018 indicated that Uganda's economy has continued to register higher growth rates compared to other African countries. Uganda has substantial natural resources, including fertile soils, regular rainfall, and sizeable mineral deposits of copper and cobalt, oil and gas, among others. Agriculture is the most important sector of the economy, employing over 80% of the workforce. The economy grew by 6.1% in the financial year (FY) 2017–2018, with a strong services sector and a rebound in agriculture from the previous year's drought. Coffee is the major export crop and accounts for the bulk of export revenue.

Since 1986, the government, with the support of foreign countries and international agencies, has acted to rehabilitate and stabilize the economy. It has done so by undertaking currency reform, raising producer prices on export crops, increasing prices of petroleum products and improving civil service wages.

36. Uganda, as one of the least developed countries, belongs to the low Human Development Index (HDI) group of countries, the majority of whom are in Sub-Saharan Africa (SSA). The common feature in all these countries is the high level of poverty. Eradicating poverty is the greatest global challenge facing the world today. It is also an indispensable requirement for sustainable development.

37. One of the challenges Uganda faces is how to create a resilient, dynamic, integrated, diversified and competitive economy.[43] A dynamic economy provides the basis for availing resources to fulfil major national objectives like human development and poverty eradication, among others. Right from independence in 1962 to date, Uganda's economic growth has been characterized by a mixed picture. The 1960s up to 1972 witnessed a strong economy. From 1973 to the mid-1980s, the economy collapsed due to mismanagement and civil wars.[44] Since 1987, Uganda has implemented economic stabilization and structural adjustment programmes.

42. NBU, Uganda Country Study on Costs, Benefits and Unmet Needs of Biological Diversity Conservation (Kampala: National Biodiversity Unit, Department of Environment Protection, Ministry of Natural Resources, 1992).
43. MoFPED, The Poverty Eradication Action Plan (PEAP II) (Kampala, Uganda, 2001).
44. A. Bigsten & S. Kayizzi-Mugerwa, Is Uganda an Emerging Economy?, OECD Project 'Department of Economics, Göteborg University, May 1999. https://www.oecd.org/countries/uganda/2674943.pdf (accessed 11 Jan. 2022).

These have reversed Uganda's economic decline, facilitated the rehabilitation of productive and social infrastructure and reduced inflation and financial imbalances while also increasing national output.

38. The total GDP has been on a consistent increase from 1986 to 2000, despite having suffered from deteriorating terms of trade. Uganda's economy continued its recovery and grew by 6.1% in FY 2017–2018. These growth rates are quite significant by global and even developing country standards. The agricultural sector, defined as consisting of crops, livestock, forestry and fisheries, is the main contributor to GDP. However, the proportion of this contribution has been declining and stood at 42% in 2001, reflecting the modernization of the country's economy. Agriculture accounted for about 20% of GDP in FY 2017–2018 and 43% of export earnings. The Uganda Bureau of Statistics estimates that about 70% of Uganda's working population is employed in agriculture.[45] While the economic growth throughout the 1990s had been remarkable, the rate has been lower than the target of 7%. This was due to the vulnerability of the economy to external shocks. The slowdown had a negative impact on the well-being of Ugandans, particularly the poorer segments of society. These are affected immensely by internal and external shocks and also have minimal coping mechanisms.

39. Despite the above scenario, the well-being of Ugandans improved when measured in terms of incidence of consumption or headcount poverty. According to a 2016 poverty assessment, poverty in Uganda reduced significantly between 2006 and 2013. The number of Ugandans living below the poverty line declined from 31.1% in 2006 to 19.7% in 2013. In the districts where insurgency persists, people have been displaced from their villages and are crowding in camps, often living in appalling environmental conditions.[46] In 2001, about 50% of the combined population of the Gulu and Kitgum districts (and more than 76% of the Gulu district population alone) was internally displaced.[47] This meant reduced acreage under cultivation. This led to lower agricultural production and, so, low incomes.

40. It is significant to note that poverty reduction has occurred across all regions of the country. In the last ten years, Poverty reduced by 18% points in the central region; 19% points in the northern region; 22% points in the eastern region; and 24% points in the West. The northern region remains the poorest part of the country. This reflects adverse weather conditions, a high dependency ratio and growing population pressures that contribute to land fragmentation and soil degradation. However, the region has seen significant progress in other dimensions of welfare, including education, health, housing conditions and access to information.

45. Uganda Bureau of Statistics, *supra* n. 24.
46. MoFPED, *Uganda Poverty Status Report, 2001 – Milestones in the Quest for Poverty Eradication* (Kampala, Uganda, 2001).
47. *Ibid.*

41. For instance, Uganda has made some progress in fighting illiteracy, with current literacy levels at 76%.[48] Education is funded by both private and government means with free primary and secondary education. This is through the universal primary and secondary education system. Over 90% of the population attains a primary education.[49]

42. There was also the adoption of the National Development Plan I (NDP 1), which was initiated in 2010–2011 to eradicate poverty in Uganda. It replaced the Poverty Eradication Action plan (PEAP). The NDP 1 focused on primary growth sectors that provide direct products and services. These include agriculture, tourism, oil and gas, manufacturing, forestry, mining, and information and communications technology (ICT). Second, it focused on the complementary sector, which provides infrastructural support to the products. These include transport, energy and water, trade and financial services.[50] In June 2015, the GoU and United Nations Developmental Assistance launched the NDP II to guide Uganda's path to poverty eradication. The main goal of the NDP II is to propel Uganda to the middle-income status with a GDP per capita of USD 1,003.[51] The GoU also presented the NDP III in 2020, whose goal is 'Increased household incomes and improved quality of life'. This goal is to be achieved under the overall theme of 'Sustainable Industrialization for inclusive growth, employment and sustainable wealth creation'. The Plan has laid out eighteen programmes, including mineral and energy development, that comprehensively cover the development issues Uganda faces. By 2025, the effective implementation of these programmes is expected to lead to: an average economic growth rate of 7%, an increase in income per capita to USD 1,300, a lower poverty rate to 15.4%, reduced income inequality (Gini-coefficient) to 0.39; and further improve health and education outcomes of the population.[52]

§4. Aid and Economic Activities in Uganda

43. In simple terms, foreign aid is the flow of official resources from rich countries to developing nations. In theory, foreign aid is presumed to be assistance intended to redress or correct capital deficiencies or inadequacies (financial, physical, and human) existing in poor nations. The expectation is that it will play two critical roles. The first is that it can be a means of inducing policies, which lead to

48. United Nations Development Programme. 'The Uganda 2013 Millennium Development Goals Progress Report'(2013).
49. World Bank. 'Quality of Uganda's Education and Health Services Possess Serious Risk to Long Term Economic Progress' (November 2013). https://www.worldbank.org/en/news/press-release/2013/11/19/quality-uganda-education-and-health-services-poses-serious-risk-long-term-economic-progress.
50. International Monetary Fund, 'National Development Plan (2010/11-2014/15)' http://www.npa.go.ug/wp-content/uploads/2020/08/NDP2.pdf.
51. Republic of Uganda, Second National Development Plan 2015/16-2019/20) (NDPII).
52. The National Development Plan (NDPIII, 2020).

improved performance. That is, aid can be the mid-wife of well-planned programmes for promoting improved performance necessary for economic development.

44. Foreign aid (grants and concessional loans) has been an important factor in the economy of Uganda. More so during the 1990s, when the country needed resources to put in place recovery programmes and overcome the socioeconomic downturn of the 1980s. As is the case for several other Sub-Saharan economies, Uganda's economy is aid-dependent. For example, from 1990 to 1998, Uganda's aid accounted for over 60% (nearly reaching 80% in 1993) of the government's total expenditure.

45. The absolute level of external assistance is projected to remain high, rising from USD 560 million in 1996–1997 to USD 1,100 million in 2015–2016. By the end of the 1990s, aid funding accounted for 55% of total expenditure. This figure still represents a high level of aid dependency that is undesirable for the following reasons:

- aid decreases the level of control the government has over domestic expenditure allocation;
- aid dependency reduces the sense of policy ownership, which can result in weak implementation and poor policy performance;
- aid dependency creates biases in the decision-making process that can lead to heavily distorted allocation of resources;
- and aid can be an extremely unstable source of finance owing to the instability of its character.

46. Through generous aid inflows, Uganda, unfortunately, is now more indebted than ever before. Uganda's relatively large external debt increased from USD 2,590 million in 1991 to about USD 3,620 million in March 2002. The debt has increased by 22%, rising from UGX 33.99 trillion as of 30 June 2017 to UGX 41.51 trillion as of 30 June 2018.[53] Over the last ten years, the government has allocated over UGX 16.871 trillion to the energy sector. This was 16.57% of Uganda's GDP as of June 2018. Some of this money has been borrowed and invested in the construction of dams with the view that electrification will address poverty and other challenges in Uganda.

47. The obvious alternative to foreign debt is a higher level of domestic investment. Expressed as a percentage of GDP, Uganda's domestic investment was very low in 1980, much lower than the African average and the comparable rates for Kenya and Tanzania. Since then, though, Uganda has made remarkable progress, and the domestic investment was slightly below 20% in 2000, up from about 7% in

53. D. Nabiruma, 'Minister Kasaija's reassurance on Uganda's debt burden is erroneous' (29 Jan. 2019, African Centre for Media Excellence). http://ugandajournalistsresourcecentre.com/op-ed-minister-kasaijas-reassurance-ugandas-debt-burden-erroneous/ (accessed 12 Jan. 2022).

1980.[54] However, domestic investments as a percentage of GDP declined for Africa and in Kenya and Tanzania over the same 1980–2000 period. As a result, by 2000, Uganda's domestic investment rate surpassed those of Tanzania and Kenya and was just slightly less than the African average.

§5. Social and Cultural Characteristics

48. Ugandans are classified by ethnic groups as listed in the Constitution of the Republic of Uganda. They are basically of three main ethnic groups – Bantu, Nilotic and Nilo-Hamitic – that constitute most of the population. The Bantu are the majority and include the Baganda, who are about three million members (18% of the population), constitute the largest single ethnic group, the Basoga at about 9%.[55] The people of the Southwest comprise 30% of the population. They are five major ethnic groups in the Southwest: the Banyankole and Bahima, 10%; the Bakiga, 8%; the Banyarwanda, 6%; the Banyoro, 3% and the Batoro, 3%.[56]

49. Residents of the North, largely Nilotic, are the next largest group, including the Langi, 6% and the Acholi, 4%. In the Northwest are the Lugbara, 4%, and the Karimojong, 2%. These occupy the considerably drier, largely pastoral territory in the Northeast. Europeans, Asians, and Arabs make up about 1% of the population, with other groups accounting for the remainder. Uganda's population is predominantly rural, and its density is highest in the Southern regions. Until 1972, Asians constituted the largest non-indigenous ethnic group in Uganda. In that year, the Idi Amin regime expelled 50,000 Asians who had been engaged in trade, industry and various professions. In the years since Amin's overthrow in 1979, Asians have slowly returned. About 3,000 Arabs of various national origins and small numbers of Asians live in Uganda. Other non-indigenous people in Uganda include several hundred Western missionaries and a few diplomats, as well as business people.

50. When Arab traders moved inland from their enclaves along the Indian Ocean coast of East Africa and reached the interior of Uganda in the 1830s, they found several African kingdoms with well-developed political institutions dating back several centuries. These traders were followed in the 1860s by British explorers searching for the source of the Nile River. Protestant missionaries entered the country in 1877, followed by Catholic missionaries in 1879.

51. The 2014 National Housing and Population Census indicated that in the last ten years, Catholics and Anglicans declined, yet Muslims, Pentecostals, Seventh-Day Adventists and traditionalists increased in number. Catholics reduced from 41.6% in 2002 to 39.3% (over 13.5 million), and Anglicans reduced from 36.7% to 32.0% (over 11 million) of the then total population of 34.6 million. Muslims increased from 12.4% in 2002 to 13.7% in 2014, and the Pentecostals increased

54. ADB, *African Development Report 2001* (Abidjan, Cote d'Ivoire, 2001).
55. Uganda – Ethnic Groups, https://www.africa.upenn.edu/NEH/u-ethn.html (12 Jan. 2022).
56. *Ibid.*

from 4.7% to 11.1%. The Seventh-Day Adventists increased from 1.5% to 1.7%. The traditionalists reduced from 1.0% to 0.1%. Orthodox remained at 0.1% and Baptist at 0.3%. Others are at 1.4%.

§6. Energy Scenario in Uganda

52. The energy sector is one of the key sectors in the Ugandan economy. On the one hand, the sector provides a major contribution to treasury resources (e.g., fuel taxes, VAT on electricity, levy on transmission bulk purchases of electricity, licence fees and royalties) and foreign exchange earnings (power exports). On the other hand, significant public investment has been injected into the sector. After liberalization, the power subsector is now attracting the largest private sector investments in the country. Therefore, the sector is not only a vital input into other sectors but also promises to be a large source of employment for Ugandans.

53. The MEMD is responsible for the sector. It deals specifically with energy policy formulation, implementation and monitoring. The sector comprises the following supply subsectors: power, petroleum, new and renewable sources of energy and atomic energy. Uganda's per capita energy consumption of 0.3 tons of oil equivalent (TOE) or 12.72 GJ is among the lowest in the world. Few people have access to modern energy supplies such as electricity and petroleum products. The energy consumption stands at about 5 million TOE/year, of which 94% is biomass (wood, charcoal and agricultural residue). Wood fuel is the dominant energy source accounting for 80% of the total energy consumed in the country. Wood fuel is consumed either as charcoal (largely consumed in urban areas) or firewood (mostly used in rural areas).

54. Energy is the major component of the country's infrastructure and is very closely linked to development because it supports both economic activity and social development. In sectors such as agriculture and manufacturing, it is a major input in the production process. At the household or domestic level, energy contributes towards human welfare, health and environmental amenities. Energy also contributes significantly to financing public expenditures. In the case of Uganda, petroleum taxes provide about 25% of total fiscal revenues, while revenue from electricity taxes contributes around 1%. The energy sector also contributes to export earnings amounting to over USD 11 million (1997) or 2% of export earnings. Uganda also earned USD 25.64 million (UGX 96 billion) from electricity exports in the year ended August 2020, according to details from the Bank of Uganda (BoU). However, the earnings fell by 95% compared to what the country earned in the same period ending August 2019.

55. Uganda is richly endowed with abundant energy resources which are fairly distributed throughout the country. These include hydro, biomass, solar, geothermal, peat and fossil fuels. The energy resource potential of the country includes an estimated 2000 MW of hydropower, 450 MW of geothermal, 460 million tonnes of biomass standing stock with a sustainable annual yield of 50 million tons, an average of 5.1 kWh per square metre per day of solar energy, and about 250 million TOE of peat. In addition, Uganda has discovered an oil reserve of about 6.5 billion barrels. Of these, 1.4 billion barrels are estimated to be economically recoverable. The overall renewable energy power generation potential is estimated to be 5,300 MW.

56. As of 2010, the country had a total energy consumption of approximately 11 million TOE. This consumption was partially met by a number of energy resources, including solar power, biomass and fossil fuels. Biomass is the most important source of energy for 97% of the population. It provides for 90% of the total primary energy consumption in the form of firewood, charcoal or crop residues. This dependence on biomass is one of Africa's highest.

57. Electricity contributes only 1.1% to the national energy balance (121,000 TOE), while oil products (mainly used for vehicles and thermal power plants) account for 8.9%. The sector, however, draws on the country's scarce hard currency resources, especially in the importation of petroleum products and energy equipment and external debt servicing in relation to the power subsector, which also uses a large portion of the project aid the country receives. The oil import bill in 1994–1995 was about USD 65 million or 15% of the value of earnings from exports. The energy sector investment in the government's RDP 1993–1996 was USD 231.71 million or 14.6% of the total plan, of which USD 215.5 million or 93% was donor funded.

58. Despite Uganda's vast hydropower potential of over 2000 MW, less than 10% of this potential is exploited. Neglect of the energy sector, as of all areas of infrastructure, is a legacy of almost twenty years of political turmoil. Also, civil strife and economic decline, which curtailed commercial energy supplies, depressed efficiency in energy production and use. It also restricted the choice of energy sources, led to a high import bill for petroleum and an inadequate institutional framework for energy resource management. The net result has pressure on the natural resource base, mainly forests, leading to degradation.

59. Meeting the energy demand of a growing economy on a sustainable and efficient basis and improving the living standards of the people is a priority of the government. The main challenge in the energy sector, therefore, is how to develop Uganda's considerable hydroelectric potential (and possibly its petroleum resources), simultaneously increase the biomass resource base and use the present resources efficiently. This challenge has been taken up by the government as evidenced by strategies and policies that have been recently developed. The overall policy goal of the government for the energy sector, as stated in the 2002 policy, is to meet the energy needs of the Ugandan population for social and economic development in an environmentally sustainable manner.[57]

---

57. Energy Policy for Uganda, 2002.

60. A number of advances have been made in the recent past to ensure adequate and reliable supplies of energy to the economy. Efforts to introduce stopgap measures using thermal generation in order to reduce load-shedding are now underway.

Uganda currently has one of the lowest per capita electricity consumption in the world, with 215 kWh per capita per year (SSA's average: 552 kWh per capita, World average: 2,975 per capita).[58] Energy demand is determined by economic activities, geographical conditions and demographic characteristics. Therefore, as a measure of economic development, Uganda's indicator above serves to confirm the country's very low level of development. In terms of structure, Uganda's annual consumption of energy is principally biomass and primarily wood fuel. Biomass accounts for 94%, petroleum products 5% and electricity 1%. Thus, consumption of modern energy amounts to only 6% of the total. Figure 1 below shows Uganda's Energy Demand.

Figure 1 Energy Demand in Uganda

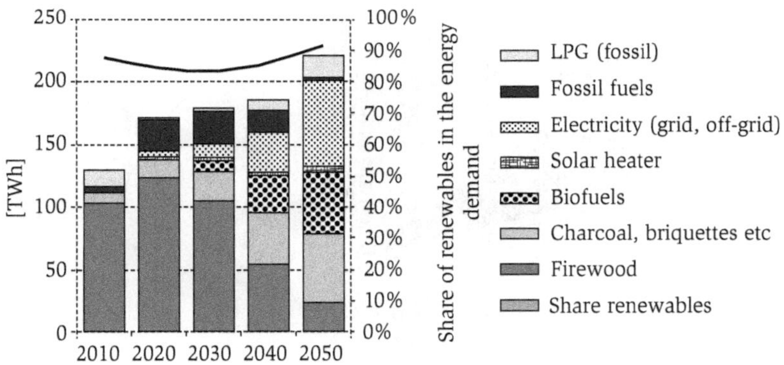

Energy demand in Uganda (bars) and the share of renewables in the energy system (line) -- renewable energy scenario

Source: World Wide Fund for Nature (WWF), October 2015- Uganda Country Office, Kampala*)*

Table 1 shows Uganda's energy consumption per sector. The biggest use is household, followed by commercial, industrial and transport. Figure 2 shows that the primary energy source in Uganda is fuel wood at 79.1%, petroleum products at 9.1%, charcoal at 5.8%, biomass residues at 4.7% and is lowest at 1.3%.

58. PWC. http://www.pwc.com/en_UG/ug/assets/pdf/uganda-budget-2013.pdf.

Table 1 Energy Consumption by Sector (Percentage)

Demand	*Portion of Overall Energy Supply (%)*	*Portion of Electricity Supply (%)*
Household	66.2	25.7
Commercial	14.3	14.9
Industrial	12.8	59.4
Transport	6.2	0.0

Source: MEMD, 2014.

Figure 2 Primary Energy Source in Uganda

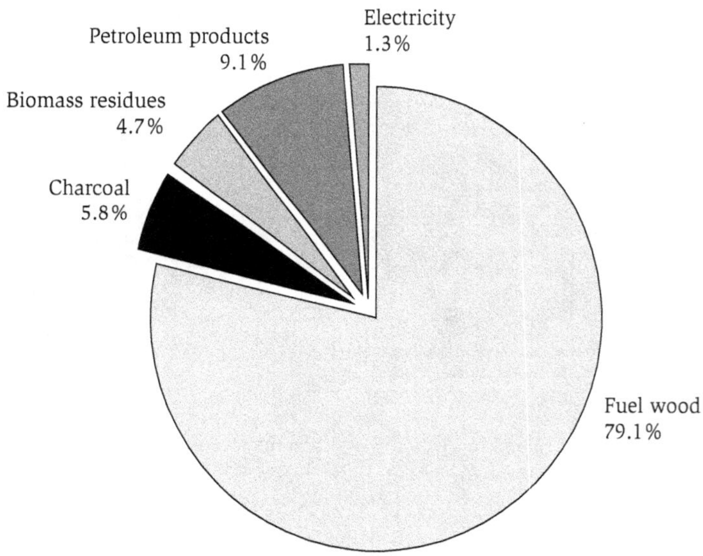

Source: Business Scouts for Development, (2021) "Sector brief: Renewable Energy" < https://www.giz.de/en/downloads/giz2022-en-sectorbrief-uganda-renewable-energy.pdf>

Part I. Energy Demand and Supply in Uganda

61. The Ministry of Energy and Minerals handles energy management in the country. It covers all energy subsectors: hydro, biomass, petroleum and renewable. It has the mandate of setting broad sector policies and strategies. The distribution of petroleum is in the hands of several companies, which are mostly sister companies to international conglomerates. Below is a synopsis of the state of the principal energy subsectors.

§1. Electricity

62. The electricity supply system in Uganda was first developed during the 1950s and 1960s. This development came with the construction of the Owen Falls Hydropower Station. It was later renamed Nalubaale Power Station.[59] The station has ten generators with a total installed capacity of 150 MW. It was later refurbished and upgraded to 180 MW, and a new one, Kiira, with a capacity of 200 MW.[60] With the liberalization of the economy and the disbanding of the electricity utility company (Uganda Electricity Board (UEB)), both Nalubaale and Kiira hydropower stations are leased to Eskom (U) Limited under a twenty-year concession agreement. The two hydropower stations form the backbone of the electricity supply network in the country.

63. Foreign investment in the Electricity sector has increased. This has coincided with the government's priority of increasing Uganda's energy production. The government recently commissioned the 183 MW Isimba Hydro Power Dam, while the 600 MW Karuma Hydro Power Dam is slated to be commissioned by 15 June 2022. The addition of these dams is projected to provide Uganda with about 380 MW of excess power generation capacity.

64. Despite these projects, Uganda has one of the lowest electrification rates in Africa. In urban areas, 55% of Ugandans have access to electricity. But, access drops to 10% in rural areas and is only 19% nationwide. Uganda has approximately

59. https://www.uegcl.com/power-plants/nalubaale-power-station/ (accessed on 7 Feb. 2022).
60. A. Fashina, M. Mundu, O. Akiyode, L. Abdullah, D. Sanni, & L. Ounyesiga. The Drivers and Barriers of Renewable Energy Applications and Development in Uganda: A Review. *Clean Technol.* 2019, *1*, 9–39. https://doi.org/10.3390/cleantechnol1010003 (accessed 7 Feb. 2022).

2,260 km of transmission lines, which the government aims to double.[61] Some existing generation capacity cannot be distributed. This is because investment in transmission is still insufficient. More investment is also needed to enable the export of electricity to the region. Uganda's Electricity Regulatory Authority (ERA) regulates licensing, generation, transmission and distribution. Uganda's power tariffs are set on a quarterly basis, and the average tariff to consumers is USD 0.17/kWh. It is USD 0.11/kWh for industrial users, with the first fifteen units of power subsidized. Umeme Company Limited is the largest energy distributor in Uganda, with 97% of all electricity in the country.[62] The main categories of users are:

(1) residential (55%),
(2) commercial/general (25%),
(3) industrial (20%)
(4) and street lighting (1%).

65. Average per capita consumption rate is 44 kWh per year. In the Kampala-Entebbe area, the average consumption rate is 170 kWh per inhabitant, while in the outlying areas is 10 kWh per year. About 72% of electricity is consumed by 12% of the population living in the Kampala–Jinja–Entebbe area.

66. However, generally, electricity demand has grown at an average of 10% per annum. This has resulted from significant GDP growth of over 6% during the past two decades. The increased demand for electricity has, in the past years, led to heavy load-shedding since the supply has not increased proportionally. Table 2 presents the energy and electricity demand for the main consuming sectors.

Table 2 The Energy and Electricity Demand of the Main Consuming Sectors

Sector	*Energy Demand (%)*	*Electricity Demand (%)*
Residential	67.09	24.24
Commercial	13.35	11.16
Industrial	11.86	64.60
Transport	7.25	–
Agriculture	0.45	–
Total	100	100

Source: Ministry of Energy and Minerals Development, Annual Report 2012.

61. Uganda Country Commercial Guide. https://www.export.gov/apex/article2?id=Uganda-Energy (accessed 7 Feb. 2022).
62. https://www.export.gov/apex/article2?id=Uganda-Energy>https://www.usaid.gov/powerafrica/uganda (accessed 7 Feb. 2022).

67. Uganda imports energy to the tune of 1,075,356 TOE and exports up to 6,589 TOE (Ministry of Energy and Minerals Development, Energy Balance of Uganda 2010). There used to be daily electricity shortages of up to 130-190 MW. Nonetheless, these have recently decreased as a result of the commissioning of the Bujagali and Isimba power stations. As of April 2019, the national generation capacity was 1,177 megawatts of electricity. To achieve the targets of this Vision, Uganda will develop and generate modern energy to drive the industry and services sectors. It is estimated that Uganda will require 41,738 MW by 2040, thus increasing its electricity per capita consumption to 3,668 kWh.[63] Other sources of energy in Uganda are thermal power plants and cogeneration. These are mainly accountable for the increase in total grid electricity energy supply from 1,609 GWh in 2006 to 2,456 GWh in 2010.[64] Table 3 shows the electricity generation by company.

63. Ministry of Energy and Mineral Development, 'Energy and Mineral Development Sector: Sector Development Plan 2015/16–2019/20' http://npa.go.ug/wp-content/uploads/2018/01/Energy-Sector-Development-plan-Final.pdf (accessed 27 Dec. 2022).
64. Ministry of Energy and Mineral Development, 'Energy Balance of Uganda 2010' (MEMD, 2010) https://energyandminerals.go.ug/ (accessed 2 Jan. 2023).

Table 3 Electricity Generation by Company in Gigawatt Hours

Category	*2009*	*2010*	*2011*	*2012*	*2013*	*2014*	*2015*	*2016*	*2017*
Hydro Generators									
Bujagali Electricity Company	–	–	–	–	1,673.90	1,661.30	1,462.00	1,560.80	1,667.10
Eskom (U) Limited	1,268.70	1,266.60	1,361.80	1,293.10	1,263.40	1,229.90	1,303.40	1,397.80	1,505.90
Ems-Mpanga	–	–	67.3	78.8	101.2	81.8	76.7	71.8	54.2
Kasese Cobalt Company Limited	59.8	49.8	56.2	58.5	59.6	59.4	64.1	58.8	61.5
Muvumbe Hydro(U) Limited									15.4
Ecopower-Ishasha	–	–	22.6	28.9	29.1	22.8	24.2	23.3	16.4
Tronder Power Limited	15.8	63.8	80.9	77.6	67.8	92.5	77.2	60.2	4.3
Tibet Hima (U) Limited	33.2	29.1	28.6	27.5	19.2	27.6	30	31.6	22.8
Hydromax	–	–	–	–	74.4	68.4	33.1	55.1	15.8
Thermal Generators									
Electro-Maxx (U) Limited	–	82.6	73.1	73.9	0.5	56.3	63.2	61.5	128.4
Jacobsen (U) Limited	276.7	380.2	399.2	153.5	1.6	37	25.5	4.7	47.4
Bagasse Generator									
Kakira Sugar Works	81.9	80.3	58.1	85.3	116.4	127.6	162.3	148.8	49.7

Category	*2009*	*2010*	*2011*	*2012*	*2013*	*2014*	*2015*	*2016*	*2017*
TOTAL	1,736.10	1,952.30	2,147.0	1,877.0	3,407.30	3,464.50	3,321.70	3,474.40	3,588.80
Annual change (%)		12	10%	-13%	82%	2%	-4%	5%	3%

Source: ERA, Date of last update: 2018-09-24.

The consumption pattern in Uganda is divided into residential, commercial and industrial, and street lighting. The detailed consumption structure is shown in Table 4.

Table 4 Number of Customers by Category in 2011–2017

Year	*2011*	*2012*	*2013*	*2014*	*2015*	*2016*	*2017*
Domestic	429,831	456,248	540,694	640,025	797,205	910,522	1,058013
Commercial	38,364	42,874	52,940	61,518	72,266	85,406	95,704
Industrial	2,020	2,263	2,528	2,746	3,054	3,146	3,245
Street Lights	327	369	359	348	311	306	303
Total	470,542	501,754	596,521	704,637	872,836	999,380	1,157,265
Annual Change (%)		6.60	18.90	18.10%	23.90%	14.50%	15.80%

Source: Ministry of Energy and Minerals Development, Date of last update: 2018-05-25.

Uganda is well endowed with hydrological resources for power generation, and most of this is concentrated in the White Nile. Table 5 shows key power stations in the country sites.

Table 5 Key Power Stations

S/n	*Plant/Source*	*Capacity (MW)*
1.	Kiira (Large Hydro Power Station)	200
2.	Nalubaale (Large Hydro Power Station)	180
3.	Bujagali (Large Hydro Power Station)	250
4.	Jacobsen Namanve (Thermal Power Plant)	50
5.	Electro-Maxx-Tororo (Thermal Power Plant)	50
6.	Kakira Sugar Works Ltd (Cogeneration)	22
7.	Kinyara sugar Works (Cogeneration)	7.5
8.	Kilembe Mines Ltd (Small Hydro)	5
9.	Tronder Power Bugoye (Small Hydro)	13
10.	Eco Power Ishasha (Small Hydro)	6.5
11.	Africa EMS Mpanga (Small Hydro)	18
12.	HydromaxBuseruka	9
13.	Kasese Cobalt Company Ltd	10.5

Source: MEMD Strategic Investment Plan 2014/2015–2018/2019.

68. In addition, Uganda underwent a comprehensive power sector reform programme in 1999. As a result, the UEB was disbanded in 2001 into three separate legal entities: (1) a generation company, the Uganda Electricity Generation Company Ltd (UEGCL), (2) a transmission company, the Uganda Electricity Transmission Company Ltd (UETCL), and (3) a distribution company, the Uganda Electricity Distribution Company Ltd (UEDCL). Furthermore, the ERA was established in 2000, while the Rural Electrification Agency (REA) was established in 2003. As a result, these entities were privatized. Eskom Uganda was awarded a twenty-year concession for the management of UETCL's assets. Umeme was awarded a twenty-year concession for the distribution Company UEDCL. UETCL remained under the management of the state. It operates the high-voltage transmission network and serves as the bulk supplier to the distribution company.[65]

69. Private companies like Kilembe Mines Ltd, Tronder Power and Kasese Cobalt Company Ltd have their own smaller hydropower plants. These are Mubuku I (5.4 MW), Mubuku II (14 MW) and Mubuku III (10.5 MW). These stations were initially built to supply their own industrial activity. However, due to the interruption in the copper and cobalt production activities, the companies entered into a contract with the Uganda Electricity Transmission Company in 2003 to sell power to the grid. Furthermore, there are other power stations like Eco Power (6.4 MW) and Africa Energy Management Systems, Mpanga (18 MW). Three other small hydropower stations include Kuluva (120 kW), Kagando (60 kW) and Kisiizi (300 kW). These supply electricity to isolated hospital grids. The German Agency for International Cooperation (GIZ) is in the process of developing small hydropower schemes in Bwindi (64 kW) and Suam (40 kW).[66]

70. Uganda still faces an acute electricity supply shortage. In 2009 only 140 MW (380 MW were installed at the time) could be used as a result of the low water levels of Lake Victoria. The other cause of the persistent electricity supply problems is the gap between the growing demand for electricity and the new generation capacity. To alleviate this problem, the government procured emergency thermal generators resulting in increased electricity tariffs. A new hydro facility has been developed at Bujagali and has been operational since February 2012. This installation generates approximately 250 MW. Before Bujagali became operational, 150 MW thermal capacities had been added in order to bridge the gap until the beginning of 2012.

71. As of May 2019, the total installed capacity of Uganda's energy was 1182.2 MW, having increased from 984.0 MW as of the end of December 2018. This growth was due to the commissioning of Isimba Hydro Power Plant (183 MW), Emerging Power U Ltd (Mayuge Solar PV) – 10.0 MW and the Sindila (Butama) HP – 5.25 MW during the period January to March 2019. About 7.5 MW of the

65. https://www.era.go.ug/index.php/sector-overview/uganda-electricity-sector (accessed 7 Feb. 2022).
66. Uganda Energy Situation, https://energypedia.info/wiki/Uganda_Energy_Situation (accessed 7 Feb. 2022).

installed capacity was accounted for by Off Grids that generated and sold their own electricity.[67] Figure 3 shows the installed capacity of Uganda's power generation.

Figure 3 Installed Capacity of Uganda's Power Generation

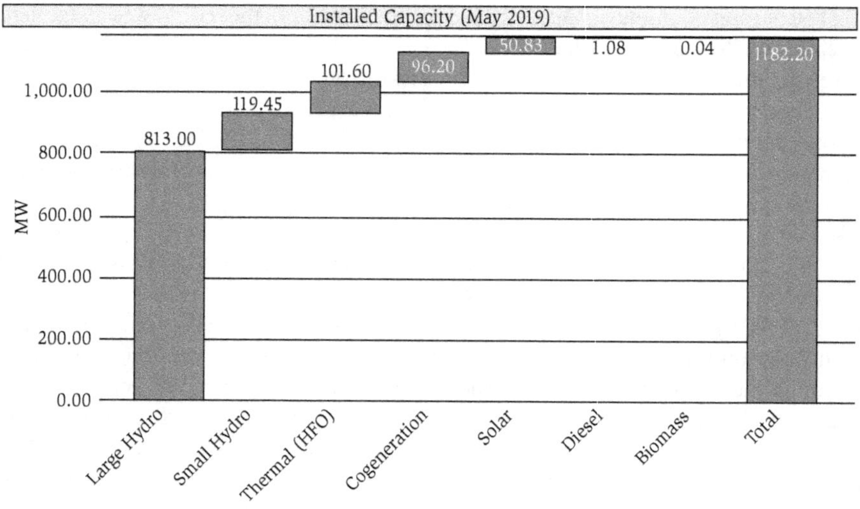

Source: Electricity Regulatory Authority, 2019.

§2. Bagasse

72. Bagasse technology uses sugarcane waste to generate electricity. Three Bagasse Power Plants generated and sold power to the Uganda Electricity Transmission Company Limited (UETCL) in 2018. These were KSW, Sugar and Allied Industries Limited (SAIL), and Kinyara Sugar Limited. The Bagasse Plants generated 206.5 GWh, the majority of which (175.2 GWh) was from KSW. Table 6 shows the power generation from bagasse in GWh.

67. Uganda Technology Needs Assessment Report For Mitigation November 2019. https://tech-action.unepdtu.org/wp-content/uploads/sites/2/2020/04/technology-needs-assessments-mitigation-uganda.pdf (accessed 7 Feb. 2022).

Table 6 Power Generation from Bagasse

Plant/Year	*2014*	*2015*	*2016*	*2017*	*2018*
Kakira	243.3	162.3	148.8	126.1	175.2
Sail Kaliro	–	–	20.8	15.9	25.6
Kinyara	–	–	7.9	7.8	5.7
Total	243.3	162.3	177.5	149.8	206.5

Source: Electricity Regulatory Authority 2018.

73. To realize greater bagasse potential, it is necessary to adopt modern conversion technology in the plants like cogeneration and also to use all the bagasse generated in the factories. However, indicative costs of plant modifications and other necessary investments have not been determined. It should be noted that this is a renewable resource of energy and is exploited by other countries at relatively higher levels. For example, 20% of electricity generation in Mauritius is from bagasse.

§3. GEOTHERMAL

74. The exploration of geothermal resources in Uganda is still at the reconnaissance and exploration stage. Geothermal energy resources in Uganda are estimated at 450 MW. Exploration for geothermal energy has been in progress since 1993. This was with support from the African Development Bank (ADB), International Atomic Energy Agency (IAEA), Iceland and German Federal Institute for Geosciences and Natural Resources (BGR). Iceland has financed two pre-feasibility studies, and BGR has financed one. There are three potential areas along the western branch of the East African Rift Valley which have been identified for detailed exploration. The three potential areas are Katwe-Kikorongo, Buranga and Kibiro.[68] Based on recent assessments, they have all been ranked as potential targets for geothermal development. The combined capacity from the three sites is about 100 MW. The three sites have been licensed to private developers (a three-year exploration licence based on the Mining Act of 2003). The current study results indicate that the temperature level varies between 150 C° and 200 C°, which is sufficient for electricity generation and for direct use in industry and agriculture.[69] The rest of the geothermal areas of Uganda are at a preliminary level of investigation. MEMD is planning to develop a Geothermal Policy and, subsequently, a Geothermal Act.

68. G. Bahati & J. F. Natukunda. (2008). Status of Geothermal Exploration and Development in Uganda. https://orkustofnun.is/gogn/unu-gtp-sc/UNU-GTP-SC-07-43.pdf (accessed 7 Feb. 2022).
69. Uganda Energy Situation, *supra* n. 66.

§4. Wind Power

75. Based on wind data collection done by the Department of Meteorology, Ministry of Water, Lands and Environment, at eleven sites over three years (1989–1992), wind speeds in most areas of Uganda are moderate, with an average speed not exceeding 3 m/s. In some areas with complex terrain, the wind may however speed up due to slopes of hills, escarpments and tunnelling effects.

76. In mountainous areas like the southwestern part towards the border with Rwanda (Kabale, Kisoro, Ntungamo) and in the area around Mt. Elgon, the average wind speed goes up to about 4 m/s. Measurement carried out under the Alternative Energy Resource Assessment and Utilisation Study at two sites for five months (June–September 2003) indicated that the average wind speed at Kabale and Mukono at 20 m was 3.7 m/s.[70] This study concluded that the wind energy resource in Uganda is insufficient for large-scale electricity generation. However, the wind resource may be suitable for special applications, such as water pumping in remote areas and for small-scale electricity generation in mountainous areas. It is possible that some sites could have enough wind speeds to generate a substantial amount of electricity. Preliminary investigations in the Karamoja region (North Eastern Uganda) and along the shores of Lake Victoria have shown that there could be potential for the production of electricity on a medium scale. In all, Uganda's wind power potential has not yet been tapped into and exploited.

77. All wind measurements which have been carried out so far are for meteorological record purposes (general weather data). This data cannot serve to document wind energy's potential as the standard height for the location of measuring equipment is, in this case, 2 m above the ground. Yet, for ideal measurements, they should be higher. More to that, the sensors used are often placed close to obstacles, a situation which may distort readings. As such, there is a need to compile wind data with the intention of monitoring wind speeds for energy use.

§5. Solar Energy

78. Uganda is endowed with favourable solar irradiation of 1,825 kWh/m^2 to 2,500 kWh/m^2 per year. This isolation is highest at the equator but varies from place to place away from the equator. It is highest in the dryer areas (northeast) and lowest in the mountainous areas (southwest) of the country. Solar radiation is also influenced by cloudy weather.[71] The average solar radiation in Uganda is 5.1 kWh/m^2/day. The data indicate a yearly variation (max month/min month) of only about a maximum of 20% (from 4.5 to 5.5 W/m^2), which is due to the location near the equator. The insolation is highest in the dryer area in the northeast and very low in

70. Final Energy Report Uganda. https://www.rvo.nl/sites/default/files/2019/02/Final-Energy-report-Uganda.pdf (accessed 7 Feb. 2022).
71. A Study on the Use and Viability of Solar Energy in Uganda. https://www.nape.or.ug/publications/energy/38-solar-enegy-viability/file (accessed 7 Feb. 2022).

the mountains in the east and southwest. Some of the completed solar power stations include; Soroti Solar Power Station (10 MW), Tororo Solar Power Station (10 MW), Kabulasoke Solar Power Station (20 MW), Mayuge Solar Power Station (10 MW), and Busitema Solar Power Station (4 MW).

79. The solar power system market in Uganda has steadily grown over the last fifteen years, with new players, including foreign investors, entering the market. The lack of grid access in rural areas and the growth of telecoms, which facilitates mobile payment and monitoring systems, are structural factors that have benefited off-grid solar development. Policy measures such as tax exemptions for equipment for solar and wind generation and subsidies for end-users have also supported the expansion of the sector.[72] The market is mainly served by the private sector, with estimated sales of about UGX 10,000/year throughout Uganda, not only for residential but also for productive (mostly water pumping) and social uses (hospitals and schools).[73] From its traditional direct use for drying foodstuff and clothes, solar energy is also being used with appropriate technology for cooking food, water heating, refrigeration, lighting, telecommunications, etc., in households, offices, hotels, schools and other organizations in Uganda. However, the scale at which solar energy is being used for purposes other than drying clothes and foods in Uganda is still very small. The use of the sun's radiation to generate electricity and heat energy for lighting and cooking is increasing greatly. It also has the potential to reduce the current demand exerted on the existing national grid-based power and consequently eradicate the negative impacts caused by the over-harvesting of biomass resources by the masses.

§6. Wind Energy

80. In Uganda, wind speeds in most areas are moderate, with an average speed not exceeding 3 m/s. In some areas with complex terrain, the wind may however speed up due to slopes of hills, escarpments and tunnelling effects. In mountainous areas like the southwestern part towards the border with Rwanda (Kabale, Kisoro, Ntungamo) and in the area around Mt. Elgon, the average wind speed goes up to about 4 m/s. Measurement carried out under the Alternative Energy Resource Assessment and Utilisation Study at two sites for five months (June–September 2003) indicated that the average wind speed at Kabale and Mukono at 20 m was 3.7 m/s. This study concluded that the wind energy resource in Uganda is insufficient for large-scale electricity generation.[74]

---

72. Final Energy Report Uganda, supra n. 70.
73. MEMD. Uganda's Sustainable Energy for All (Se4all) Initiative Action Agenda. https://www.seforall.org/sites/default/files/Uganda_AA_EN_Released.pdf (accessed 7 Feb. 2022).
74. Final Energy report Uganda, *supra* n. 70.

§7. Nuclear Energy

81. This is a form of energy released from the nucleus, the core of atoms, made up of protons and neutrons. This source of energy can be produced in two ways: fission – when nuclei of atoms split into several parts – or fusion – when nuclei fuse together. Inside nuclear power plants, nuclear reactors and their equipment contain and control the chain reactions, most commonly fuelled by uranium-235, to produce heat through fission. The heat warms the reactor's cooling agent, typically water, to produce steam. The steam is then channelled to spin turbines, activating an electric generator to create low-carbon electricity.

82. Nuclear energy is one of the most coveted cost-effective, reliable and clean energy options. However, it has challenges that include a demand for highly-skilled human resources. Since 2012, Uganda has indicated its willingness, determination, and intention to develop nuclear power for peaceful means using locally available uranium deposits. The Integrated Nuclear Infrastructure Review (INIR) mission reviewed in December 2021 the status of nuclear infrastructure development using Phase 1 criteria of the IAEA's Milestones Approach, a comprehensive method to assist countries that are considering or planning their first nuclear power plant which split the activities necessary to establish the infrastructure for a nuclear power programme into three progressive phases of development. To diversify its energy mix, which is now mainly based on hydroelectricity, Uganda has taken steps towards the introduction of nuclear power. It drafted an energy policy that includes nuclear power and established a Nuclear Energy Programme Implementing Organisation (NEPIO).[75] An Inter-Governmental Agreement (IGA) between Uganda and Russia on peaceful use of nuclear energy was signed on 17 September 2019 in Vienna. Negotiations with potential nuclear power project developers are ongoing.[76]

§8. Petroleum Consumption and Supply

83. The downstream petroleum supply industry operates under the overall policy of a free market. The Petroleum Supply Act was enacted and came into effect at the end of 2003. Imports of principal petroleum products (petrol, diesel and kerosene) in 2004 totalled 571,749 m^3. Government revenue from duty on the products amounted to about UGX 251 billion. Total sales of petroleum products in 2004 amounted to 646,839 m^3. The 2004 total sale was made up of 186,285 m^3 of petrol, 260,978 m^3 of diesel, 49,340 m^3 of kerosene, 79,131 m^3 of aviation fuel, 53,313 m_3 of fuel oil, 4,500 m^3 of cooking gas (Liquefied Petroleum gas (LPG), 6,391 m^3 of lubricants and 6,901 m^3 other petroleum products. Table 7 shows sales of petroleum products by type, excluding aviation fuel, over the period 2006–2010 in m^3.

75. IAEA Completes Ugandan Nuclear Infrastructure Review. https://www.world-nuclear-news.org/Articles/IAEA-completes-Ugandan-nuclear-infrastructure-revi (accessed 7 Feb. 2022).
76. MEMD. The 2020 Energy Sector Performance Report. http://www.energyandminerals.go.ug/site/assets/files/1081/2020_performance_review_report.pdf (accessed 7 Feb. 2022).

Table 7 Sales of Petroleum Products

Year	*Petrol*	*Kerosene*	*Diesel*	*LPG*	*Total*
2006	198,125	42,897	417,449	5,800	664,271
2007	185,272	33,321	427,225	7,150	652,968
2008	239,855	59,248	499,688	8,272	807,063
2009	225,684	42,590	511,604	8,599	788,477
2010	287,390	57,392	600,846	7,838	953,466
Percentage Change					
2009	–6	–28	2	4	–28
2010	27	35	17	–9	70

Source: Ministry of Energy and Mineral Development 2010.

84. There is a steady increase in the demand for petroleum products driven mainly by economic growth. Apart from the recorded increase in demand, there is also a strategic need to ensure the availability of reliable supplies at all times. The latter is particularly pertinent because Uganda imports all its requirements, and it is a landlocked country. Product marketing and distribution are within the private sector with several companies involved: Shell (30.3% of market share); Total (19.2%); Caltex (16.6%); Gapco (8.8%), Petro (U) 6.5%; Kobil 6.1%; others 12.5%.

85. The distribution system consists of over 300 retail outlets (service stations), most of which have been improved and upgraded by the oil companies. A number of other distributors are joining this competitive market.

86. Traditional oil companies still dominate the petroleum market, with Shell, Total and Caltex controlling about two-thirds of the market. However, they lost some of their market shares to the newly licensed companies, which have gained significant market shares. The newer companies with the fastest growing market shares included Kobil (U) Ltd, Petro (U) Ltd, Hared Petroleum Ltd, Petrocity Enterprises Ltd and MGS/Mogas.

The oil companies import finished products through the ports of Mombasa in Kenya (70% of the supply) and Dar es Salaam in Tanzania (30%). From Mombasa, the products are transported by pipeline through Nairobi to terminals in Eldoret (about 110 km from the Uganda border) and Kisumu (on Lake Victoria, about 90 km from the Uganda border). The pipeline is owned and operated by the Kenya Pipeline Company (KPC). KPC requires that Kenyan companies own all products transported in the pipelines. Consequently, the Kenyan sister companies of the Uganda oil companies must be in the supply chain. Plans are underway to extend the Eldoret part of the pipeline to Kampala. MEMD, Uganda, has been carrying out aggressive promotion of Kenya–Uganda Oil Pipeline Extension project.

87. Physical data on the KPC show that the terminal at Mombasa has a storage capacity of 70,000 m^3 for clean products. The Mombasa–Nairobi pipeline is 14 inches, has a capacity of 10,000 m^3 per day and could double the capacity if one additional pumping station were built. The Nairobi to Eldoret and Kisumu pipeline is 8 inches and splits up into 6-inch pipes, one to Eldoret and one to Kisumu. The capacity from Nairobi is 5,000 m^3 per day. Export potential is 2,200–2,500 m^3 per day. The remainder is reserved for western Kenya. The current need for Uganda is 550 m^3 per day, assuming 30% of the total is supplied for Dar es Salaam.

88. Local Pump prices of petrol, kerosene and diesel are high when compared to neighbouring Kenya and Tanzania; that is, by 2014, they were UGX 3,727, 2841 and UGX 3,304, respectively, with the possibility of increasing relatively fast (MEMD, 2014). The retail price in Uganda ranges from four to five times its Cost, Insurance, and Freight (CIF) landed cost at the seaboard in Kenya and Tanzania. The principal reasons for the high prices are the high inland transportation costs from the seaboard – about one-third of the CIF Kampala cost of the product and high wholesale and retail costs because of the small size of the market. Another is the high taxes levied on petroleum. The tax rates of the respective CIF prices range from 175% for petrol, 130% for diesel and 90% for kerosene. This has led to rampant smuggling. It is estimated that about 10% of the petrol, kerosene and diesel consumed in Uganda is illegally imported. As a result, the government introduced the biocode programme, which was instituted to detect smuggled and adulterated fuel on the market.

89. In 2004, a total of 571,749 m^3 of officially imported fuel was marked compared to 536,158 m^3 in 2003. And 4,052 fuel samples were collected and analysed. Only 0.03% of the samples were found below specification compared to 0.4% in 2003, indicating the high quality of fuel consumed and a vast decline in adulterated fuel. By 2014, the Total petroleum imports were marginally higher compared to 2013 by 9.7%. By commodity, total petroleum imports fell by 8.4% in kerosene but rose by 13.4% in petrol and 8.2% in diesel. Overall, petroleum imports have risen by 48.7% since 2007. The total import bill in 2014 was UGX 5,012 billion, the highest in the last seven years, while Government revenue totalled UGX 993 billion. Government revenue peaked in 2009 at UGX 1,216 billion, while its lowest was recorded in 2007 at UGX 450 billion.

I. Oil and Gas Exploration and Development in Uganda

90. Efforts to find potential petroleum in Uganda started as far back as the 1920s. The efforts were first documented by a government geologist, E.J. Wayland, in the publication 'Petroleum in Uganda' in 1925. This included reporting the existence of oil seepages in Uganda.[77]

77. PAU, History of Petroleum Exploration in Uganda. https://www.pau.go.ug/history/#:~:text=In%201925%2C%20Petroleum%20Potential%20of,both%20Uganda%20and%20DRC%20sides (accessed 10 July 2022).

91. In the period between 1936 and 1956, the first shallow stratigraphic wells were drilled by the African–European Investment Company.[78] The first deep well, Waki B-1 well, was drilled in 1938 in Butiaba, Buliisa. Over twenty shallow wells were drilled in Kibiro and Kibuku areas for geological correlation. Geological surveys carried out during the 1940s and 1950s established the presence of sedimentary sequences of clays and silts.[79]

92. In the period between 1945 and 1980, there was limited activity because of World War II and changes in policies of colonial rule. East Africa was zoned for agriculture and west Africa for Oil Exploration by the Colonial master, and post-independence political uncertainties and instability in the country.[80]

93. Consistent and more efforts commenced in 1983 with the acquisition of 9,578-line km of aeromagnetic data that identified three depot centres along the entire length of the Graben and have been going on. Later, in 1985, the Petroleum Exploration and Production Act was enacted. The World Bank Credit also moved in to support Petroleum Exploration Promotion.[81]

94. There were more developments in the 1990s. A cooperation agreement was signed between Uganda and the Democratic Republic of Congo for joint exploration and development of common fields.[82] In the same year, there was formation of the Petroleum Exploration and Production Department (PEPD) which carried out geological and geophysical surveys in areas identified by aeromagnetic data. Data acquired was used to promote Albertine Graben for investment. In 1991, the PEPD commenced ground geological and geophysical data acquisition. In 1993, the Petroleum Exploration and Production Regulations were drafted. This was followed by signing the first Production Sharing Agreement (PSA) between Petrofina Exploration Uganda and Government over the entire Albertine Graben. The Petroleum Unit in the Geological Survey and Mines Department (GSMD) of the Ministry transformed into the PEPD. PEPD commenced a follow-up of ground geological and geophysical surveys in areas identified by the aeromagnetic data. Data acquired was used Subdivide the Graben into nine smaller Exploration Areas. In 1997, there was licensing of exploration Area 3 (Semliki Basin) to Heritage Oil and Gas Limited, and in 1998, Heritage acquired the first 2D seismic data on 170-line km in Uganda.

95. The decade of 2000 was significant because of the development that took place. In 2001, Hardman Resources and Energy Africa was licensed to do exploration in the northern Lake Albert Basin, which is known as Exploration Area 2.[83] Between 2002 and 2004, there was drilling of the first deep wells in the basin to encounter oil and gas. This was done by Heritage and Energy Africa. In 2005, Exploration Area 5, also known as the Rhino Camp Basin, was licensed to Neptune

78. *Ibid.*
79. *Ibid.*
80. *Ibid.*
81. *Ibid.*
82. *Ibid.*
83. *Ibid.*

Petroleum. There was drilling of the Mputa-1 well by Hardeman and Energy Africa in the Kaiso-Tonya area. The first deep wells (Turaco-1, 2, 3) that were drilled by Heritage in the Semliki Basin between 2002 and 2004 (in Western Uganda) did have positive results in terms of encountering some hydrocarbons. This restored the hope of those that had invested their time, money and, indeed, their lives in this sector.

96. The Constitution was amended by the Constitution (Amendment) Act 11 of 2005, which provides that all minerals and petroleum in, on or under any land or waters in Uganda are vested in the government on behalf of the Republic of Uganda. In 2006, Hardman Petroleum, now Tullow Oil, made its first commercial discovery well in the Kaiso-Tonya area. Mputa-1 well was drilled in December 2005, and on 6 January 2006, it struck oil and was declared the first commercial discovery in Uganda. A year later, in 2006, Uganda confirmed commercial petroleum resources. In 2007, Dominion Petroleum was licensed to Exploration Area 4B (Lakes Edward and George Basin). In 2008, the Cabinet approved the National Oil and Gas Policy for Uganda its implementation commenced. In 2012, the Oil and Gas Revenue Management Policy was approved. The key legislation to regulate petroleum, the Petroleum (Exploration, Development and Production) Act 2013 and the Petroleum (Refining, Conversion, Transmission and Midstream Storage) Act, were enacted. The Public Finance Management Act 2015 handles petroleum revenue management. The Income Tax Act was amended in 2018. No person can lawfully carry out any exploration or development operations on petroleum in or upon any land in Uganda without a licence.

97. Three main oil sedimentary basins were identified in the West of Uganda. The Western basins have sediments of around 4,000 metres in depth and are potential prospects for petroleum discoveries. Aeromagnetic, gravity and surface geological surveys have been conducted. Promising seismic surveys or exploratory drilling have been undertaken. Product sharing is in place, and the Ministry has prepared a promotional package to attract companies to explore Uganda. In January 1997, Heritage Oil and Gas Ltd of the United Kingdom was awarded a petroleum exploration licence in one of the three main sedimentary basins near Lake Albert. Heritage completed drilling Turaco-2 well in February 2004. The well, which deviated from a depth of 1,460 metres of Turaco-1, reached a total depth of 2,963 metres. The data acquired from the well indicated the presence of two hydrocarbon zones. In 2003, Hardman Resources N.L. (Hardman) and Energy Africa Limited acquired 2D Seismic data over Lake Albert and has since been successful in identifying oil resources in the area.

98. In 2001, the exploration of EA 3 Semliki Basin was licensed to Heritage, while EA 2 (Northern Lake Albert Basin) was licensed to Hardman. From 2002 to 2004, there was drilling of Turaco-1, 2 and 3 wells in the Semliki Basin. From 2003 to 2004, there was acquisition of seismic data over Lake Albert. In 2005, Exploration Area 5, the Rhino Camp Basin, was licensed to Neptune Petroleum. In 2006, there was the first discovery of oil in the Kaiso-Tonya area (Mputa-1 well), and in 2007, the exploration Area 4B was licensed to Dominion Petroleum. In 2007–2011, there was more acquisition of seismic data and drilling of wells in all licensed areas.

In April 2013, Uganda Government and three oil companies – Tullow Oil, Total and China National Offshore Oil Corporation (CNOOC) agreed to build a refinery with a capacity of 30,000 BPD.

99. Exploration activities involved the completion of Kingfisher 2D Ocean Bottom Cable (OBC) seismic testing, which was concluded on 8 January 2014, and the East Nile 3D seismic survey in May 2014 in Kingfisher and Packwach areas, respectively, plus the drilling of Rii-2A and Waraga-3 in EA 1 and EA 2, respectively. By the end of 2014, the cumulative seismic data acquired in the country was 3,766.466 km^2 of 2D Land; 3,291.66 km^2 of 2D Marine; 578.64 km^2 of 2D Transitional Zone; 1,346.26 km^2 of 3D Land and 261.8 km^2 of 3D Marine seismic with a total cost of USD 111,997,896.

100. A cumulative total of 118 onshore wells were drilled in the Albertine Graben by the end of 2014, with 83 of them being appraisal wells while 35 were exploration wells. Kingfisher-2 still ranks highest with flow rate of 13,830 barrels of oil per day, and Jobi East-6A with lowest flow rate of 4.3 barrels of oil per day so far. Only 2 gas wells have been tested so far, i.e., Turaco-3 and Nzizi-2. The two wells flowed gas at 60 million and 14.13 million standard cubic feet of gas per day, respectively. The gas in Turaco-3 was heavily contaminated with carbon dioxide (CO_2). The current Stock Tank Oil Initially in Place (STOIIP) estimate in the Albertine Graben stands at 6.5 billion barrels, and 1.4 billion barrels of this is estimated to be recoverable. The Non-associated Gas Initially in Place (GIIP) stands at 499 Billion Cubic Feet (BCF), and the associated gas is estimated at 173 BCF. A total of 40,385 barrels of non-flared crude oil is currently being stored at Ngiri-2 and Kasamene-1 well sites as well as Tangi camp. A commercial plan to dispose of the crude is not yet in place.

101. Following the enactment of the Petroleum (Exploration, Development and Production) Act 2013 PEDP Act, and the Petroleum (Refining, Conversion, Transmission and Midstream Storage) Act 2013 RCTMS Act, the first production licence was issued to CNOOC in 2013 over the Kingfisher field and a memorandum of understanding on commercialization signed between the government and licensed oil companies. The first production licence was issued to CNOOC in 2013. Tullow Uganda Operations Pty Limited and Total were issued with five and three licences, respectively, in August 2016.

102. In February 2015, the GoU announced the first open competitive licensing round for the Blocks. Armour Energy Limited of Australia, WalterSmith Petroman Oil Limited, Niger Delta Petroleum Resources Limited of Nigeria and Oranto Petroleum International Limited were the four shortlisted firms with whom the GoU negotiated and signed other production-sharing agreements.

103. In 2016, six production licences were issued to Tullow Uganda Operation, and three Production licences were issued to Total E&P. In 2016, the government granted eight oil production licences to Tullow Uganda Operations Pty Ltd and Total E&P Uganda B.V. By 2017, a total of nine production licences had been issued in Uganda. Full-scale production has been earmarked for 2025, and currently, progress is being made on the oil roads, crude oil pipeline, refinery, central processing facility and other installations.

104. The oil companies currently licensed in the country to undertake petroleum exploration, development and production are as follows: China National Offshore Oil Corporation Uganda Limited (CNOOC Uganda Ltd), which is operating in the Kingfisher Discovery Area. Total E&P Uganda B.V. is operating in Exploration Areas 1 and 1A, and seven petroleum discoveries have been made in this area. These are: Ngiri, Jobi, Rii, Jobi-East, Mpyo, Gunya and Lyec. Tullow Uganda Operations Pty Ltd is operating in Exploration Area 2, and this area has a total of nine discoveries, and these are Ngege, Kasamene, Kigogole, Wahrindi, Ngara, Nsoga, Mputa, Nzizi, and Waraga. Three exploration licences were awarded to Armour Energy Ltd and Oranto Petroleum Limited for Kanywataba and Ngassa (Shallow and Deep) fields, respectively.

105. In 2010, the Uganda Government proposed to construct a refinery after a feasibility study demonstrated that it would be economically viable. In December 2013, the government shortlisted several firms to build the refinery, but the tender was not awarded until 2015. RT Global Resources (RTGR), a Russia-led consortium, was selected as the Preferred Bidder, and the other, led by SK Engineering of South Korea, was ranked as the second and Alternate Bidder. The winning consortium (RTGR) pulled out, prompting a hasty second bidding round in June 2017, which a few months later suffered the same fate.

106. In 2017, the GoU selected the Albertine Graben Refinery Consortium to negotiate the Project Framework Agreement (PFA) for the development of the oil refinery. The plan for the development of the refinery is in line with the Uganda National Oil and Gas Policy (2008) which provides for value addition and development of necessary infrastructure in the oil and gas sector. The PFA for the project was signed on 10 April 2018. After several engagements, AGRC's USD 17 million Pre-FID Performance Bond was issued and confirmed by the GoU on 7 September 2018. The PFA thus became effective, and the Pre-FID activities, such as the FEED, Environmental and Social Impact Assessment (ESIA) and geotechnical studies for the refinery development commenced in September 2018. The project structure has since changed, with the GoU now favouring a public-led as opposed to a private-led partnership. Once completed, the refinery is expected to produce 60,000 barrels of oil per day. The project includes the development of a 60,000 barrels of oil per day (bopd) refinery in Kabaale, Hoima District and a 211-kilometre multi-products pipeline from Kabaale to a distribution hub in Namwambula, Mpigi District.

107. To export crude oil from Uganda, the construction of the East African Crude Oil Pipeline (EACOP) has been proposed. The Pipeline is a 1,443-km crude oil export infrastructure that will transport Uganda's crude oil from Kabaale–Hoima in Uganda to the Chonoleani Peninsular near Tanga in Tanzania for export to the international market. This major export system (296 km in Uganda and 1,147 km in

Tanzania) comprises of 24" insulated buried pipeline, six pumping stations, two pressure reduction stations and a marine export terminal.

108. In 2020, the Extractives Industries Transparency Initiative (EITI) Board approved Uganda's application to join the EITI.[84] As a member of the EITI, Uganda is required to publicly disclose information, such as contracts, beneficial owners, revenues and payments, including payments related to the environment

109. The government, in April 2021, approved the Resettlement Action Plan (RAP) for the EACOP project in the Ugandan section. This approval paves the way for the completion of the land acquisition processes, compensation of Project Affected Persons (PAPs) and resettlement of PAPs. The EACOP traverses ten districts in Uganda; Hoima, Kikuube, Kakumiro, Kyankwanzi, Mubende, Gomba, Sembabule, Lwengo, Rakai and Kyotera.

110. In February 2022, Total Energies EP Uganda, CNOOC Uganda Limited, the Uganda National Oil Company (UNOC), and the Tanzania Petroleum Development Corporation (TPDC) announced that they had reached the Final Investment Decision (FID) for the upstream oil production projects and the EACOP. The Ugandan government expects developing the oil sector will require several billion dollars of infrastructure investment to build and support a refinery, two central processing facilities, and the 1,445 km EACOP – the world's longest heated pipeline. In 2018, the AGRC – a US-led group of companies including General Electric, YAATRA Africa, and the Italian engineering firm Saipem – won the right to finance, build, and operate a planned USD 3.5 billion oil refinery. The FID for the refinery is projected for mid-2023. In June 2021, Total announced it had made a conditional award of USD 2 billion to a consortium led by US-McDermott International and Chinese-Sinopec for engineering, procurement, construction, and commissioning (EPCC) for the development of thirty-one well beds and a central processing facility of the Tilenga onshore oil field that will generate up to 200,000 barrels per day.

111. The construction of pipeline EACOP has recently generated debate in both regional and international fora. The debate has centred on its impact on the environment and people, with activists arguing that EACOP will adversely affect the environment as well as displace people. The activists have campaigned against its construction and consequently that the crude oil discovered in Uganda be a stranded asset (remain in the ground). However, the Governments of Uganda and Tanzania have defended the project as one that is necessary for the development of both countries. They further assert that it is being executed in a sustainable manner with the highest standards possible in resettling PAPs.

84. Uganda became the EITI's 54th member country and the 26th in Africa.

§9. GAS

112. Gas is a group of hydrocarbon-based gases derived from crude oil refining or natural gas fractionation. They include ethane, ethylene, propane, propylene, normal butane, butylene, isobutene, and isobutylene.

113. For the convenience of transportation, these gases are liquefied through pressurization.[85] Since the commercial discovery of oil in Uganda, less has been said about the vast potential of natural gas reserves that coexist alongside the 3.5 billion barrels of oil.[86] In hydrocarbon-rich grounds like the Albertine Graben stretch, where oil exploration is taking shape, the presence of natural gas is high and is usually found in the natural rock formations along with underground water and oil. When natural gas is refined, it produces Compressed Natural Gas (CNG), Liquefied Natural Gas (LNG) and LPG, all used differently for domestic purposes like cooking, heating and automobile fuel.

114. For now, the Uganda government plans to use the current gas reservoirs for the generation of large-scale electricity supply to add to the current power supply of 504 megawatts. The amount of gas reserves is not yet ascertained because appraisal of the discoveries is still ongoing, but Uganda has about 93 billion cubic feet of non-associated gas from the fields of Nzizi, Ngiri, Kasamene, Kigogole, Ngege, Jobi-Rii, Ngassa, Nsoga and Jobi-East. In an ideal reservoir, there are two types of gas resources: associated (dissolved and gas cap) and non-associated gas (sometimes referred to as free gas); however, most of Uganda's discoveries are associated gas – located at the tip or within oil fields. The available associated gas could amount to about 192 million standard cubic feet – located in fields like Mputa, Waraga, Kingfisher and Nzizi. Other wells, including Kasamene, Kigogole, Nsoga, Wairhindi, Ngara, Lyec, Mpyo, Gunya, Ngiri, Jobi-Rii and Jobi-East have also been found to have some embedments of natural gas.

In a nutshell, Uganda's gas potential has not been exploited yet, but once exploited, the country shall soar to an unimaginable great economic height.

§10. BIOMASS

115. Biomass is the predominant energy type used in Uganda. It accounts for 90% of the total energy consumption in the country and grew by approximately 3.6% between 1995 and 2000. Key forms used are firewood, charcoal, and shrubs. Grass, farm residues and wood wastes are used in regions facing significant wood scarcity. Charcoal is mainly used in urban areas, while firewood, agro-residues and wood wastes are widely used in rural areas. Whereas these resources are widely used for energy generation, most of the traditional biomass energy technologies, which include wood and charcoal stoves, ovens and kilns used in Uganda, are inefficient.

---

85. Index Mundi, 'Uganda's Uganda Liquefied Petroleum Gases Production by Year' http://www.indexmundi.com/energy.aspx?country=ug&product=lpg&graph=production (accessed 9 Feb. 2022).
86. Dailymonitor, 'What lies ahead for Uganda's gas' https://www.monitor.co.ug/uganda/business/prosper/what-lies-ahead-for-uganda-s-gas-1543976 (accessed 19 March 2022).

116. Firewood is used mainly with three-stone stoves in rural households for cooking and for food preparation by commercial vendors in urban areas. Less than 9% of all households use efficient wood stoves. Although some institutions like schools and hospitals still use firewood, their stoves are most often more advanced. Charcoal is mainly used in a metallic stove, traditionally known as a '*sigiri*'. Use of improved charcoal stoves with a ceramic insulation lining is increasing. The conversion of firewood to charcoal uses mainly earth mounds and pits, which give an average conversion efficiency of about 10–15%. Efforts to train charcoal makers in efficient ways to make charcoal have had a limited impact. Most of them still make it on an individual and traditional basis.

117. The household sector is the biggest consumer of energy (87.8%), of which 98.0% is biomass-based energy. The consumption of biomass energy is expected to remain high because of the high cost of modern energy. Other factors include inefficient use of wood fuel, a high population growth (2.5% per annum) and a general lack of awareness by the community about natural resource conservation. This has contributed to the deforestation of Uganda's forests and bushlands. Currently, almost 1.2% of the total area of Uganda is degraded forest. The situation has been made worse by the inability of electricity companies to supply reliable and cheap electricity hence excessive charcoal use. Biomass, principally wood fuel and charcoal, is the most important energy source in Uganda quantity-wise. This is mainly because the country has a favourable physical and ecological regime. Recent work under the National Biomass Study puts the annual sustainable supply of biomass at 29 million tonnes, which is equivalent to approximately 8 million tonnes of oil. This is divided as shown in Table 8.

Table 8 Sustainable Biomass Supply

Biomass Type	*Sustainable Harvest (Million Tonnes)*	*%*
Tree biomass	26.3	51
Bush	10.5	21
Papyrus and reed	4.5	9
Farm-level vegetal waste, stalks of maize, sorghum, cotton stalks, etc.	6.2	12
Agro processing vegetal waste, bagasse	1.4	3
Grass, forbs	1	2
Sub-total	51	100

Source: Uganda Biomass Energy Strategy, 2013.[87]

87. MEMD (2013). Biomass Energy Strategy (BEST) Uganda.

118. Biomass energy in Uganda is found in different forms: tree biomass, bush biomass and Agricultural areas. Tree biomass is estimated to be about 20%, while bush biomass comprises 30%. The balance is agricultural areas, mainly coming from fallow land and arable land. Tropical high forests supply 2% but are not a significant source of wood fuel or charcoal because of being located away from high population areas. The annual yield from crop residues is estimated to be 5 million tonnes, 90% of which is from farmland, although most crop residues are not burnt in households.

The use of residues is also more widespread in industries. For instance, the sugar industry uses bagasse, and some clay factories use coffee husks. Dung production is estimated to be 3 million tonnes, which is equivalent to 2.8 million tonnes of air-dry wood. No dung is, however, being used as fuel in the country.

119. Wood fuels provide energy for cooking and water boiling for most rural and many urban homes. They are also important for rural industry, especially in the production of building materials, such as bricks, and commercial enterprises in urban areas, such as restaurants and bakeries.

120. The reliance on wood fuels is expected to continue for many years to come. This is due to the high prices of petroleum fuels and the limited availability of electricity. The above is particularly so for rural households, which use wood fuel for cooking (96%) and lighting (10%). Even in urban areas, wood fuel is used for cooking by 91% of the population, electricity and gas 8% and paraffin 1.5%, while the figures for lighting homes are 40% (electricity) and 59.5% (paraffin). Yet heavy dependence on firewood and charcoal is not only a health hazard, especially for those living in poorly constructed houses, but also impacts heavily on the environment. The total wood fuel and biomass consumption of 16 million tonnes in 1994 was divided as shown in Table 9.

Table 9 Estimate of Consumption of Wood Fuels and Biomass 1994 ('000 Tonnes)

Location	*Crop Residues*	*Collected*	*Purchased*	*Charcoal*	*Total Wood*
Rural	981	11,257	151	304	12,963
Urban (non-Kampala)	19	245	197	944	1,404
Kampala	1	47	69	1,424	1,542
Total	1,001	11,819	417	2,672	15,909

Source: Uganda Energy Assessment, ESMAP 1996.

121. Biomass energy estimates for 2014 were UGX 4,618 billion nationally. The demand was estimated at 44.2 million tonnes. Specifically, firewood demand was estimated at 28.2 million tonnes, agro residue demand at 3.5 million tonnes, charcoal at 1.8 million tonnes, and charcoal wood equivalent at 16 million tonnes.

122. It is clear from Tables 8 and 9 that the estimated sustainable supply of biomass is almost twice the level of demand for Uganda as a whole. However, wood fuel supply problems exist in a localized manner. In particular, supplies of woody biomass are not adequate to meet demands in major urban centres. Wood has to be imported from other regions. Countrywide, however, using a demand growth of 3% per year, a supply surplus is forecast to persist well into the next century. Industrial biomass consumption in Uganda is higher than in other countries in the region. Limited availability and high prices of petroleum and electricity have stimulated biomass demand. Presently, in final energy terms, the Ugandan industry consumes twice as much biomass energy (in TOE or GJ) as petroleum products and over five times as much electricity.

123. Uganda's commercial sector consumes twenty times as much biomass as all other forms of energy combined (also in final energy terms). Key industries which rely primarily and sometimes exclusively on biomass include tea production, construction industry, including brick, tile and lime, tobacco curing, refining sugar/ jaggery and fish smoking.

§11. Cogeneration and Fossil Fuels

124. There is considerable potential for cogeneration in the sugar processing industry as well as textile manufacturers, beer industry, cement industry, and foods and beverages industry. The potential in the sugar industry alone is currently estimated to be over 100 MW, while for other industries, it could be over 50 MW. Cogeneration contributes to power generation as well as to the goal of energy efficiency.

§12. Other Renewables

125. Other than woody biomass, Uganda is richly endowed with renewable energy resources such as solar. Renewable energy development has received much attention in Uganda, and many pilot exercises have taken place. However, only a small fraction of these resources is utilized due to problems such as lack of coordination, little exchange of information and experiences, limited follow-up and very limited monitoring and evaluation. With regard to photovoltaics (PVs), the private sector is a major player in the development of solar resources in Uganda. It is estimated that over 3,500 PV units are installed in households by the private sector. Many of these are used for rural household lighting and livestock fencing, among other things. In addition, non-governmental organizations (NGOs) have installed hundreds of solar systems for activities like refrigeration, lighting and water pumping. The rapidly expanding tourism sector has also boosted the use of PVs in and around parks and reserves. Solar water heating units have been installed in a number of such places.

Part II. Role of Government Institutions in the Administration of Energy Law and Policy

§1. The Ministry of Energy and Mineral Development

126. The mandate of the MEMD is to establish, promote the development, strategically manage and safeguard the rational and sustainable exploitation as well as utilization of energy and mineral resources for social and economic development. The roles and functions of the Ministry are to acquire processes and interpret technical data in order to establish the energy and mineral resource potential of the country and to create an enabling environment in order to attract investment in the development, provision and utilization of energy and mineral resources. Third, it is to inspect, regulate, monitor and evaluate activities of private companies in the energy and mineral sectors so that the resources are developed, exploited and used on a rational and sustainable basis, finally, to provide policy guidance and ensure effective development, exploitation and management of energy and mineral resources.

127. The MEMD consists of one technical directorate, which is made up of three departments, namely: the Energy Resources Department, the PEPD and the GSMD. The support services of the Ministry consist of Finance and Administration Department, Sectoral Planning/Policy Analysis Unit and the Resource Centre. As a result of the unbundling of UEB, three other parastatals, namely, Uganda Electricity Generation Company Limited (UEGCL), UETCL, and Uganda Electricity Distribution Company Limited (UEDCL), were created. These companies operate under the policy guidance of the Ministry. The GoU plans to transfer these organizations to the Ministry.

128. The mandate of the Energy Resources Department is to promote and coordinate the development of energy resources. It is also to ensure an adequate supply of energy and promote efficient utilization of energy for social and economic development. The objectives of the department include creating an enabling environment. This is to attract investment in the development, provision and use of energy resources, ensuring the rational development of sustainable and efficient use of energy resources; promoting, facilitating and harmonizing standards as well as regulations concerned with energy; ensuring compliance with set standards, laws and policies, as well as competitiveness in the energy sector, strategically managing energy resources in the national interest, promoting export of energy resources and facilitating the development of suitable renewable energy resources for use in Uganda.

129. The Energy Department is headed by a commissioner, under whom there are three Assistant Commissioners. Each commissioner heads a division. These divisions include; new and renewable sources of energy, electric power and energy efficiency. There are several functions of the energy department, which include:

(a) formulation and review of national policies on energy;
(b) preparation of national plans for the development, supply and utilization of energy resources;
(c) identification of suitable new energy sources to be developed for use in Uganda;
(d) mobilization of finances and technical assistance for the development of energy resources;
(e) coordination and supervision of government projects on the development of energy resources;
(f) coordination of the plans and activities of local government in relation to energy;
(g) promotion of energy resources development and coordination of the efforts of the various institutions involved in this function;
(h) provision of technical help to local government in energy-related activities;
(i) provision of technical advice as may be required by the various institutions involved in energy resources development;
(j) monitoring and advising on energy supplies to ensure sufficiency and availability;
(k) making forecasts of petroleum products requirements in the country and working out strategies for satisfying the requirements;
(l) monitoring and guiding the activities of oil companies to ensure compliance with national policies, legislation, standards and plans;
(m) monitoring and guiding the operations of hydroelectric power companies to ease compliance with national policies, legislations and plans;
(n) monitoring and guiding the utilization of energy in the country to promote and ensure efficiency and compliance with policies, standards and plans, and also to minimize wastage as well as the degradation of the environment;
(o) inspection, monitoring and coordination of the activities of local government in the area of energy development, utilization and conservation;
(p) where necessary, providing technical assistance, support supervision or training so as to ensure implementation of national policies and adherence to performance standards relating to energy;
(q) initiation of policy and legislation to atomic energy;
(r) setting of standards relating to atomic energy in general and radiation in particular;
(s) initiation and review of international agreements on the use of atomic energy;
(t) monitoring the implementation of agreements, policies and standards on the use of atomic energy;

(u) maintaining an up-to-date information base on energy resources and controlling and managing disasters caused by or related to energy resources.

130. The government has an important role to play by ensuring that new and renewable sources of energy are effectively developed and applied. The New and Renewable Sources of Energy Division also has the following functions:

(i) identifying suitable new sources of energy to be adopted or developed for use in Uganda;
(ii) encouraging specialized institutions to research into and develop new and renewable sources of energy;
(iii) mobilizing resources and technical help for the development of new and renewable sources of energy;
(iv) coordinating the activities of the various institutions and the local government in relation to new and renewable sources of energy;
(v) coordinating and supervising government projects on the development of new and renewable energy resources; and
(vi) provision of technical assistance to local government and other organizations involved in the development of new and renewable energy sources.

131. The mandate of the Energy Efficiency Division is to ensure the efficient utilization of energy in all sectors of the economy. This includes industry, commercial buildings, institutions, households, transport and agriculture. The main functions of the division are: providing advice and technical guidance to energy users with the aim of improving the efficiency of utilization; including advice on substitution of energy sources for better efficiency; monitoring, directly or through agents, the efficiency of energy utilization in all spheres of activity; providing advice and technical guidance to energy users on the minimization of environmental pollution arising from energy use and setting efficiency standards for the utilization of various types of energy sources and for various modes of utilization.

132. The specific activities undertaken by the Energy Efficiency division include energy awareness campaigns, collecting energy consumption data from all sectors, carrying out energy audits and surveys and capacity building in academic institutions. The Energy Efficiency Division carries out awareness campaigns in the following ways. First, by producing and distributing energy awareness materials, organizing and conducting awareness workshops for industrialists, hoteliers, small-scale industries, institutions, radio and Television programmes and the energy efficiency week. The division also has the responsibility of collecting and maintaining data on energy consumption. These data are important for making the annual national energy balance. The division is also responsible for energy audits.

133. An energy audit is a detailed analysis of energy used in an organization. It involves a structured review of how energy is purchased, managed and used, with the aim of identifying potential savings. Either the division or the individual firm may initiate the energy audits. The division selects a sector depending on the perceived need. A few firms in the sector are audited, and the findings are normally used to create awareness in that sector. However, a firm interested in undertaking an energy audit may express its interest to the ministry in writing. Depending on the availability of time and funds, the energy audit is conducted at an appropriate time. An energy audit involves the following steps: assembling all energy bills for the previous years, identifying the main uses for energy around your site, calculating energy used per operation/unit production, checking how well energy is used against industry standards, identifying possible energy saving opportunities/measures, evaluating the cost and payback period of each measure and prioritizing the opportunities identified.

134. Electricity, especially hydroelectricity, remains a major source of power for industries, institutions and urban areas in general. The actual production and supply of electric power are being divested to autonomous and private companies. The Ministry, however, has a big role to play at the national level. The main objective of the Electric Power Division is to ensure sufficient, reliable and low-cost electricity supply in the country. The functions of the division are:

(a) identification of opportunities for the development of electric power supplies, and encouraging the private sector and other institutions to take up the development;
(b) monitoring and coordinating the operations of various electric power development, production and supply organizations;
(c) providing technical guidance where necessary and possible to ensure adequate and reliable supply of electric power throughout the country;
(d) mobilizing resources and technical assistance for the development of electric power supplies;
(e) coordinating and supervising government projects on the development of electric power supplies and providing technical and operational support as may be required by the ERA.

135. The GSMD aims at establishing, promoting the development, strategically managing and safeguarding the rational and sustainable utilization of mineral resources for economic and social development. Its mandate is to collect, collate, process, analyse, archive and disseminate geoscience data, monitor operators and enforce regulations in the mineral sector and develop and maintain professionals capable of generating and utilizing available geoscience data. In addition, it is required to promote and ensure rational development and utilization, in a safe and sustainable environment, of mineral resources for the socioeconomic enhancement of the people of Uganda. The objectives of GSMD are to systematically collect, interpret, preserve and disseminate geological information that is required to maintain the national geoscience database; maintain a body of expertise that can use this data to advise the government, the private sector and the general public; carry out geological investigations and promotional activities to attract investment in exploration and development of mineral resources; carry out engineering geology investigations and monitor earthquakes and other related natural disasters such as landslides and volcanoes and advise the public on remedies; provide effective and reliable laboratory services in the mineral sector for institutional and public use and to administer the Mining Act and Regulations; and provide advisory services to miners on mining methods and environmental protection.

136. GSMD has four operational divisions, namely: (1) geological surveys, (2) mines, (3) geoscience data and (4) laboratory. The Geological Survey Division, among other things, collects and interprets the geological data, identifies economic mineral prospects and produces maps and reports relevant to the promotion of exploration and exploitation of Uganda's mineral resources. The operational sections are mapping, exploration, drilling, remote sensing, geophysics and the national seismological network project. The Mines Division issues licences for the exploration and exploitation of the identified mineral occurrence. It is also responsible for the administration of the Mining Act and Regulations to ensure proper management of the mineral resources and preservation of the environment through appropriate mining methods. The Geoscience Data Division preserves and disseminates the geoscience data of the department. It offers a technical link of the department to the local and foreign investors in the mining sector. It operates documentation, cartography and computer sections. Finally, the laboratory division collects/receives raw data and samples. It analyses and processes the same for interpretation. The laboratories are the assay, geochemical, spectrographic, petrographic and mineral dressing.

§2. The Electricity Regulatory Authority

137. The ERA was established under the Electricity Act 1999 and is the authority responsible for regulating and licensing the generation, transmission, distribution, sale, export, import and distribution of electrical energy in Uganda. ERA sets licence conditions and ensures compliance to licence conditions by Licensees. ERA ensures that utilities earn a reasonable rate of return on their investments necessary to provide a quality service at affordable prices to electricity consumers.

§3. The Rural Electrification Agency

138. REA is a semi-autonomous body established in accordance with section 62 of the Electricity Act. REA was established by the Minister of Energy and Mineral Development through Statutory Instrument 2001 no. 75, to operationalize Government's Rural Electrification (RE) function under a public-private partnership. REA is the Secretariat of the Rural Electrification Board (REB), which manages the Rural Electrification Fund (REF). The REB is the governing body of the REA and provides subsidies to support RE projects.

§4. The Uganda Electricity Transmission Company Limited

139. UETCL was incorporated as a limited liability company in 2001 in accordance with the Companies Act Cap 110 (as repealed by the Companies Act 2012) and the Public Enterprise Reform and Divestiture Act. The existence of UETCL is provided for in the Electricity Act Cap 145, which provided for unbundling the vertically integrated UEB into successor Companies and establishment of the ERA. Among its other licences, the UETCL is licensed to: construct, own and operate installations for high-voltage transmission of electricity; coordinate the power supply system to obtain instantaneous balance between the generation and consumption of electricity; and purchase power to provide continuous and economic supply of electricity to meet the load requirement for customers served directly or indirectly from high-voltage transmission grid (HVTG) facilities.

§5. Uganda Electricity Distribution Company Limited

140. UEDCL is a limited liability company incorporated in Uganda under the Companies Act and started operations on 1 April 2001. UEDCL owns the distribution infrastructure operating at 33 kV and below. It is responsible for the retail of electricity, including metering and billing of consumers. UEDCL buys bulk power from UETCL in accordance with the terms set in a Power Purchase Agreement. UEDCL granted a concession (2005–2024) to Umeme (a venture by Eskom and Globeleq) to manage and operate the national distribution grid. Besides Umeme, ERA issued licences to new electricity distribution companies, and the total number of distribution companies now stands at eight.

The distribution companies are:

(i) Umeme Limited,
(ii) West Nile Rural Electrification Company (WENRECo),
(iii) Uganda Electricity Distribution Company Limited (UEDCL),
(iv) Bundibugyo Electricity Cooperative Society (BECS),
(v) Kyegegwa Rural Energy Cooperative Society (KRECS),
(vi) Pader-Abim Community Multi-Purpose Electric Cooperative Society (PACMECS),
(vii) Kilembe Investments Limited (KIL), and
(viii) Kalangala Infrastructure Services Limited (KIS).

The above-mentioned companies are operating in various regions of the country.

§6. Uganda Electricity Generation Company Limited

141. UEGCL is a corporate body incorporated under the Companies Act and in conformity with the Electricity Act 1999. The company was incorporated in March 2001 to operate and maintain the formerly UEB's Generation Stations at Nalubaale and Kiira Power Stations. This included UEB in accordance with the Public Enterprise Reform and Divestiture Act. In November 2002, Nalubaale and Kiira were re-privatized through a long-term concession of twenty years with Eskom Enterprises (U) Ltd. The Objectives of UEGCL have since expanded to include project development. They also include the development of Hydro Power Stations and other renewable energy projects. In this regard, the company is the implementing agency of the GoU for the 183 MW Isimba and 600 MW Karuma Hydro Power Projects and Associated Transmission Lines and Substations with the mandate to deliver the projects within the cost, time and specified quality. UEGCL is also developing other small Hydro Power stations and renewable energy plants, which include the 44 MW Muzizi Hydro Power Station.

§7. UMEME

142. Umeme was formed in 2004 when the GoU leased the UEDCL to a consortium belonging to Globeleq (56%), a subsidiary of the Commonwealth Development Corporation of the United Kingdom, and Eskom of South Africa (44%). It is the largest energy distributor in Uganda, distributing about 97% of all electricity used in the country. The shares of the stock of the company are listed on the Uganda Securities Exchange (USE) and are cross-listed on the Nairobi Stock Exchange (NSE). It operates as a private company 'concession' granted by the government. The concession agreements have been amended a couple of times to reflect the changing business environment and also, to facilitate improvements in performance. The agreements set out terms, conditions and obligations of the parties to the different contracts that cover the following aspects:

- Lease and Assignment Agreement (LAA) between Umeme and UEDCL grants Umeme (as agent) a leasehold interest in the distribution network and in land, property and equipment owned by UEDCL (principal) and to be used to distribute electricity to consumers in Uganda. The agreement has a term of 20 years from the transfer date of 1 March 2005. The agreement, among others, provides conditions under which are included the Umeme received 'possession of the assets under the concession asset but not ownership' and thus has the exclusive right to use, maintain and retire the distribution network assets and related systems and has to retransfer the assets back to UEDCL after twenty years unless the contract is terminated before that date.
- The power sales agreement between Umeme and UETCL provides for the sale and the bulk supply by UETCL of electricity to Umeme for on-sale over a period of 20 years. Of interest to the performance of Umeme is that the agreement obligates Umeme to purchase power from a single buyer while granting rights to Umeme and placing limits on bulk supply tariffs and payment obligations that protect Umeme's revenues – for example, rights to withhold payments or offset revenues due to UETCL relating to the bulk supply tariff (BST).
- The support agreement between Umeme and the government (represented by the Ministry of Finance as the principal) stipulates that government support and obligation to pay Umeme for energy arrears not covered by government entities so as to keep the company financially viable and government commitment and obligation to pay a buy-out amount in the event of contract termination resulting from either political, regulatory or early termination by government or at the end of the concession. Specifically, the payment must be made in dollars not later than 270

days following the receipt or issuance of any termination notice or 90 days following the final resolution of any dispute. In case of natural termination of the concession, the government is obligated to pay the buy-out amount not later than 30 days following the last day of the concession term. There have been public concerns that the buy-out amount condition is steep for a government that is persistently struggling to finance its growing budget and a perception that government is increasingly beholden to Umeme since it is not in a position to pay.

- Licences for the Supply and Distribution of Electricity within a defined geographic area (1 km off the existing grid) in specific towns of Uganda subject to certain conditions.

143. In all four of the above licences, Umeme is contracted as the agent by the respective institutions – principals on behalf of the GoU, to raise funding and to deliver quality electricity services to customers.

§8. Electricity Disputes Tribunal

144. Electricity Disputes Tribunal (EDT) was established by the Electricity Act 1999 Part XIII as a body concerned with the arbitration of cases in the electricity sector. Any stakeholder, who may not be satisfied with ERA's decisions, can appeal to the tribunal. The tribunal is at liberty to hear and determine all matters referred to it relating to the electricity sector. However, such jurisdiction does not include a trial of any criminal offence committed under the law or the hearing of any dispute that a licensee and any other party may have agreed to settle in accordance with the agreement binding them. In the exercise of its jurisdiction under the Act, the tribunal has all the legal authority of the High Court. Persons dissatisfied with the decisions of the tribunal can, within thirty days from the pronouncement of the tribunal's decision, appeal such decision to the High Court.

Some of the consumer grievances within the mandate of the tribunal include: violations of the rights of electricity consumers; trespass to private property without compensation by agents of Umeme; denial of access to affordable and reliable electricity; delay in allotment/release of power connection; reduction/addition in load (power surges); loss due to voltage fluctuations/power cuts/ interrupted/inadequate power supply; discriminative load-shedding patterns; restoration of connection; complaints regarding refunds; reasonableness of service line charges; illegal disconnection; theft or unauthorized load connection.

§9. The Petroleum Authority of Uganda

145. The Petroleum Authority of Uganda (PAU) is a statutory body established under the Petroleum (Exploration, Development and Production) Act 2013. Its roles and functions of the PAU are described in Part III of the Petroleum (Exploration, Development and Production) Act 2013 and Part II of the Petroleum (Refining, Conversion, Transmission and Midstream Storage) Act 2013, together with section 7.2.4 of the National Oil and Gas Policy. The main function of the PAU is to monitor and regulate the exploration, development and production of petroleum in Uganda. Specifically, it is mandated, among other things, to monitor and regulate petroleum activities including reserve estimation and measurement of the produced oil and gas, advise the Minister in the negotiation of petroleum agreements and in the granting and revocation of licences, assess tail-end production and cessation of petroleum activities and decommission participation in the measurement of petroleum to allow for estimation and assessment of royalty and profit oil or gas due to the State and be responsible for the approval of the exercise, ascertain the cost oil or gas due to licensees, ensure that licensees uphold laws, regulations, rules and contract terms, administer petroleum agreements, ensure optimal levels of recovery of petroleum resources, promote well-planned, executed and cost-efficient operations, ensure optimal utilization of existing and planned facilities, ensure the establishment of a central database of persons involved in petroleum activities, manage petroleum data and provide periodic updates and publication of the status of petroleum activities, take such action as is necessary to enforce the requirements in a licence.

146. The activities that are undertaken by the PAU include the following: reviewing submissions from the licensed oil companies, including reports on geoscience and engineering studies, annual resource reports, annual audit reports and procurement reports, review and approval of budgets and work programmes submitted by the licensed oil companies; monitoring field activities carried out by the licensed oil companies in the field; stakeholder consultations for land to be acquired and used during the development of infrastructure and production phases of the petroleum value chain, participating in developing the legal frameworks, like the Inter-Governmental and Host Government Agreement and the design aspects of the EACOP and regulating the implementation of National Content Development including aspects like employment and training of Ugandans and provision of goods and services by Ugandan enterprises.

147. The role of PAU in promoting the implementation of National Content Development provision of goods and services by Ugandan enterprises was tested in the case of A*ndrew Oluka v. Petroleum Authority of Uganda, Total E&P Uganda & CNOOC Uganda Limited.*[88] The Applicant sought a declaration that the procurement processes that were undertaken by the Respondents in respect of the EACCOP Project, the Tilenga Upstream project and the Kingfisher Development area project were done in contravention of Articles 2, 26, 40 and 244 of the Constitution and all enabling laws providing for national content in the petroleum sector. An injunction was sought to restrain the Respondents from continuing to conduct any further procurements in the petroleum sector which did not comply with national content provisions of the law and a declaration that all business income derived from the procurements under the above-named projects is taxable in Uganda. The Court dismissed the application as an abuse of process for being frivolous and vexatious and for failing to use appropriately available procedures in the oil and gas sector, and not being able to name any human right that was infringed or enforced, and

88. Miscellaneous Cause No. 252 of 2021.

it was not a matter of public interest. It is important to note this case is an indicator that there is awareness in public regarding the implementation of the local content law.

§10. The Petroleum Exploration and Production Department

148. The PEPD operates as one of the technical departments under the MEMD and is mandated to establish the petroleum potential of the country, and is therefore the key lead agency for the Project. In accordance with section 22 (1) of the National Environment Act (NEA), the authority (NEMA) shall, in consultation with the lead agency, be responsible for carrying out audits of all activities that are likely to have significant effects on the environment.

§11. The Uganda National Oil Company

149. Uganda National Oil Company (UNOC) was established under section 42 of the Petroleum (Exploration, Development & Production) Act and section 7 of the Petroleum (Refining, Conversion, Transmission & Midstream Storage) Act, both of 2013. It was incorporated under the Companies Act of 2012 as a limited liability company wholly owned by the GoU. It is a separate commercial entity responsible for state participation in the licences and other related business aspects. UNOC has the mandate to handle the state's commercial interests in the petroleum subsector, manage state participation in petroleum activities, and manage the marketing of the country's share of petroleum received in kind, among others.[89] It is mandated to hold a 15% participating interest as a GoU nominee or on behalf of the State in the nine Petroleum Production Licences covering fields that are planned to be developed as part of the Tilenga and Kingfisher Projects.[90]

§12. The National Environment Management Authority

150. National Environment Management Authority (NEMA) is a semi-autonomous institution established in May 1995 under section 4 of the NEA Cap. 153 (now section 8 of the NEA 2019) as the principal agency in Uganda charged with the responsibility of coordinating, monitoring, regulating and supervising environmental management in Uganda. In the energy context, NEMA is responsible for regulating the impact of energy investments on the environment. NEMA awards certificates of environmental clearance following review and approval of Environmental Audits, ESIA Reports and RAPs.

---

89. PEDP Act ss 42 & 43.
90. UNOC, https://www.unoc.co.ug/upstream/ (Accessed 3 Feb. 2019).

§13. The Directorate of Water Resources Management

151. The Directorate of Water Resources Management (DWRM: This is under the Ministry of Water and Environment and is responsible for managing the water resources of Uganda in an integrated and sustainable manner in order to secure and provide water of adequate quantity and quality for all social and economic needs for the present and the future. It is the body that issues Surface Water Abstraction and Construction Permits to Project Developers involved in developing hydro-power projects. It also issues Water Discharge permits in addition to groundwater abstraction permits.

§14. Uganda Investment Authority

152. Uganda Investment Authority (UIA): This is a semi-autonomous government agency operating in partnership with the private sector and GoU to drive national economic growth and development. It guides investors in the RE sector in all matters of registering their businesses in Uganda.

Part III. Sources of Energy Law

Chapter 1. Policy Framework for Energy in Uganda

§1. Vision 2040

153. Vision 2040 is a long-term national development perspective which aims at achieving a Uganda with a prosperous people, a harmonious nation and a beautiful country. In its mission statement, it intends to achieve 'A Transformed Ugandan Society from a Peasant to a modern and Prosperous Country within 30 years'. It aspires to change the country from a predominantly low-income country to a competitive upper-middle-income country within thirty years, with a per capita income of USD 9,500. It recognizes the opportunities to include, though not limited to, oil and gas, minerals, water resources, tourism and agriculture, among others.

154. The vision acknowledges the commercial viability of oil and gas deposits in the Albertine Graben, whose reserves potential capacity is estimated at 6.5 billion barrels of oil equivalent, of which 1.4 billion barrels are recoverable. From this lies Uganda's hope to spur economic growth, create employment, foster technology transfer and generate revenues for investments. The government shall construct a refinery to enable Uganda to achieve maximum multiplier effect through stimulation and strengthening of the associated secondary and tertiary industries.

155. The government aims to strengthen the policy, legal, institutional and regulatory framework to foster transparency, protect the environment and good governance in the oil and gas sector. Pipeline infrastructure shall be constructed to deliver the refined products to the domestic, regional and international markets. Other infrastructure includes roads leading to the refinery and production areas, railways, airports near refinery areas and appropriate water supply infrastructure. The citizenry shall be supported to take up opportunities through enterprise development, strengthening the private sector associated with the oil and gas industry, capacity building and establishment of local area development fund.

156. Through this vision, the government will transform human resources and build a critical mass of scientists, engineers, and technicians in the oil and gas sector and also ensure that they are equipped through the application of the latest science and technology. A specialized oil and gas research development centre shall then be established. Through this, the economy shall flourish, and development shall be achieved.

§2. Poverty Eradication Action Plan

157. Vision 2040 is the bedrock for development planning in Uganda. From it, a number of development pathways have sprung up, including the National Environment Action Plan (NEAP), Education Sector Investment Plan (ESIP), Health Sector Investment Plan (HSIP), Water Sector Development Plan (WSIP), Road Sector Investment Plan (RSIP), District Environment Action Plan (DEAP) and PEAP.

158. Energy is linked directly or indirectly with all the priority sectors. Access to adequate, affordable and sustainable energy services is necessary to fulfil most development objectives defined in the PEAP, particularly in health, education, transport, agriculture, mining, industrial production and modern means of communication. Directly, energy provides a key input in achieving PEAP pillars 1, 2 and 5. Key productive infrastructure cannot function without energy, just as the quality of human development depends on the availability of modern and efficient energy. Indirectly, energy supports PEAP pillars 3 and 4. It is important to note that the effectiveness of issues of security and governance depends on the level of development of information technology, which must rely on the reliability and development of energy sources.

§3. Uganda's Medium-Term Expenditure Framework

159. The GoU has been operating an MTEF since 1997–1998. The MTEF is a three-year rolling plan that sets out past performance, the budget for the current financial year, and the projected resources for the following two years. The MTEF guides all public expenditure decisions, including the use of resources committed by donors, so that consistency with government priorities can be ensured. Under the MTEF, resources are allocated according to government priorities and on the basis of sectoral Budget Framework Papers (BFP) and Local Government Budget Framework Papers (LGBFP). The BFPs, which are increasingly being developed using a sector-wide approach to planning (SWAP), set out sectoral priorities, sector resource requirements and the sectors' comprehensive development plans.

160. Sectoral BFPs are evaluated by the Poverty Eradication Working Group (PEWG), which scrutinizes the extent to which sectoral plans address key poverty-relevant issues, such as geographical inequality and empowerment. The PEWG is also mandated to scrutinize sectoral BFPs regarding the extent to which they address environmental considerations. In order to take forward this mandate, the PEWG has developed draft guidelines for integrating environmental concerns into BFPs to be used by BFP sector working groups starting with the 2003–2004 budget cycle.

§4. Energy Policy, 2002

161. The energy sector has historically placed emphasis on policies which address the supply of commercial sources of energy. The main goal of the National Energy Policy is to meet the energy needs of the Ugandan population for social and economic development in an environmentally sustainable way; the second objective is to increase access to modern affordable and reliable energy services as a contribution to poverty eradication. On the demand side, the main objective for households and institutions is to provide affordable energy services for households and the community. Basic services, including water supply and sanitation, health, education, public lighting and communication, improve the social welfare of the rural population. The specific objectives for this sector are to: achieve a sustainable level of energy security for low-income households so as to reduce poverty at the household level; improve efficiency in the use of biomass resources, recognize that biomass will remain a dominant source of energy, especially in the rural areas, for the foreseeable future; specifically target provision of energy for productive activities such as rural-based industries in order to directly raise incomes; and sensitize women on energy source and technology choices in order to reduce the labour and health burdens associated with biomass energy use.

162. The policy proposes to develop the use of renewable energy resources on both small and large scales. The strategies for implementing the policy include supporting the dissemination of biomass and other renewable energy technologies (RETs) to increase their positive impact on the energy balance and the environment; facilitating adequate financing schemes for RETs by establishing sustainable financing mechanisms to make them more accessible; ensuring that RET producers and importers ascribe to certified performance and technical standards; promoting geothermal energy development and exploration; and supporting efforts to develop biomass resources in agreement with the Uganda Forestry Policy and the National Forest Plan.[91]

163. The National Energy Policy recognizes the role energy supply improvement in rural areas is likely to play; hence, the need to include biomass in the realms of national energy planning. It also recognizes that wood fuel-harvesting contributes to the degradation of forests as wood reserves are depleted at a rapid rate in many regions, to environmental impacts, and to the health of end-users and the burden of collecting firewood on women and children as a result of increased use of biomass energy. In some parts of the country, wood fuel is now scarce. This could be addressed to some extent through demand-side management, which includes the use of energy-efficient devices and alternative sources. There is insufficient data on the demand and supply of biomass fuels in the country and a lack of awareness

---

91. Wabunoha et al., 'Review of Development Policies, Legislation, and Regional Processes and Frameworks That Affect the Conservation of the Great Apes in the Democratic Republic of Congo, Uganda and Rwanda, A Consultancy Report for the International Gorilla Conservation Programme' (April 2004), 53–54.

about the potential for biomass energy technologies. The policy views the reinforcement of the database on biomass, especially demand, as a major thrust for planning purposes.

164. The policy recognizes the inadequacies within government institutions to plan for and monitor the subsector and to conduct research and development. The energy policy plans to increase private sector participation through the use of smart subsidies, particularly for improvement in efficiency and technology acquisition. Emphasis would be placed on improving the efficiency of biomass use along the whole chain from production to end-use. The energy policy proposes strategies to address demand-side sectors, namely households and institutions, industry and commerce, transport and agriculture.

165. Energy efficiency is the major thrust in demand-side management. In addition, the policy proposes strategies to address the supply subsectors of power, namely: petroleum, biomass and other renewable energy. The major objective of the biomass and other renewable energy strategy is to provide focused support for the development, promotion and use of renewable energy resources for both small- and large-scale applications.

§5. The Renewable Energy Policy 2007

166. The 2007 Renewable Energy (RE) Policy for Uganda aims at making modern renewable energy a substantial part of the national energy consumption. The overall goal of the policy is to increase the use of modern renewable energy from the current 4% to 61% of the total energy consumption by the year 2017. The emphasis on renewable energy is premised on the fact that the ever-increasing cost of fossil fuels makes them too expensive for developing countries like Uganda. The (RE) policy recognizes that electricity access to rural populations and the urban poor requires special packages to make connections and services affordable. The RE policy provides for the establishment of the Rural and Urban poor Electricity Access Programme, which will enhance the ongoing procedures for community schemes, where the cost of connection to the community is subsidized. The Programme will also support the development of independent grids supplied by micro and pico-hydros and biomass gasifiers to be managed by communities and solar PV systems in dispersed remote settlements.

§6. Rural Electrification Strategy and Plan (2001–2010)

167. The Electricity Act of Uganda empowers the Minister responsible for electricity to prepare a sustainable and coordinated RE Strategy and Plan for Uganda for the approval of the Cabinet. The first RE strategy and plan, covering the period 2001–2010, was approved by the Cabinet in February 2001. The primary objective of the RE strategy is to reduce inequalities in access to electricity and the associated activities of social welfare, education, health and income-generating opportunities.

The RE strategy aimed to achieve 2010 a RE rate of 10%, meaning that 480,000 rural consumers, a net increase of 400,000 over the year 2000 figure to be serviced. The RE strategy built on and extended the thinking on RE set out in the Power Sector Restructuring and Privatization Strategy (PSRPS) of June 1999. It provided the rural complement to the privatization of UEB, which, otherwise, would have benefited mainly urban consumers.

168. The RE strategy provides for the establishment of a REA by the Minister of Energy and Mineral Development to carry out the Minister's responsibilities with regard to RE. The REA, together with the system operator, prepares a RE master plan. The master plan, which should be updated every five years, provides information on investment opportunities and potential demand. Regulation of RE projects will be the responsibility of the ERA. However, the regulation of small power projects below 2 MW will be 'light-handed' to avoid the regulatory process becoming an administrative barrier to private sector involvement. The RE strategy also sets up the modality for financing RE projects. The REF provided for in the Electricity Act is the main instrument for achieving equitable regional distribution access to electricity. In order to make RE projects commercially viable and tariffs affordable for a big number of rural communities, the Fund is utilized to buy down investment costs, risks and information barriers to public or private initiatives. The sources of money to the fund include money appropriated by Parliament; any surplus money made from the operations of ERA declared to the Minister of Finance and paid to the Fund under section 27(3) of the Electricity Act, a levy of 5% on transmission bulk purchases of electricity from generation stations; and donations, gifts and loans acceptable to the Minister of Energy and Mineral Development and the Minister responsible for finance. Currently, in place, there is the RE Strategy and Plan, 2013–2022. However, the provisions in the strategy mainly focus on matters related to RE design and construction implementation. The strategy and plan do not provide for Environment, Health & Safety (EHS) standards in RE programs. Therefore there is a need to provide for EHS standards/requirements in the RE Strategy and Plan as one of the ways of making sure that there is clear management commitment and visibility as far as EHS matters are concerned.

§7. Plan for Development of Uganda's Biomass Energy Strategy

169. This plan attempts to synchronize the energy strategies in the energy policy, the National Forest Plan and the National Environment Plan. The plan addresses elements relating to the institutional framework, human resource capacity, mobilization of financial resources and information accessibility. It is envisaged that this plan will be the basis for further development of a National Biomass Energy Strategy (NBES). An ideal biomass energy strategy should ensure that resources are used without negative social, economic and environmental consequences. This requires balancing the supply and demand of biomass energy. While the energy sector is responsible for energy supply and demand, a number of other sectors are involved in biomass energy issues, including forestry, agriculture, environment, industry, health, population, gender and education. The major objective of this initiative is to synchronize and build on the strategies from different sectors that address biomass energy demand and ensure that stakeholders in the subsector play roles based on their comparative advantage in formulating and implementing the biomass energy strategy.

170. A sustainable biomass energy strategy entails balancing supply with demand. Both supply-side and demand-side options can be implemented, and the order of priority depends on effectiveness in meeting the objective and on financial and human resource limitations. Information on demand, as well as on available biomass for energy, is a crucial part of the strategy. Projections of supply and demand derived using baseline data are useful in the selection and prioritization of the options. The national development priorities are used as overall guiding principles in prioritization. The ranking of an option is based on pre-structured criteria which take into account the various aspects of sustainability and prevailing limitations in implementing the option.

§8. The National Water Policy, 1995

171. The Water Policy, the Water Action Plan, 1995, and the Water Act now form a coherent framework for the management, protection and use of the nation's vital water resources. The overall water policy objective is to manage and develop the water resources of Uganda in an integrated and sustainable manner so as to secure and provide water of adequate quantity and quality for all social and economic needs with the full participation of all stakeholders so as not to leave the future generations any worse off than ourselves. The policy introduces an integrated, multi-sectoral approach to water resources management in the prevailing socioeconomic context. It emphasizes the importance of: (i) treating water as an economic, social and environmental good; (ii) relying on markets and pricing to determine water allocation among various sectors and user groups; (iii) involving the beneficiaries and the private sector in managing water at the lowest appropriate level; and (iv) recognizing that water is a finite resource that contributes to economic development and supports natural ecosystems.

172. Based on the government's overall policy of good neighbourliness and promotion of regional cooperation for optimal resource use, the policy principles adhered, in the regional context, to the accepted principles of international law on the use of shared water resources, without causing appreciable harm to other users. This policy takes into account economic liberalization, privatization and decentralization reforms. The policy objective is to sustainably manage and develop water resources in an integrated and sustainable manner so as to secure and provide water of adequate quantity and quality for all social and economic needs of the present and future generations with full participation of the stakeholders. It sets out water supply and sanitation policies as well as sustainable provision of accessible clean, safe water and hygienic sanitation. The advantage of the policy is that the principles of this policy are contained in the Water Act.

§9. Uganda Forestry Policy, 2001

173. The objective of the Uganda Forestry Policy is to establish an integrated forest sector that achieves sustainable increases in the economic, social and environmental benefits from forests and trees by the people of Uganda, especially the poor and vulnerable. The policy provides for the protection of Permanent Forest Estate (PFE) under government trusteeship and the development and sustainable management of natural forests on private land. This is aimed at promoting profitable and productive forests. The policy provides a wider cross-section of stakeholders' participation in the management of the forest estate. This includes local government, the private sector, local communities and farmers in the conservation and sustainable use of forest biodiversity. The policy supports conservation initiatives in forests with high biodiversity values; promotes collaboration between sectoral institutions concerned with biodiversity conservation; promotes sharing benefits derived from biodiversity among all stakeholders; addresses conflicts arising from conservation; promotes income generation out of conservation; supports capacity building to enhance knowledge on forest biodiversity, its management and potential use in future; supports the integration and coordination of methods of forest genetic and species conservation.

§10. National Environment Action Plan (NEAP), 1995

174. The environmental policy and the NEAP address all natural resources. The energy sector objective is 'to meet national energy needs through increased use of hydropower, improved efficiency of energy use, increased use of alternative energy sources, increased production of (plantation and on-farm) trees and promotion of exploration and production of fossil fuels'. The strategies outlined to achieve this objective include acquiring or developing, testing and disseminating appropriate alternative energy technologies; providing incentives (smart subsidies) for private and institutional wood fuel plantations; encouraging the private sector to establish energy plantations.

§11. National Oil and Gas Policy for Uganda, 2008

175. The National Oil and Gas policy aims at achieving the exploitation and utilization of oil and gas in a manner that contributes to poverty eradication and creating durable and sustainable social and economic capacity for the country. The objectives of the policy include national participation in the petroleum and gas industry, nature conservation and the use of revenues to create lasting value for the entire nation. This policy is intended to guide the development of Uganda's emerging Oil and Gas sector following the discovery of commercial petroleum resources in 2006. It supersedes the Energy Policy (2002) for Uganda in matters of exploration, development, production and utilization of the country's oil and gas resources. The policy provides for the administration, regulation and management of upstream petroleum and presents a basis for regulating and investing in the midstream petroleum subsectors. The policy details the production of oil and how the money from oil will be shared. It provides for the creation of institutions which will manage the oil resource and ensure that the oil revenues are used for developing social infrastructure. This calls for strategies to integrate oil revenues into capital investments in national and regional infrastructure development and basic services. Protection of the environment and conservation of biodiversity, public participation, transparency and accountability, among others, are named as the guiding policy principles.

176. The policy stresses that creation of lasting benefits shall include the use of oil and gas resources to develop durable and competitive competencies through education and infrastructure development, together with financial and social capital, which is useful beyond the life of oil and gas. The policy further avers that the activities of the current generation shall not put a burden on future generations, especially with regard to the depletion of non-renewable resources. These resources shall, therefore, also be used to provide for intergenerational equity. Sustainable resource management, as opposed to accelerated revenue generation, will, among other things, contribute to creating lasting benefits for Ugandan society.

§12. Oil and Gas Revenue Management Policy, 2012

177. The 2008 National Oil and Gas Policy required that an appropriate framework be put in place to aid the sustainable management of oil and gas revenues, and the Oil and Gas Revenue Policy was developed in 2012 for that purpose. This policy provides details on how the anticipated revenues shall be managed and integrated into the existing government systems with a view to mitigating the overall impact of these revenues on the economy. The policy requires the highest standards of transparency and accountability in the management of oil and gas revenues and gives the institutional and governance structures to be used to achieve this. Lastly, to promote harmony and social cohesion, the policy provides a mechanism for the sharing of royalty revenues with the local governments within the oil-producing region.

§13. National Climate Change Policy, 2015

178. The overarching objective of the policy is to ensure that all stakeholders address climate change impacts and their causes through appropriate measures while promoting sustainable development and a green economy. Specifically, it aims at identifying and promoting common policy priorities to address climate change, adaptation policy responses, promoting mitigation policy responses and monitoring detection, attribution and prediction of climate change in Uganda. It also aims at supporting the integration of climate change issues into planning, decision-making and investments in all sectors and trans-sectoral themes through appropriate institutional arrangements and legal framework and facilitating the mobilization of financial resources to address climate change in Uganda.

179. The goal of the policy is to ensure a harmonized and coordinated approach towards a climate-resilient and low-carbon development path for sustainable development in Uganda. The overarching objective of the policy is to ensure that all stakeholders address climate change impacts and their causes through appropriate measures while promoting sustainable development and a green economy.

180. The adaptation Policy Priorities are relevant to the energy sector. These include forestry to ensure sustainable management of forestry resources so that they can continue to provide global services, including mitigating climate change while supporting the sustainable development needs of communities and the country and energy to promote sustainable energy access and utilization as a means of sustainable development in the face of uncertainties related to climate change.

181. The mitigation Policy Priorities that are relevant to the energy sector are as follows: (a) In Forestry by protecting and promoting carbon sinks by continuing and stepping up efforts targeted at effective forest management and making a deliberate departure from 'business as usual' by formulating sectoral policies that address issues associated with increased unit productivity in plantation forestry. (b) Promoting and developing afforestation and reforestation programmes in non-forested areas and intensifying afforestation and reforestation efforts in other areas. (c) In land Use by promoting and enforcing urban and rural planning of settlements and Control and monitoring land development and other land-use changes in a sustainable manner so as to better manage GHG sources and sink, Reduced Emissions from Deforestation and Forest Degradation+ (REDD+) and continue to actively promote joint REDD+ efforts involving the public and private sectors. (d) Wetlands by promoting a balance between conservation and sustainable use of wetlands to reduce GHG emissions. (e) In agriculture, by mainstreaming climate change mitigation issues, promote and improve the management of natural resources in order to ensure resilient, productive and sustainable agricultural systems with reduced GHG emissions. (f) Energy Generation by supporting and accelerating the implementation of the Renewable Energy Policy (REP) in order to promote and develop new clean energy technologies and reduce GHG. (g) Energy Utilization by promoting conservation and efficient utilization of energy to reduce GHG emissions, especially at consumer levels (industries, households, commercial and institutional buildings), encouraging the use of alternative fuels instead of heavily relying on biomass. (h) Transport by promoting the development, approval and effective implementation of a long-term national transport policy and plan that will take GHG mitigation concerns into account, assessing the effect of a gradual shift to the use of less carbon-intensive fuels (including CNG, ethanol and LPG) in vehicles instead of relying heavily on gasoline and diesel fuels, promoting modes of transport that take into account GHG emission reduction. (i) Waste Management Promote sustainable use of solid and liquid wastes for energy generation and other uses, such as fertilizers (after sorting). (j) Industrial Sector by promoting cleaner production processes in industries to contain the increase in GHG emissions. (k) Cross-cutting Priorities: Technology transfer and the large-scale diffusion of clean, low-carbon technologies put in place functioning institutions that can manage and coordinate issues related to the transfer, deployment and diffusion of technology, including the promotion of the capacity development necessary to support the implementation of clean and low-carbon technologies and encourage technological development to address the problem of climate change in sectors of economic development with high emissions.

182. The priority for the energy sector is to promote sustainable energy access and utilization as a means of sustainable development in the face of uncertainties related to climate change. The specific strategies for tackling this sectoral policy priority will include the following:

(i) Promote and participate in water resource regulation so as to ensure the availability of water for hydropower production;
(ii) Promote and participate in water catchment protection as part of hydroelectric power infrastructure development;
(iii) Diversify energy sources by promoting the use of alternative renewable energy sources (such as solar, biomass, mini-hydro, geothermal and wind) that are less sensitive to climate change;
(iv) Promote energy-efficient firewood cook stoves and solar and LPG cookers;
(v) Conduct research to determine the potential impacts of climate change elements like rainstorms on the country's power supply chain.

Chapter 2. Legal Framework for Energy in Uganda

§1. The Constitution of the Republic of Uganda 1995, as Amended

183. The Constitution, as the supreme law, provides the legal and regulatory framework in the country. It provides for all aspects pertaining to land, the environment and other related aspects. Objective XXVII (iii) provides a duty for the state to promote and implement energy policies that ensure that people's basic needs and those of the environment are met, thus laying the foundation for sustainable energy development.

184. Article 244 of the Constitution of Uganda vests the ownership and control of minerals and petroleum in the Government on behalf of the citizens of Uganda. The Government therefore holds all resources in trust for the people of Uganda. The Constitution also empowers Parliament to make laws regulating the exploration and exploitation of minerals and petroleum.

§2. The Petroleum (Exploration, Development and Production) Act 2013

185. The Act operationalizes Article 244 of the Constitution and the National Oil and Gas Policy of Uganda. Section 4 of the Act vests petroleum resources in the Government on behalf of the people. The Act seeks to establish institutions to manage petroleum resources and regulate petroleum activities, including licensing, exploration, development, production and decommissioning.

186. According to section 66 of the Act, when a discovery is made, the licensee is required to notify the Government and submit a technical evaluation. The licensed Oil Company appraises the discovery and determines the extent of the discovery and the characteristics of the crude oil therein by drilling an additional well and/or undertaking well-testing. Following the completion of appraisal and interpretation of the data acquired during appraisal, the company applies for a production licence and this application is supported by a Field Development Plan (FDP), which details how the company intends to produce and transport the petroleum in the discovery; and a Petroleum Reservoir Report (PRR) that describes the technical understanding of the reservoir below the surface. These reports are reviewed by Government and discussed with the company until an agreement is reached and a production licence is issued. The company then prepares the field for production by drilling injection and production wells and also putting in place other surface facilities for production and processing of crude oil.

187. The Act has three regulations made there under:

(1) The Petroleum (Exploration, Development and Production) Regulations 2016: The regulations operationalize requirements enabled by the Petroleum (Exploration, Development and Production) Act 2013.

(2) The Petroleum (Exploration, Development and Production) (Health, Safety and Environment (HSE)) Regulations 2016: The regulations define requirements pertinent to management of health safety and environment in upstream oil and gas operations. Requirements are provided for risk assessment and management; occupational health and safety; accident prevention; community health and safety; occupational hazards; electrical installations; working environment; safety appliances, equipment materials, devices and clothing; fire and explosion protection; emergency preparedness; safety requirements for plants and equipment; medical facilities and first aid services; and incident handling, investigation, recording and reporting.

(3) The Petroleum (Exploration, Development and Production) (National Content) Regulations 2016:

These regulations promote the development of capacity within Uganda for the provision of goods and services in the oil and gas sector. Among other stipulations, the regulations require licence holders to submit procurement forecasts, prioritize Ugandans during procurement of goods and services, and submit plans for training and recruitment of Ugandans.

Under Regulation 5, PAU is required to supervise, coordinate and monitor the development of national content in petroleum activities, develop and operate the national content evaluation system for licensees, operators, contractors and subcontractors and assist Ugandan companies, Ugandan citizens and registered entities to develop their capabilities and capacities to further the development of national content in petroleum activities.

Regulation 7 requires the licensee, within twelve months after the grant of a licence, to submit to the PAU a national content programme stating proposals for the employment and training of Ugandans, the required quality, health, safety and environment standards for goods and services to be procured, the transfer of technology, knowledge and skills to Ugandan companies.

Regulation 10 requires every licensee, operator, contractor and subcontractor to reserve the contracts for goods and services specified in the Schedule to be supplied by Ugandan companies, Ugandan citizens and registered entities. Regulation 11 requires PAU to develop a national supplier database for petroleum activities. It shall publish the list of Ugandan companies, Ugandan citizens and registered entities that are qualified to provide goods, works and services for petroleum activities in the national supplier database by 31 December of each year.

Under Regulation 13, national content shall form part of the bid evaluation criteria, and in all circumstances, national content shall be allocated at least 10% of the total evaluation score, which shall be rated wholly or substantially on employment and training of Ugandan citizens, utilization of local goods and services and the proposals for technology transfer maintain an office in a community in Uganda where the licensee has significant activities.

Regulation 15 requires that all contracts whose total budget exceeds USD 1,000,000 and are to be executed in Uganda shall contain a labour clause mandating the use of a minimum percentage of Ugandan labour in specific categories as may be stipulated by the Authority.

Regulation 16 requires the licensee shall to develop and submit to the Authority for approval a transparent policy and plan for the training and employment of Ugandans, specifying the required minimum qualifications. That Ugandan citizens shall be given priority for employment in any petroleum activity executed by any licensee and take into consideration the promotion of participation of specific groups, including women, persons with disabilities and persons from different geographical areas or ethnic backgrounds.

Regulation 17 requires that the licensee shall, within twelve months after the grant of a licence by the Minister, and on each subsequent anniversary of that grant, submit to the Authority for approval, a detailed plan for recruitment and training of Ugandan citizens in petroleum activities.

Regulation 18 requires that the licensee shall provide training and knowledge transfer through different means including: (a) internships and attachment of Ugandan citizens in petroleum activities; (b) support of the industry enhancement centre, including health, safety and environment and quality standards; (c) support of existing institutions in Uganda by providing knowledge and technology; (d) mentorships; (e) scholarships; (f) sending resource persons to training institutions for purposes of knowledge and technology transfer; and (g) where necessary, establishing training centres. (4) The licensee shall, upon request by the PAU, provide industrial training for students and support to educational institutions. Regulation 20 requires the licensee shall submit to the PAU for approval a succession plan for all positions not held by Ugandan citizens.

Regulation 21 requires every licensee, contractor or subcontractor shall apply for a recommendation from the Authority prior to making any application for work permits for expatriates to the Government ministry, department or agency responsible for immigration.

Regulation 22 prohibits the licensee, contractor or subcontractor from employing an illegal immigrant.

Regulation 23 requires that every licensee shall submit to the Authority for approval an annual plan satisfactory to the Authority, setting out details and initiatives aimed at promoting the effective transfer of technology, technical know-how and skills relating to petroleum activities from the licensee to the Government of Uganda, Ugandan companies, Ugandan citizens and registered entities.

Regulation 24 requires the licensee, where necessary, to carry out research and development in Uganda or elsewhere as may be approved by the PUA.

Regulation 27 requires the licensee shall communicate its national content policy, programme, targets and procedures to its contractors and subcontractors and ensure that the contracts signed with contractors and subcontractors have the provision for national content. (2) A licensee shall ensure that its contractors and subcontractors comply with the licensee's national content policy.

Regulation 28 provides for Reporting by contractors and subcontractors. (1) A licensee shall ensure that contractors and subcontractors are contractually bound to report on national content compliance to the licensee and, upon request by the Authority, directly to the Authority. (2) A licensee shall report to the Authority, on a quarterly basis, in respect of its monitoring and enforcement of compliance by contractors and subcontractors. (3) A licensee shall allow the Authority or an authorized officer access to their records for the purposes of assessment and verification of national content compliance reported to the licensee or the Authority by the contractor or subcontractor.

Regulation 30 requires that, where possible, the PAU may require a contractor, subcontractor and any other entity engaged in petroleum activities in Uganda to carry out fabrication and welding activities in Uganda.

§3. The Petroleum (Refining, Conversion, Transmission and Midstream Storage) Act 2013

188. The Act establishes the legal framework for sustainable management of the midstream oil and gas sector.

§4. The Petroleum Supply Act of 2003

189. The Act provides for the supervision and monitoring, importation, exportation, transportation, processing, supply, storage, distribution and marketing of petroleum products. This Act and the rules made under it have been repealed or revised:

(i) Petroleum Supply (General) Regulations 2009: The Regulations provide detailed application procedures for petroleum construction permits, obligations of a holder of a permit or license, and quality control of petroleum products;
(ii) The Petroleum (Spirit) (Licensing, Testing and Possession) Rules (149 – 1): These rules provide specifics on the licensing, testing, and storage of petroleum spirit;
(iii) The Petroleum (Spirit) (Conveyance by Road) Rules (149 – 3): These rules provide specifics on licensing and conditions for transporting petroleum spirit by road.

§5. The Public Finance Management Act 2015

190. The Act provides for fiscal and macroeconomic management, among other things, to establish the Petroleum Fund and the collection and deposit of revenues into and the withdrawal of revenue from the Petroleum Fund and for the management of the Petroleum Revenue Investment Reserve and to provide for the financial reports, annual reports and annual plans of the Petroleum Fund and the Petroleum Revenue Investment Reserve.

§6. The East African Crude Oil Pipeline (EACOP) (Special Provisions) Act, No 25, 2021

191. The purpose of the Act is to facilitate the implementation of the East African Crude Oil Pipeline Project in Uganda and to implement the obligations of Uganda under the Intergovernmental Agreement and the Host Government Agreement and for related matters

192. Section 5 makes provisions for the transportation tariff. Thus the tariff to be charged by the project company for the provision of transport and related services in relation to the EACOP system shall be in relation to petroleum produced at the existing Uganda oil fields. The system in relation to which the tariff charged by and paid to the project company is equal to the tariff for petroleum produced at the existing Uganda oil fields reaches 1,046,000,000 barrels, an amount equal to USD 12.77 per barrel and adjusted each year starting from the first anniversary of the date of the first commercial delivery of petroleum at the exit point of the EACOP system at an annual increase of the lower of the US consumer price index and 2% per annum.

193. Section 5 specifies the title to petroleum. The Ugandan State participant shall hold the legal and beneficial ownership of petroleum allocated to it arising from the 15% state participating interest in applicable petroleum agreements at the exit point from the upstream project at Kabaale to enable it to exercise its rights and perform its obligations.

194. Section 8 provides for payment in which the State or the Uganda National Oil Company is a shipper; they may pay the transportation tariff charged by the project company for the provision of transport and related services by way of payment-in-kind, the details of which will be agreed in agreements for the transport of petroleum. The project company may acquire petroleum in connection with any payment-in-kind arrangements agreed with the State or the Uganda National Oil Company, in their capacity as shippers, for the payment of the transport tariff under the agreements for the transport of petroleum and sell the petroleum to other shippers or third party purchasers.

195. Section 11 provides that the EACOP project shall constitute public works, and thus, the Uganda Land Commission (ULC) or other relevant state authority shall grant land rights to enable the project company to undertake all project activities. Where land has been identified for implementation of project activities, compensation of PAPs and acquisition of the land shall be done in accordance with the laws of Uganda and the Host Government Agreement. Each land rights instrument issued to the project company by the relevant state authority shall enable the project company to undertake all the required project activities, including owning the EACOP system and granting security over the land rights and the EACOP system placed, on, under or in the land and be in effect for sixty-six years, or in the case of short-term requirements, for a shorter period of time corresponding to the duration of the relevant project activities.

196. Section 12 requires that the national content regime be applicable to the EACOP project in accordance with the existing legal framework.

197. Section 36 makes provisions for decommissioning. It requires that decommission shall be conducted in accordance the all the relevant laws. The PAU is required to coordinate with the relevant Tanzanian state authority to assist the project company in achieving the harmonization and coordination of the decommissioning plan and the decommissioning activities across Uganda and Tanzania and cooperate and coordinate with the relevant Tanzanian state authority in the process of approving each version of the decommissioning plan submitted by the project company to ensure that a uniform, consistent and harmonized decommissioning plan is approved for the EACOP project. The project company shall be responsible for the costs related to the implementation of the decommissioning plan. The project company, the Minister and the relevant Tanzanian state authority shall together choose from among the financial institutions indicated in the decommissioning plan either a single financial institution to act as escrow agent and account bank or a financial institution to act as escrow agent and a second financial institution to act as account bank, in which case the escrow agent shall hold the decommissioning fund in trust. The project company shall make transfers to the decommissioning fund as follows from the date falling five years after the first oil date and until the date falling ten years after the first oil date; the project company shall make annual transfers to the decommissioning fund in accordance with the Host Government Agreement for decommissioning works approved in the latest decommissioning plan and from the date falling ten years after the first oil date, the project company shall make transfers to the decommissioning fund in accordance with the Host Government Agreement. Under section 42, the project company shall have the right to receive and use electrical power generated from excess associated gas by the upstream project at Tilenga or Kingfisher for pumping, heating and other operational purposes solely in connection with the transport of petroleum through the EACOP system, including the right to construct and operate any necessary infrastructure, in accordance with arrangements jointly agreed with the ERA; and the project company shall have the right to use petroleum in the EACOP system for the purposes of electricity generation and process heating for pumping, heating, terminal operations and other operational purposes solely in connection with the transportation of petroleum through the EACOP system, on terms and conditions to be agreed with the shippers.

198. Section 43 provides that the project company may make excess capacity in the EACOP project's fibre optic network available to third parties on the basis of no cost to the user and no liability for the project company in accordance with the arrangements agreed with the relevant state authority.

199. Section 44 makes provisions for the fiscal regime applicable to the EACOP project. Section 44 and Schedule 2 provide the following fiscal regime: *(a) Corporation Tax*: a ten-year income tax exemption for tariff income earned by the East Africa Crude Oil Company Limited (Project Company) from owning and running the EACOP system. *(b) Capital Gains Tax:* no gain or loss, or deemed gain or loss arising solely as a result of a change in the direct or indirect ownership of the Project Company in respect of the deemed disposal of the assets of the Project Company is to be included in the chargeable income of the Project Company. *(c) Branch Profit Tax:* no branch profits tax is to be imposed on the Project Company on the basis that the Project Company is and remains a resident of Uganda for the duration of the EACOP project. *(d) Disposals of interests in the Project Company by a Project Participant*: a direct or indirect disposal of an interest in the Project Company must be taxed in accordance with Ugandan law and must consider the allocation %age to determine the tax. *(e) Domestic and Foreign Tax Credits:* a domestic tax credit can be offset against any domestic income tax imposed on a project participant, and any excess credit may be refunded on application within sixty days if the domestic tax credit exceeds the total corporate income tax for that year. Further, foreign tax credit can be offset against any foreign income tax, including the foreign equivalent of any withholding tax or branch profits tax, with the excess credit carried forward indefinitely for use against corporate income tax on foreign source income in a subsequent fiscal year. *(f) Exclusion of Part IX A of the Income Tax shall not apply to the Project. (g) Withholding tax on interest payments:* no withholding tax will arise on payments of interest to any other finance party. *(h) Withholding tax on technical services:* payments made to non-residents by the Project Company and level 1 contractors for the supply of technical and other services provided directly and exclusively for the EACOP project will attract a withholding tax of 5%. *(i) Withholding tax on dividends:* No withholding tax shall be imposed on payments of dividends by the Project. *(j) Other Withholding Tax considerations*: no withholding tax should arise on Payments to the Project Company of tariff from owning and operating the EACOP system, the import of goods and Payments for the purchase of an asset, payments for the supply of petroleum for the Payments made, or deemed to be made, by the Ugandan head office to the Tanzanian permanent establishment in connection with project activities; or The amount of any payment allocated to the Tanzanian permanent establishment. *(k) Value Added Tax Considerations:* The supply of transportation and incidental services by the Project Company through the EACOP system be a zero-rated supply. VAT will be imposed on the import of goods and services provided directly and exclusively for the EACOP project by the Project Company, a level 1 contractor or a level 2 contractor. No VAT is imposed on any import, sale for export or export of petroleum; and d. No VAT is imposed on supplies or deemed supplies between the Project Company and the Tanzanian permanent establishment or the Project Company and the United Kingdom permanent establishment. *(l) Import, Customs and Excise Duty:* no customs or import duties are to be imposed on equipment and inputs, and engineering plant, excluding motor vehicles, capital goods and temporary importation of any motor vehicles that are for the direct and exclusive use in the EACOP Project except for motor vehicle registration fees. Further, the customs, import, export or excise duties will not be an economic cost to the EACOP project. *(m) Transit Fee:* no transit fee or any other charge of a similar nature shall be imposed on the EACOP project, the petroleum transported or the sale or export of petroleum. *(n) Stamp Duty*: No stamp duty is chargeable on any instrument of transfer of shares in the Project Company that is incorporated in the United Kingdom. The Act also limits the stamp duty on any transfer or other acquisition of land rights in relation to the EACOP Project to UGX 500,000. The Stamp duty on an instrument entered into by the Project Company as security for any financing agreement or an instrument effecting the transfer, novation, assignment or sub-participation of any interest of a finance party in a financing agreement is limited to UGX 10,000. *(o) National Social Security Fund (NSSF):* The Project Company's level 1 contractors and their respective employees who are not ordinarily resident in Uganda from making contributions to NSSF. *(p) Other taxes and charges*: Local government rates, trade licence fees, investment licences, and fees for the issuance, maintenance or renewal of project authorizations shall not exceed a total of USD 100,000 per calendar year.

§7. The Electricity Amendment Act 2022

200. The Act provides for the generation, transmission, distribution, sale and use of electricity; and licensing and control of activities in the electricity sector. This Act was amended recently by the Electricity Amendment Act No. 4 of 2022. It establishes the ERA, whose functions include issuing licences for the generation, transmission, distribution or sale of electricity and for ownership or operation of transmission systems. Several regulations made thereunder include:

(i) The Electricity (Primary Grid Code) Regulations 2003: The regulations provide the guidelines and procedures for the licensees of the electric power system to operate the Uganda power system.
(ii) The Electricity (Safety Code) Regulations 2003: The regulations establish mandatory safety precautions applicable to electrical systems and to associated plants and apparatus under their ownership or control.
(iii) The Electricity (Installation Permits) Regulations 2019: The regulations require any person or company involved in electricity installation to obtain valid permits issued by the Installations Permits Committee. The permits vary in classes.
(iv) The Electricity (Reporting and Record Keeping) Regulations 2019: The regulations provide for a licensee to keep reports and records relating to the legal, technical, financial, hydrological, environmental and other relevant issues relating to the operation of the licensee.
(v) The Electricity (Quality of Service Code) Regulations 2020: The regulations seek to regulate licensees' activities relating to the generation, transmission, system operation, bulk supply, distribution, sale, import and export of electricity so that those activities are carried out in a fair and reliable manner.
(vi) The Electricity (Isolated Grid Systems) Regulations 2020: The regulations regulate generating stations constructed, owned and operated for commercial purposes of a capacity not exceeding 0.5 MW.
(vii) The Electricity (Approval and Verification of Investments) Regulations 2020: The regulations require approval and verification of all investments of licensees by the Investment Authority.

§8. The Atomic Energy Act 2008

201. The Act regulates the peaceful application of ionizing radiation; establishes the Atomic Energy Council; and provides for the safety and protection of individuals, society and the environment from the dangers of ionizing radiation, among other functions. The Act regulates the handling, use, transportation and disposal of radioactive materials and devices emitting ionizing radiation.

202. The regulation under the Act is the Atomic Energy Regulation 2012, which seeks to specify minimum requirements for the protection of individuals, society and the environment from the dangers resulting from ionizing radiation and provide for the safety and security of radiation sources.

§9. The Explosives Act, Cap 298 and the Explosives Rules, S.I. 298-1

203. This Act and the rules regulate the manufacture, storage, sale, importation, exportation, transportation, and use of explosives in Uganda.

§10. The National Climate Change Act 2021

204. The purpose of the Act is to give the force of law in Uganda to the United Nations Framework Convention on Climate Change, the Kyoto Protocol, and the Paris Agreement; to provide for climate change response measures; to provide for participation in climate change mechanisms; to provide for measuring of emissions, reporting and verification of information; to provide for institutional arrangements for coordinating and implementing climate change response measures; to provide for financing for climate change; and for related matters.

205. Part II of the Act provides climate Change response measures that include developing a Framework Strategy on Climate Change within one year after the commencement of this Act, develop a Framework Strategy on Climate Change for Uganda shall guide Government in planning and budgeting for financing and monitoring of climate change programs and activities.[92] This will be reviewed every five years or earlier as may be deemed necessary.

206. In developing the Framework Strategy, the Department responsible for climate change in the Ministry responsible for climate change shall take into account the available scientific and indigenous knowledge on climate change, the specific resilience and adaptation needs of the vulnerable and marginalized communities, gender and human rights issues, the need to ensure food security, the need to promote sustainable development in Uganda, the loss and damage occasioned by climate change on ecosystems, communities and humankind, the status and trends of the human population in Uganda, the requirements of the NDP relating to climate

92. *Ibid.*, s. 5.

change, the expected outcomes of the implementation of climate change responses and measures and the obligation of Uganda under the Convention, its Protocol and the Agreement.

207. The Framework Strategy on Climate Change shall specify the impacts, risks and risk trends of climate change and the assessment of the impacts, risks and risk trends, specify the mitigation and adaptation priorities to be applied, specify the measures to be adopted to strengthen resilience and to reduce vulnerability to climate change, specify the mechanism for achieving climate-resilient development and low greenhouse gas emissions, and its financing, identify the most vulnerable areas, including the ecosystems and communities without resilience to the impacts of climate change and their variability and extremes, identify the differential impacts of climate change on gender and the vulnerable and marginalized communities, indicate the research and development programmes to be undertaken for enabling the response to climate change, provide for the education, public awareness and training in climate change matters, for all agencies of Government, and the public, provide for the dissemination of information on climate change and specify the plans, policies, programmes and actions of Government for responding to climate change.

208. The Act provides for the National Climate Change Action Plan: (1) The Department shall, within one year after the commencement of this Act and in accordance with the Framework Strategy on Climate Change, develop a National Climate Change Action Plan. (2) The Climate Change Action Plan shall indicate (a) the actions to be undertaken to assess and manage the impacts, risks, risk trends and vulnerability to climate change; (b) the responses, measures and actions to be undertaken for achieving adaptation to and mitigation of climate change; (c) the measures and actions to be undertaken to conserve and enhance sinks and reservoirs of greenhouse gases.

209. Part III of the Act requires Uganda to participate in the climate change mechanisms such as compliance emissions trading mechanisms, voluntary emissions trading mechanisms, non-market approaches referred to in article 6 of the Agreement, cooperative approaches referred to in article 6 of the Agreement; and any other climate change mechanism as may be prescribed by regulations.

210. Part IV makes provisions for measuring emissions, reporting and verifying information. The targeted greenhouse gas emissions, the reductions of those targeted greenhouse gas emissions and the removal of the targeted greenhouse gases from the atmosphere shall be measured or calculated in tonnes of carbon dioxide equivalent. The amount of greenhouse gas emissions and the removal of greenhouse gases for a period shall be determined every two years in accordance with the internationally acceptable reporting practice under the Convention, its Protocol and the Agreement. The net emissions for the period, in relation to the targeted greenhouse gas, means the amount of emissions of that gas for the period, reduced by the amount of removals of that gas for that period. The measurements of the national reference level, the targets, emissions, removals and net emissions shall indicate the different measurements of each lead agency in the national inventory referred to in section 13(1). A lead agency shall develop a baseline of carbon dioxide and other targeted greenhouse gas emissions.

211. Section 22 empowers the Minister responsible for the Environment in consultation with the Minister responsible for finance to provide incentives to persons engaged in implementing response measures for adaptation and mitigation.

212. Section 26 promotes litigation on climate change. Thus a person may apply to the High Court for relief against the Government, an individual or a private entity whose action or omission threatens or is likely to threaten efforts towards adaptation to or mitigation of climate change. The High Court may, in addition to any other orders it may deem appropriate, make orders to prevent, stop or discontinue the act or omission that is the subject of the application, compel the Department, lead agency or any person to take measures to reverse the act or perform the act that was omitted or provide compensation to a person that has suffered loss or damage as a result of the act or omission. The Act further promotes public interest litigation. Thus, a person may apply to the High Court under subsection (1) notwithstanding that person cannot prove that the act or omission of the Department, lead agency, individual or private entity has caused or is likely to cause personal harm or injury to that person or any other person.

§11. The Mining and Minerals Act 2022

213. The Act is aimed at strengthening the administrative structures for the effective management of the mineral subsector, providing for the acquisition, management and dissemination of geological information; regulating the licensing and participation of commercial entities in mining operations, providing for Government participation in mining operations, providing for value addition with a view of promoting local growth by reaping benefits across the whole value chain; to provide for an open, transparent and competitive process of licensing, creating a conducive environment for the promotion of exploitation of Uganda's mineral potential; providing for sustainable mineral marketing strategies by setting up buying and auctioning centres, providing for the formalization of artisanal and small scale mining; to provide for national content development in mining operations; providing for the regulation and management of geothermal resources, providing for efficient and safe mining operations, providing for decommissioning of mining infrastructure providing for payments arising from mining operations and repealing the Mining Act 2003; and for related matters.

214. Section 2 provides that Act applies to all activities, operations and transactions related to the prospecting, exploration, mining, development, exploitation, research and beneficiation of minerals, including the processing, smelting, refining of minerals and trading of mineral substances and the extraction of geothermal resources for direct use.

215. Section 4 requires every person involved in mining and minerals operations or any other person performing functions, duties or powers to give effect to the principles and safeguards of environmental management prescribed under the NEA 2019 and any other written law.

216. Section 9 provides that the entire property in, and control of, all minerals in, on, or under any land or waters in Uganda are and shall be vested in the Government, notwithstanding any right of ownership of or by any person in relation to any land in, on, or under which such minerals are found. In other words, it shall hold mineral rights on behalf of and for the benefit of the people of Uganda.

217. Section 15 provides five types of mineral rights that may be granted. These are: (i) prospecting licence, (ii) exploration licence, (iii) retention licence, (iv) large-scale mining licence, medium-scale mining licence, small-scale mining licence, and (v) artisanal mining licence.

218. Section 21 establishes a Uganda National Mining Company whose functions are: to manage the State's strategic commercial interests in the mineral subsector, to optimize value to its shareholders, to participate in accordance with the terms of mineral agreements in joint ventures in which it holds an interest on behalf of the State, to participate in meetings of the operating committees in furtherance of its participation in the respective joint operating agreements, to study and propose new mining ventures locally and internationally and to undertake the exploration and mining operations in the best interest of the State where private entities are unwilling to do so.

219. Section 27 provides that role of local governments shall be to integrate publicly available mineral deposit information provided by the Directorate into their development plan and participate in the implementation of mining policies, laws and mineral-related activities in collaboration with the Directorate, monitor and regulate the exploitation of minerals in collaboration with the Directorate in a manner prescribed by regulations, create awareness of mining activities within their areas of jurisdiction in collaboration with the Directorate, facilitate dialogue between the local communities or PAPs and mineral rights holders, participate in the resolution of disputes arising from mineral-related operations in collaboration with the Directorate and receive reports and plans of the companies operating in their jurisdiction every six months.

220. Section 28 provides that Minister for mineral development may enter into an agreement that include minimum exploration or mining operations to be carried out and the work plan determined for purposes of such operations, the minimum expenditure in respect of exploration or mining operations, financial obligations, production-sharing arrangements where minerals have been ascertained and quantified, the manner in which exploration or mining operations shall be carried out, the processing of any mineral or group of minerals found, obtained or mined by the holder of a mineral right in the course of exploration or mining operations, the basis on which the market value of any mineral or group of minerals in question may from time to time be determined, project financing and insurance arrangements, environmental management obligations, health and safety obligations, requirements for local content, including the use of local labour and goods, community benefit sharing and community development, including the obligation to conclude community development agreements with the affected communities, the establishment of culturally relevant local dispute resolution mechanisms, resolution of disputes through arbitration mechanisms, the right of the Minister to withdraw or cause to be relinquished portions of the licence area covering land that has been earmarked by Government for a public infrastructure project, at no cost to Government, the protection of the land rights or any customary rights of any of the registered owner, customary owner, lawful occupant or bona fide occupant of the land in the area subject to a mineral right a

221. Section 29 requires the responsible Minister to develop or cause to be developed a model mining agreement or other model agreements as may be entered into by Government under this section which shall be submitted to Cabinet for approval.

222. Section 31 introduces a competitive licensing regime for brownfields (existing mining projects) and retains a first come, first served model for greenfields (new mining projects).

223. Section 94 provides for the establishment of areas for artisanal mining to allow for artisanal operations.

224. Section 105 provides for the application for prospecting licence for geothermal resources for direct use.

225. Section 120 requires a person to acquire a licence from the Minister responsible for Mineral Development to process, smelt, refine, cut, blast, polish or trade in minerals or possess commercial quantities. Other licences required section 123 to include Mineral Processing Licence and Mineral Smelting Licence under section 124.

226. Under 175 rights in waters and wetlands, all rights in wetlands and in the waters of any spring, stream, river, watercourse, pond or lake on or under public land are vested in the Government; and no such wetlands or water shall be obstructed, dammed, diverted, polluted or otherwise interfered with, directly or indirectly, except in accordance with the Water Act, and the NEA 2019.

227. Section 176 provides that every application for a mineral right or licence for beneficiation shall indicate whether the applicant intends to utilize for prospecting, exploration, mining or beneficiation operations any water existing within the boundaries of his or her mineral right or licence for beneficiation, to utilize any natural source of water existing at the site to which mining or beneficiation products are conveyed for washing or treatment and to obtain and convey to the area of his or her mineral right or licence for beneficiation, from any natural water supply outside the boundaries of the mineral right or licence for beneficiation, such specified volume of water as may be required for the relevant operations, to occupy any land that may be required for the construction of a dam, reservoir or pumping station and for the conveyance of such water to the area where the water is utilized, by means of pipes, duets, flumes, furrows or otherwise, and for such conveyance to have a right of passageway or to construct any works necessary for the collection, storage or conveyance of such water.

228. In section 179, all minerals obtained or mined in the course of prospecting, exploration or mining operations shall be subject to the payment of royalties on the gross value of the minerals produced based on the prevailing market price of the minerals at such rates as shall be prescribed by the Minister in collaboration with the Minister responsible for finance by statutory instrument.

229. Section 212 requires a holder of a mineral right, licence or permit to preserve in as far as is possible, the natural environment, minimize and control waste or undue loss of or damage to natural, geological, biological, cultural, or archaeological resources, prevent and where unavoidable, promptly treat pollution and contamination of the environment and take no steps which may unnecessarily or unreasonably restrict or limit further development of the natural resources of the mineral right, licence or permit area or adjacent areas. The holder is also required to put in place measures to prevent pollution from occurring during operations, including by use of the best available techniques and best environmental practices and also take the necessary action to stop further pollution and minimize the impacts of the pollution on human health and the environment, give notice of the pollution to the Minister, the National Environment Authority and any other relevant lead agency in accordance with the NEA 2019, take steps to mitigate any damage or nuisance resulting from the pollution or from measures to counteract it, take steps to clean up and restore the environment as near as possible to its original state, and pay compensation for the damage caused in accordance with the NEA 2019 and any other applicable written law.

230. Section 217 requires a holder of a mineral right, licence or permit who intends to close or abandon the mine or operation or a major part of the mine or to decommission a facility or processing plant shall submit a decommissioning plan to the responsible Minister before the mineral right, licence or permit expires or is surrendered or before the use of a facility is terminated permanently.

231. Section 230 requires a holder of a mineral right, licence or permit to ensure that the mining operations and licensed activities are conducted in a manner that enables a high level of safety to be maintained and further developed in accordance with technological developments, best mining industry practices, the Occupational Health and Safety Act 2006 and any other applicable written law. The holder is also required to identify the hazards and evaluate the risks associated with any work performed in the course of mining operations or activities carried out under the mineral right, licence or permit which constitute a hazard to the health of persons employed for the purposes of that work and the steps that need to be taken to comply with the provisions of this Act and regulations made under this Act; and prevent the exposure of the persons referred to in paragraph to the hazards.

232. Sections 179 and Schedule 2 Royalty from minerals shall be shared as follows: Government – 70% Local Governments – 15%, Sub-county or Town Council – 10% and Owners, lawful occupants or bona fide occupants of land subject to mineral rights – 5%.

§12. Regulatory Framework Concerning Electricity

233. The legal and regulatory framework for the Uganda energy sector is based on the Electricity Act and various regulations and is complemented by a policy framework that includes the Energy policy 2002 and the renewable energy policy, which was completed in 2007.

Chapter 3. The Electricity Amendment Act 2022

234. The Electricity Act was enacted in 1999, amending the previous Electricity Act of 1964. The Act has recently been amended by the Electricity Amendment Act No. 4 of 2022. It provides for the establishment of the ERA and its functions, powers and administration. It also makes provision for the generation, transmission, distribution, sale and use of electricity. It streamlines the licensing and control of activities in the electricity sector and makes provision for plant and equipment and for matters relating to safety. It also liberalizes and introduces competition in the electricity sector. The Act repeals the Electricity Act and provides for a successor company after the UEB.

§1. The Electricity Regulatory Authority

235. Part II of the Act establishes the ERA, which shall be a body corporate with perpetual succession. The authority can acquire property, sue or be sued in its name. It is comprised of five members of high moral character and proven integrity and competence. The members are appointed by the minister. Its membership is professional as the chairperson shall be qualified and experienced in management, economics or the electric power sector, while each of the other members shall be qualified in either engineering in electricity, law, administration and management, finance or economics, energy industry or environmental matters.

236. The Act under section 7 provides for the security of tenure for the members to be five years and eligible for reappointment though they shall not be appointed for more than two terms. Such members are entitled to remuneration in the form of allowances as the minister may, with the approval of the Cabinet, specify in the instrument of appointment. Membership can be terminated upon the resignation of any such member by giving sixty days' notice of their intention to do so. The minister has powers to remove a member from office if they are adjudged bankrupt, they become public officers, members of parliament, a minister or member of a local government council, convicted of an offence involving fraud or dishonesty or sentenced to a term of imprisonment for six months or more by a court of competent jurisdiction, has been absent without leave of the Authority for more than three consecutive meetings of the Authority, where they are permanently incapable of performing their duties as members and where they behave in a manner unbecoming of the office of a member. Such a member shall be notified in writing by the minister and given an opportunity to explain to the minister.

237. The Authority is mandated to do the following as provided for under section 10; issue licences, receive and process applications for licences, prescribe terms and conditions of licences, modify licences, make and enforce directions to ensure compliance with licences to establish a tariff structure and to investigate tariff charges, approve rates of charges, terms and conditions of electricity services, develop and enforce standards for the generation, transmission and distribution of electricity among others. These functions shall be performed in an open and objective, fair and reasonable, non-discriminatory manner and promoting fair competition.

238. The Authority may appoint special committees to inquire and advise it on such matters within the scope of the authority's functions and perform such duties as the Authority may delegate to it. The authority has the discretion to co-opt a person to assist it on any matter if it is satisfied that their qualifications are likely to assist it, and such a person may take part in the Authority's proceedings. ERA shall be independent in the performance of its functions and duties and exercise of its powers and shall not be subject to the direction or control of any person or authority.

§2. The Secretariat and Staff of Authority

239. The Secretariat shall consist of the chief executive officer (CEO) and other staff. Under section 19, the CEO shall be appointed by the Authority from among persons of high standards of integrity and maturity and who have substantial qualifications or experiences in administration, economics, finance, law, management, environment or technical knowledge relating to the electricity industry. The services of the CEO may be terminated by the Authority for abuse of office, misconduct, physical or mental incapacity, mismanagement or incompetence.

240. The Act under section 20 gives the functions of the CEO to include the day-to-day management of the affairs of the Authority and implementation of the policy decisions of the Authority, and control of the staff of the Authority.

§3. Finance of the Authority

241. The Authority's funds shall consist of money appropriated by Parliament for the purposes of the Authority, fees prescribed by the Authority for processing of licence applications, a levy not exceeding 0.3% on the revenues received from generated electric energy, money borrowed by the Authority and grants from government, gifts or donation from other sources acceptable to the minister and the minister responsible for finance.

242. The Authority has the power to open and maintain the operation of the bank accounts under section 24. All money received shall be banked as soon as practicable after being received and only be withdrawn with the Authority's consent. The Authority has the power to borrow money from any source as may be required for meeting its obligations or for the discharge of its functions. The surplus funds may be applied for the payment or discharge of its expenses, obligations or liabilities incurred in connection with the performance of its functions or exercise of its powers under the Act and for the payment of any remuneration or allowances. The funds may also be invested in fixed deposits with a bank approved by the Authority, in treasury bills and securities of the government or in such other manner as may be approved by the Authority after consultation with the minister.

243. The Authority shall keep proper accounts of its income and expenditure and records. A statement of account of the Authority shall be prepared for every financial year in a form approved by the minister responsible for finance and submitted to the Auditor General for auditing. After auditing, the report so produced shall be presented to parliament.

§4. Licensing under the Act

244. This is addressed under part V where the Act creates a requirement for notification of the Authority by a person intending to establish a project for which a licence is required. The notification must be in the prescribed form as provided for under section 29. The notice shall consequently be published in the Gazette and in at least one national newspaper of wide circulation containing a summary of the notice. The Authority shall then invite directly affected parties and affected public agencies to make comments on the notice.

245. Under section 33, an application for a licence is made to the Authority, and the application shall contain the legal and financial status of the applicant, technical and economic description of the project, the planned time of commencement and completion of the construction of the project. The Authority is under a duty to process all applications expeditiously, not later than one hundred days.

246. The Authority shall put into consideration the energy needs of the country, region or community and the impact of the operations of the undertaking on the social, cultural and recreational life of the community, among other things provided for under section 37 of the Act. The grant of a licence can be refused, and in this case, the authority has to give its reasons for refusal to grant the licence. The licence, once granted, can be revoked where it is satisfied that the licensee is not operating in accordance with the terms and conditions of the licence as espoused in section 42 of the Act.

247. The licence terms and conditions can be modified if the benefits of the public interest of such modification significantly exceed the disadvantages of the licensee. Notice before modification has to be given to the licensee. The modification can be initiated either by the authority or by an application from the licensee. The licence shall remain in force for as long as specified in it though it shall not exceed forty years from the date of issue. The licence is renewable by an application to this effect within three years before expiry. The Act prohibits the transfer of a licence without the written consent of the Authority.

248. It is prohibited under the Act for any person to generate, transmit or distribute electricity for the purpose of giving a supply to any premises, sell electricity to any premises or export or import electricity except under the authority of the Act.

§5. Rural Electrifications

249. The government is under an obligation to promote, support, and provide RE programmes. This it does through public and private sector participation as provided for under section 62. Consequently, the minister is mandated to prepare a sustainable and coordinated RE strategy. She/he also plans for the approval of parliament. An annual report has to be submitted to parliament on the progress of this plan.

A fund shall be established known as the 'Electricity Development Fund', and the money shall be administered in accordance with the Act. The minister shall maintain a national RE database to assist in the monitoring of progress and establishment of the targets of RE. There is an REB that oversees the management of the 'Electricity Development Fund' as amended by section 17 of the Act of 2022. The Minister shall lay before Parliament approved annual estimates of revenue and expenditure drawn from the fund in accordance with section 13 of the Public Finance Management Act 2015.

§6. Use of Land for Installations

250. Under section 67, a licensee authorized by the Authority either generally or on a particular occasion may place or maintain electric supply lines over or upon any land. The licensee shall not acquire any more rights than those of the user of the land in question. And they shall do as little damage as possible to the land and to the environment and shall ensure prompt payment of fair and adequate compensation.

251. The Act provides for the giving of thirty days' notice to the ULC or a district land board of the intention to enter upon such land under the control of these authorities. The owner of the land where a licensee has placed an electric supply line may apply to the authority giving convincing reasons to have it altered. Any aggrieved person about the decisions of the authority may, within thirty days after such a decision has been taken, appeal to the tribunal.

252. Compensation under section 70 shall be determined as if the land has been acquired under the Land Act and the Land Acquisition Act. Such a claim for compensation shall be lodged with the authority within one year of the date of the act of the operator which gave rise to the claim. The Act under section 71 further provides for compulsory acquisition of the land. This is if a licensee considers that he or she requires the acquisition of the land or interest in land greater than the right of use necessary for the purpose of providing or maintaining electricity supply lines. The licensee may, with the approval of the authority, request action by the minister responsible for land under this section and the authority shall not unfairly withhold or delay its approval.

§7. Inspection

253. Section 72 is to the effect that every licensee shall, at the end of every financial year, prepare and submit to the authority, in a form prescribed by the authority, a report on the operations and services of the licensee and to the extent to which the conditions of the licence are being followed. The inspectors may be appointed by the authority for the purposes of verifying compliance by a licensee with the Act.

254. The authority may investigate any licensee or system operator who commits any act or omission in breach of fair competition. Any person with a complaint relating to a breach of fair competition against any licensee of the system operator shall lodge it with the authority. Also, any licensee found in breach of fair competition shall pay such amount of compensation to the consumer for any loss caused to him or her, as the authority may determine.

§8. Tariffs

255. The Act provides under section 75 that the tariff structure and terms of supply shall be in accordance with the principles of tariff calculation and terms of supply prescribed by the authority taking into account the licensee's total revenues from tariffs covering all reasonable costs and a reasonable rate of return. Every application for a license shall contain a proposal for the terms of supply and for fixing the tariffs, including total tariff revenues.

256. A licensee shall not, in fixing tariffs and terms of supply, show undue preference or discrimination among customers similarly situated having regard to the place and time of supply, the quantity of electricity supplied, the consumer load and power factor and the purpose for which the supply is taken. The holder of a generation licence shall pay to the district local government, in which the renewable energy-generating station is situated, a royalty agreed upon by the licensee and the district local government, as per section 18 of the Amendment.

§9. Rights and Duties of Consumers

257. Section 76 states that consumers shall comply with safety regulations made by the authority, and whoever fails to do so commits an offence. The licensee is under a duty to supply, but there are exceptions to this in section 79. These include where the supply of electricity is already being given to the premises by another licensee, who is prevented from doing so by circumstances beyond their control or it is not reasonable in the circumstances to do so, among other reasons. Consequently, a person who refuses a supply of electricity by a licensee may make a complaint to the Authority, which shall take such action against the licensee as it deems necessary in accordance with the Act.

§10. Electricity Dispute Tribunal

258. The tribunal is established under section 93 and is to be chaired by a person appointed by the Judicial Service Commission, and such a person must qualify to be a judge of the High Court. Other members shall be appointed by the minister on the recommendation of the Public Service Commission. To be appointed a member of a tribunal, a person should be of high moral character and proven integrity and proven experience in at least one of the following areas:

- technical knowledge either in the generation,
- transmission or distribution of electricity,
- law or administration,
- finance or economic,
- energy industry or environment.

259. The members' tenure of office is five years, as per section 97, but they are eligible for reappointment. A member shall take the Oath of Allegiance and the Judicial Oath before assuming their duties. Termination of membership may be upon resignation of a member by a notice in writing delivered to the minister. The minister may also remove a member from office who is unable to perform the functions of his or her office arising from infirmity of body or mind, misbehaves or conducts themselves in a manner unbecoming of the office of a member of the tribunal and incompetency among other grounds as set out under section 101.

260. The Act requires a member of the tribunal with any interest, pecuniary or otherwise, that could conflict with the proper performance of his or her functions to disclose the interest to the parties to the proceedings and shall not take part in the proceedings. The quorum of the tribunal is three, and the chairperson shall, at all times, preside over the sittings unless he or she is absent, and then the deputy chairperson shall preside over proceedings. The tribunal may seek technical advice from persons whose specialized knowledge or experience may assist it in its proceedings. The tribunal shall, under section 109, have jurisdiction to hear and determine all matters referred to it relating to the electricity sector. In the exercise of its functions, the tribunal shall have the powers of the High Court. Consequently, its judgments and orders shall be executed and enforced in the same manner as those of the High Court. The tribunal has the power to review its judgment and orders upon its own motion or upon application by an aggrieved party. Appeals from the tribunal are addressed to the High Court.

261. A member of the Authority or of a committee is not personally liable for any action done or omitted to be done by them in good faith without negligence for the purpose of carrying into effect the provisions of this Act. This cover extends to the staff as well as long as they act in good faith in the exercise of their duties.

§11. Offences and Penalties

262. Part XII deals with Offences and Penalties. Under section 82, any person who tampers with or adjusts any installation or part of an installation, or manufactures or imports or sells any equipment so as to cause or to be likely to cause harm to human life or damage to any equipment or other property commits an offence and is liable on conviction to a fine not exceeding fifty currency points or to imprisonment for a term not exceeding five years, or both. Any person who, without the consent of the licensee or ERA, affixes or causes to be affixed any advertisement, bill or notice or any paper against or upon or otherwise defaces any building, post or bracket or other equipment or the enclosure thereof used for or in connection with any electrical installation commits an offence and is, on conviction, liable to a fine not exceeding ten currency points. Any person who by any rash or negligent act or omission causes injury or damage to any person or property in respect of any installation or equipment or part thereof commits an offence and is liable on conviction to a fine not exceeding thirty currency points or to imprisonment for a term not exceeding three years, or both. Any person who damages any meter or other instrument used on or in connection with any licensed installation for recording the output or consumption of energy commits an offence and is liable on conviction to a fine not exceeding twenty currency points or to imprisonment for a term not exceeding two years, or both.

263. Any person who in any manner dishonestly obstructs electrical energy, consumes electrical energy, uses electrical energy, or alters the index of any meter or other instrument used on or in connection with any installation for recording the output or consumption of energy, or prevents any such meter or instrument from duly recording the output or consumption of energy, commits an offence and is liable on conviction to a fine not exceeding thirty currency points or to imprisonment for a term not exceeding three years, or both. Any person who uses, works or operates, or permits to be used, worked or operated any installation commits an offence and is liable on conviction to a fine not exceeding 300 currency points and to a further fine not exceeding five currency points for every day or part of a day during which the offence continues after conviction.

264. Any person who supplies energy from an installation to or for the use of any person commits an offence and is liable on conviction to a fine not exceeding 200 currency points and to a further fine not exceeding five currency points for every day or part of a day during which the offence continues after conviction.

265. Section 83 is to the effect that a licensee who without lawful excuse fails to comply with any term or condition of the licence commits an offence and is liable, on conviction, to a fine not exceeding ten thousand currency points and in the case of a continuing contravention, to an additional fine of five hundred currency points for every day or part of a day during which the offence continues. Where an offence committed by a body corporate is proved to have been committed with the consent or connivance of, or to be attributable to any neglect on the part of a director, manager, secretary or other similar officer of the body corporate or any person who was purporting to act in any such capacity, he or she, as well as the body corporate, commits that offence and is liable to be prosecuted and punished accordingly. Where the authority is satisfied that a licensee: (a) has contravened or is contravening any term or condition of a licence; or (b) has failed or is failing to achieve any standard of performance prescribed under this Act, regulations or a licence, the authority may impose on the licensee a fine not exceeding five thousand currency points as per section 83B of the amendment of 2022. Any unauthorized line or work may, after conviction of the licensee, be removed by order of ERA, and if the order is not complied with, the reasonable costs of removal may be recovered from the licensee. A person who, negligently and without lawful authority, extinguishes or damages any public lamp or defaces any post, bracket or other means of support of a public lamp commits an offence and is liable on conviction to a fine not exceeding twenty thousand currency points or imprisonment not exceeding ten years or both under section 326 of the Act of 2022: (1) A person commits an offence when they: (a) cuts, removes, takes away or transfers any electric supply line, material, meter or public lamp from a tower, pole or any other installation or site where it may be stored or situated including during transportation, without the consent of the licensee or the owner; (b) stores or otherwise keeps in his or her premises, any electric supply line, material, meter or public lamp without the consent of the licensee or owner; (c) moves from one place to another any electric supply line, material, meter or public lamp without the consent of the licensee or owner; (d) without authorization connects any meter, indicator or apparatus with any electric supply line through which electricity is supplied by a licensee or disconnects a meter, indicator or apparatus from any electric line; (e) without authorization reconnects any meter, indicator or apparatus with any electric supply line or other works being the property of a licensee when the electric supply line has been cut or disconnected; (f) lays or causes to be laid or connects up any works for the purpose of communicating with any other works belonging to a licensee; or (g) damages any meter, indicator, or apparatus belonging to a licensee or alters the index of any meter, indicator or apparatus or prevents any meter, indicator or apparatus from duly registering. (2) A person who commits an offence under subsection (1) is liable, on conviction, to a fine not exceeding fifty thousand currency points or imprisonment not exceeding twelve years or both. (3) A person convicted of a subsequent offence under this section is liable to a fine not exceeding one hundred thousand currency points or imprisonment not exceeding fifteen years or both. (4) A person who receives stolen electric supply lines or materials knowing or having reason to believe the same to be stolen property, commits an offence and is liable, on conviction, to a fine not exceeding fifty thousand currency points or imprisonment not exceeding fifteen years or both.

266. It is also an offence to wilfully or negligently cause energy to be diverted from its proper course or to be wasted; or break, throw down, cause to fall or damage any supply line, post, pole, or other equipment, installation or any part thereof, as the case may be, connected with the supply of energy, the culprit is liable on conviction to a fine of twenty thousand currency points or imprisonment not exceeding ten years or both this is provided for under section 24 of the Electricity Act as amended.

The new Act further inserts an offence under section 86A and provides that (1) A person who (a) taps, makes or causes to be made any connection with overhead, underground or underwater lines or cables or service wires or service facilities of a licensee; (b) tampers with a meter, installs or uses a current reversing transformer, loop connection or other device or method which interferes with accurate or proper registration, calibration or metering of electric current; or (c) damages or destroys an electricity meter, apparatus, equipment or wire or causes or allows any of them to be so damaged or destroyed as to interfere with the proper or accurate metering of electricity, to abstract, consume or use electricity, commits an offence and is liable, on conviction, to a fine not exceeding twenty thousand currency points or imprisonment not exceeding ten years or both.

No person should, without the lawful permission of ERA or the licensee, as the case may be, undertake any work or engage in any activity in the vicinity of any electrical installation or part of the installation in a manner likely to interfere with any electrical installation or to cause danger to any person or property. Any person who contravenes this provision commits an offence and is liable on conviction to a fine not exceeding twenty currency points or to imprisonment for a term not exceeding two years, or both. No person should install any electrical wiring or extension to existing wiring on any premises without first obtaining an installation permit issued by ERA:

> 89. General penalty. A person convicted of an offence under this Act for which no penalty is expressly provided is on conviction, liable to a fine not exceeding fifty thousand currency points or imprisonment not exceeding twelve years or both and in case of a continuing offence, to a fine not exceeding five hundred currency points for every day or part of a day during which the offence continues.

Section 90 provides that a person convicted of an offence against the Electricity Act for which no penalty is expressly provided is, on conviction, liable to a fine not exceeding ten currency points and in case of the continuation of the offence to a fine not exceeding one currency point for every day or part of a day during which the offence continues after conviction.

267. Any person who removes, destroys or damages, whether wilfully or otherwise, any installation or any part of an installation or a public lamp, post, bracket or other means of support of a public lamp, or other instrument used in connection with any installation for recording the output or consumption of energy is, in addition to any penalty to which he or she may be liable under the Electricity Act, liable to pay full compensation for the damage he or she has done and the compensation is recoverable by civil action or suit before any court.

268. A person who knowingly provides false or incorrect information to the Authority commits an offence. A person convicted of an offence may be held liable for any loss or damage caused by the offence and may be ordered by the court, in addition to any penalty imposed by the court for the offence, to pay an amount of compensation for the damage. Such an order of court may be enforced as if it were a judgment in a civil action or suit before a court.

269. The new Act protects persons who are members of the tribunal or employees of the tribunal in respect of any act done or omitted to be done in good faith in the discharge of any function under this Act from prosecution or any proceedings regarding the same (section 112A).

270. Besides the Electricity Act, which is the major legislation on electricity in Uganda, there are other legislations of importance which are as follows:

- The Electricity (Primary Grid Code) Regulations. SI No. 24 of 2003,
- The Electricity (Safety Code) Regulations. SI No. 22 of 2003,
- The Electricity (Tariff Code) Regulations. SI No. 23 of 2003,
- The Electricity (Licence Fees) Regulations SI No. 20 of 2003,
- The Electricity (Licence Fees) (Amendment) Regulations SI No. 3 of 2014,
- The Electricity (Installation Permits) Regulations 2019,
- The Electricity (Reporting and Record Keeping) Regulations 2019,
- The Electricity (Quality of Service Code) Regulations 2020,
- The Electricity (Isolated Grid Systems) Regulations 2020, and
- The Electricity (Approval and Verification of Investments) Regulations 2020.

Chapter 4. The Electricity (Installation Permits) Regulations 2019

271. These regulations were made under section 119 of the Electricity Act. The regulations relate to the installation, alteration or repair of any conductor or apparatus or system of wiring in or upon premises, connected or intended to be connected to a supply of electricity. The regulations establish the Installations Permits Committee with a representative constitution of three persons representing the Authority, one person representing a holder of a distribution and supply licences, one representative from the Engineers Registration Board, a representative of the Uganda consumer protection association and one person representing the Vocational Training Institute; with such representation and the power to make its own rules and procedures. Therefore, the committee is competent to execute its duties and functions under the regulations.

272. The regulations under Regulation 10 make mandatory provisions for the requirement of permits, and no person shall practice as an installation person unless they have a permit to this effect. Further, the permits referred to in the regulations are personal, and therefore each person must have their own permit, and the company permit shall not pass as a general permit for the company's employees. Before acquiring a permit, it must be satisfied that the person possesses the qualifications stated in the regulations under Regulation 11, which include any of the following:

- a university degree in a relevant field of study,
- a higher technician diploma,
- an ordinary technician's diploma,
- a master craftsman certificate,
- a craftsman's certificate or intermediate certificate, or any other related technical qualification recognized by the committee and such qualifications shall determine the class of permit to be issued by the committee.

273. The permits are classified as follows under Regulation 14 into class A for carrying out all and any kind of class of electrical installation, including high voltage, B which is for carrying out installation work of medium voltage, C for carrying out installation work not exceeding low voltage of 415 V, D for carrying out installation work not exceeding low voltage of 240 V, and Z which is for specialized fields like switchgear installation, centralized cooling and refrigeration installation of generator sets, solar systems and electrical installation systems and designs.

274. The permits are applied for in writing to the committee, and it is a statutory requirement to exhibit the same at the work premises. Permits are issued upon satisfaction of certain conditions laid down under Regulation 15, which include the applicant being at least 18 years, fit and proper to conduct business, have knowledge of the latest edition of the rules and regulations, they should have suitable premises from which to conduct the business, should have suitable instruments to be able to carry out the recognized tests on the type of installation.

275. The permits are not absolute and can therefore be cancelled or the renewal refused where it is satisfied that the person has failed to comply with any conditions contained in these regulations. The regulations make a requirement for the submission to a licensee of a Completion of Installation report upon completion of any installations.

276. Complaint's mechanism is addressed under Regulation 23, where any person aggrieved by any action of the committee concerning the refusal or cancellation of a permit may appeal to the Tribunal established under the Act. Under Regulation 25, it is an offence to cause or permit any electrical installation work to be carried out on one's premises in contravention of these regulations, and consequently, such person is liable on conviction to a fine not exceeding two hundred currency points or imprisonment not exceeding twenty-four months or both.

Chapter 5. The Electricity (Licence Fees) (Amendment) Regulations SI No. 99 of 2014

277. These Regulations set the licence fees charged by ERA under sections 10 (c), 10 (n) and 119 of the Electricity Act. The fees are detailed in the Schedule to the Regulations and are in four parts, namely:

(1) the Grid (National) Connected systems,
(2) isolated grid systems,
(3) import/export of electricity and application fees,
(4) application and approval fees.

Table 10 and Table 11 present the detailed fee structure under the Regulations and Isolated Grid Systems, respectively.

Table 10 Grid (National) Connected Systems[93]

Generation-Related Licences		
Cat. I	Very Large generators 200 MW	USD 112,500 per 50 MW or part thereof
Cat. II	Large Generators 50 MW and above but less than 200 MW	USD 71,925 per 50 MW or part thereof
Cat. III	Medium generators 10 MW and above but less than 50 MW	USD 12,000 fixed plus USD 3,000 per 10 MW or part thereof
Cat. IV	Small generators up to 0.5 MW and above but less than 10 MW	USD 12,000
Cat. IV	Very small generators	
	(a) 0.5 MW and above but less than 2.0 MW	USD 6,000
	(b) Below 0.5 MW	USD 2,500
Transmission-related licences		
	(a) Transmission	USD 112,500
	(b) System operator	USD 112,500
	(c) Bulk supply	USD 112,500
Distribution-related licences		
Cat. I	Very Large distributors 200 MW or (1,600 GWh) & above	

93. NARUC, 'Ugandan Regulators Draft Isolated Grid System Regulation to Achieve Rural Electrification Goals' (NARUC, 2020). https://www.naruc.org/international/news/ugandan-regulators-draft-isolated-grid-system-regulation-to-achieve-rural-electrification-goals/ (accessed 2 Jan. 2023).

	(a) Distribution	USD 125,000 fixed
	(b) Supply	USD 125,000 plus USD 30,000 per 100 GWh or part thereof.
Cat. II	Large distributors 50 MW or (400 GWh) but less than 200 MW (1600 GWh).	
	Distribution Supply	USD 187,500 fixed USD 187,500 plus USD 30,000 per 100 GWh or part thereof
Cat. III	Medium distributors 10 MW (80 GWh) and above but less than 50 MW (400 GWh)	USD 12,0000 fixed plus USD 6,000 per 10 GWh or part thereof
Cat. IV	Small Distributors 2 MW (16 GWh) and above but less than 10 MW (80 GWh)	USD 12,000
Cat. V	Very Small Distributors (a) 0.5 MW(4 Wh) but less than 2 MW(4 GWh)	USD 3,500
	(b) Less than 0.5 MW (4 GWh)	USD 1,500

Source: National Association of Regulatory Utility Commissioners, (2020) "The National Isolated Grid System Regulations 2020" < https://www.naruc.org/international/news/ugandan-regulators-draft-isolated-grid-system-regulation-to-achieve-rural-electrification-goals/>.

Table 11 Isolated Grid Systems

Combined Generation Distribution and Sales Licence		
Cat. I	Medium generators 10 MW and above but less than 50 MW	USD 12,000 fixed plus SUD 6,000 per 25 MW or part thereof
Cat. II	Small generators	
	2 MW and above but less than 10 MW	USD 12,000
Cat. III	Very Small generators	
	(a) 0.5 MW (4 GWh) and above but less than 2 MW (16 GWh)	USD 3,500
	(b) Less than 0.5 MW (4 GWh)	Exempt
Combined Generation Distribution and Sales Licence		
Import and export of electricity		
Cat. I	At a voltage above 33 kV	

	(a) Import & Export	USD 112,500
	At a voltage of 33 kV & below	
	(a) Import	USD 12,000
	(b) Export	USD 12,000
Application and Approval fees		
	Premium for feasibility study	USD 3,000
	Licence Application	USD 3,500
	Licence Transfer Application	USD 3,500
	Application for Amendment of Licence or Modification	USD 3,500
	Application for Renewal of Licence	USD 3,500
	Permit Extension Application	USD 1000
	Application for Licence Exemption	USD 3,000

Source: National Association of Regulatory Utility Commissioners, (2020) "The National Isolated Grid System Regulations 2020" https://www.naruc.org/international/news/ugandan-regulators-draft-isolated-grid-system-regulation-to-achieve-rural-electrification-goals/.

Chapter 6. The Electricity (Primary Grid Code) Regulations, SI No. 24 of 2003

278. The Uganda Grid Code is a schedule to the Electricity (Primary Grid Code) Regulations. It provides the guidelines and procedures for the licensees of the electric power system to operate the Uganda power system. It recognizes the fact that prior to its introduction, generation licensees had concluded that PPA was at variance with its provisions. In order to avert the apparent conflict, it provided that in the event of any conflict, the PPA would take precedence only to the extent that it did not affect the security and safety provisions of the Code. All generation licensees, the grid system operator, the distribution licensees and consumers connected to the HVTG are required to comply with the Code in the course of their respective businesses. The Code is administered by the Uganda Grid Code Committee, which is empowered by ERA, which is in turn empowered to make final decisions on amendments to the Code in consultation with the committee. The Code contains rules and procedures for the efficient management of the electric supply industry in Uganda, taking into account a wide range of operational conditions that are likely to be encountered under normal and exceptional circumstances. It does not predict and address all possible operational situations.

All licensees and big consumers are required to provide requisite information to the system operator as is necessary to facilitate compliance with the Code.

In this respect, the system operator has the following responsibilities:

- to supervise the operation of the grid system;
- to coordinate the planning of the grid system with the generators, distributors and big consumers;
- to perform the monitoring and reporting function required for the effective operation of the Code and submit periodic reports to the licensees, the Grid Code Committee and ERA.

279. Other key responsibilities of the system operator are to provide service to coordinate interconnections to the grid. They also provide data to ERA to support the development and expansion plans for the grid system.

280. If circumstances arise which the provisions of the Code have not foreseen, the system operator is required to undertake extensive and prompt consultations with all affected generators, distributors and big consumers in an effort to reach an agreement as to what action, if any, is to be taken. If an agreement between the system operator and generators, distributors or big consumers cannot be reached in the time available, the system operator is empowered to determine all necessary actions to be taken. The systems operator should then notify the generators, distributors, big consumers and ERA immediately thereafter. In making such a determination, the system operator should have regard, in any event, to what is reasonable in all circumstances towards maintaining the reliability and safety of the system. Each generator, distributor and big consumer is required to comply with all instructions of the system operator following such a determination, provided the instructions are consistent with the current technical parameters of the particular generator, distributor and big consumer as registered under this Code. The system operator should also promptly refer all such unforeseen circumstances and any such determination to ERA. In case the instructions by the system operator are outside the current technical parameters of a particular generator or distributor, the matter should be determined by ERA. The matter can then be brought before the f=grid code committee for consideration of a revision of the grid code.

§1. The Grid Code Committee

281. The Code establishes and maintains the grid code committee, whose functions include regularly reviewing the Code, reviewing all suggestions for amendments to the Code that are submitted by licensees or big consumers, submitting recommendations to ERA as to amendments to the Code that the committee believes are necessary or desirable and providing reasons for the recommendations, issuing guidance on the interpretation, implementation and performance of the Code when required to do so by ERA and considering changes that may be necessary or desirable to the Code arising out of any unforeseen circumstances. In addition, ERA may request the committee for guidance on the interpretation, implementation and performance of the Code on its own initiative or upon request by a licensee or big consumer.

282. All instructions given by the system operator and communications (between the system operator and generators, distributors and big consumers) should be given by telephone or voice recording, electronic message or by facsimile and should be confirmed within twenty-four hours. Confirmation may be by telephone, electronic message or in writing. The recording of instructions or communication given or made by telephone should be accepted as evidence of those instructions or communication. All messages sent by telephone or radio must be repeated by the receiving party to ensure that the receiving party has clearly understood such instructions. Names of the originator and recipient of such instruction or communication must be logged at relevant ends. Copies or recordings of all communications given by the system operator by whatever means should be retained by the system operator for at least twelve months. Technical data and notices to be submitted to the system operator should be delivered in writing. This should be either by hand or sent by registered post, or in case of insufficient time, by facsimile transfer, and followed by the original by way of registered post or by hand.

§2. Uganda Standards and Codes of Practice

283. All installations, equipment, plant or apparatus should comply with the Uganda National Bureau of Standards (UNBS) and Codes of Practice or, in their absence, the Institute of Electrical and Electronics Engineers or British and International Electrotechnical Commission Standards. In the absence of each Standard or Code of Practice, the responsible agency should be consulted, along with ERA, to get permission for the utilization of good professional practice. Any dispute between any generator, distributor, big consumer or system operator in relation to any provision of this Code may be referred to ERA. ERA should then decide on the dispute and make an order accordingly. The practice and procedure to be followed in the determination of a dispute should be such as ERA may consider appropriate. Any directly affected person who feels aggrieved by the decision of ERA may appeal against ERA's decision to the Tribunal.

§3. Systems Operations Code

284. The System Operations Code provides guidelines, criteria and procedures to promote coordinated operation of the grid system in Uganda. The objective of the System Operations Code is to ensure that adequate and reliable electric power supply is available to the consumers of the Uganda electric power system under normal and, to as large an extent as possible, under emergency operating conditions. The reliability criteria for normal, as well as emergency conditions, are described in the System Operations Code. The System Operations Code is applicable to all generators, distributors, big consumers and the system operator in the grid system of Uganda. ERA is responsible for the ratification, interpretation, application and revision of the System Operations Code in consultation with the Grid Operations Code Committee.

§4. Operational Planning

285. Under Regulation 3(2), the operational plans include scheduling the operation of the generators to ensure reliable operating margins, scheduling operating configurations of the transmission system, developing procedures for maintaining system integrity during emergencies and planning maintenance outages with the generating plants, big consumers, transmission and distribution facilities. The operational plans for the grid system are based on the operations criteria to maintain the reliability and continuity of supply. The grid system operates sufficient generation capacity to meet its obligation to continuously balance its generation to meet the system load. Regulation 3(2) also provides for voltage control. The grid system operates capacitive, inductive, reactive generation scheduling, transmission lines scheduling, and load-shedding at proper levels to maintain system voltages within established high and low limits (+ or -6% at low voltage).[94] Each generator is required to maintain adequate MVAR reserve resources to support its voltage under credible contingency conditions.

286. Regulation 3(2) also relates to time and frequency regulation. It provides that frequency should be scheduled at 50 Hz (+ or -0.5) and controlled to that value except for those periods in which frequency deviations are scheduled to correct for

94. Reactive generation scheduling, transmission and switching and load-shedding if necessary, shall be implemented to maintain these levels.

time errors. Second, operating limits for frequency deviation and time error should be established with grid system reliability as the first priority, while each generator should participate in time error correction procedures. Finally, the grid system operator should coordinate the time error correction procedures. Each generator is required to accurately account for inadvertent interchange through daily schedule verification and the use of reliable metering equipment. In addition, each generator should be active in preventing inadvertent interchange accumulation.

§5. Operational Reserves

287. Regulation 3(3) of the National Grid Code deals with operating reserves criteria. Operating reserves consist of spinning reserves[95] and non-spinning reserves.[96] In operating its capacity, the grid system should use all of its resources to provide for a level of operating reserves sufficient to account for such factors as errors in forecasting, generation and transmission equipment unavailability, number and size of generating units, system equipment, forced outages, maintenance schedules, regulating requirements and system load diversity. The system operator should allocate sufficient spinning reserves to be distributed among the various generating units in the grid system as a contingency against loss of generation, error in demand forecast, sudden increase in demand or reduction in generation capacity.

The operating reserves should be large enough to cover the loss of the largest generating unit in the system. However, non-spinning reserves may be allocated to any generator or generating unit as long as that generating unit has not been allocated as part of the spinning reserves and can be synchronized and put online within thirty minutes.

§6. System Voltage and Reactive Power Criteria

288. Regulation 3(4)(1) covers reactive power reserve guidelines. First, the guidelines provide that where it is practicable and economic, each generator, distributor and big consumer of the grid system should meet its local reactive requirements. Generators should also carry sufficient reserve reactive capacity to protect the system voltage levels under any contingency condition. Distributors are also required to ensure sufficient reactive equipment to maintain power factor within required limits (not less than 0.9). The second reactive power reserve guideline is that reserves should be planned and applied effectively within the appropriate time interval when contingencies occur. Finally, there should be automatic voltage-regulating equipment in service at power stations set to appropriate voltage levels, which will allow the system to be self-regulating.

---

95. Spinning reserves constitute the additional output from generating plant that must be realizable in real time in order to arrest a drop of system frequency due to a loss of generation or a loss of external inter-connector or mismatch between generation and demand.
96. Non-spinning reserves constitute the output available from stand-by generating units that can be synchronized and loaded up within five minutes for a hydro and thirty minutes for a thermal plant to respond to abnormal demand increase or further generating units breakdown.

289. Regulation 3(4)(2) covers system voltage criteria. Under this, each generator and the system operator are required to coordinate the use of voltage control equipment. This is to maintain transmission voltages as specified in the connection agreement. This agreement is prepared by the system operator and generators in cooperation and approved by ERA and reactive flows to maintain system security and stability. Regulation 3(4)(3) deals with coordination by the system operator. On the basis of the expected power flows, the system operator should determine the required voltage profile of the system. Thereafter, it should allocate the MVAR generation and reactive reserve capacity required in each section of the system and generating unit to ensure the maintenance of satisfactory voltage levels in the event of loss of circuits. The system operator should also arrange the reactive output of generating units to meet the reactive requirements as economically as possible.

290. The responsibility of the generators is also set out. They are required to operate their plant to maintain the specified voltage levels and provide reactive, capacitive and inductive VARS as instructed by the system operator. Generators should also inform the system operator of any difficulties in meeting the agreed voltage levels or in providing the reactive requirements. In addition, they should also ensure that automatic voltage regulators and VAR limiters are continuously in service and inform the system operator whenever a generating unit is operating without its automatic voltage regulator or VAR limiter. Regulation 3(4)(5) covers emergency operations criteria. The objective of these criteria is to maintain stable conditions throughout the system under emergency conditions. In cases of sudden voltage fall and a corresponding sudden rise in reactive power generation, each generating unit should maintain the additional MVAR output that the units have picked up and should not reduce field current or adjust transformer taps until instructed by the system operator, except when adjustment is necessary to keep the units within their capacity limits.

291. When requested by the system operator, generating units should increase MVAR output to the capacity of the units,[97] and normal running can only be resumed on instructions from the system operator. The system operator may also ask distributors and big consumers to lock transformer tap positions or shed load when necessary in order to maintain stable voltage. In cases of sudden voltage rise and a corresponding fall in a reactive generation, generating units should not take action to recover the MVAR generation lost on the units. Field current should not be increased or transformer taps adjusted until instructed by the system operator, except when adjustment is necessary to keep the units within their stability limits.

§7. Operations Plans

292. Regulation 3(5) covers operational plans. The generators and the system operator are charged with maintaining a set of current plans, which are designed to

97. Capability output of units should be determined by rotor, stator, transformer oil and temperature limits set by the manufacturers or the maximum name plate rating output of the exciter.

evaluate options and set procedures for reliable operation through a reasonable future time period. In addition, they are responsible for using available personnel and system equipment to implement these plans. This is done to assure that grid system reliability is maintained. The objectives of the operational plans are twofold.

293. First, they are to inform all generators, distributors or big consumers whose systems are connected to the grid system of the procedures and responsibilities which are required to execute the operations plans. Second, they are to enable the system operator to coordinate operations and outages of centrally dispatched generating units taking into account transmission system outages. This is intended to provide the maximum reliability of electric power delivery at the lowest cost.

294. Clause 3(3)(3) sets out the basic operating requirements pertaining to operations plans for the grid system. In normal operations, each generator, working with the system operator, should plan its future operations to ensure that normal interconnection operation proceeds in an orderly and consistent manner. Each distributor should also provide its best estimate of demand to the system operator so that the system operator can develop the total demand forecast. In planning for emergency conditions, a set of plans should be developed, maintained and implemented by each generator and the system operator to cope with operating emergencies. These plans should be conducted with other generators and the system operator as appropriate. With regard to long-term deficiencies, each generator and the system operator should maintain comprehensive and coordinated procedures to deal with long-term capacity or energy deficiencies. Load-shedding, however, requires a distributor or big consumer coordinated by the system operator to establish a programme of manual and automatic load-shedding, which is designed to arrest frequency or voltage decays that could result in an uncontrolled failure of the grid system. The programme should be coordinated throughout the grid system to prevent unbalanced load-shedding, which may cause high transmission loading and extreme voltage deviations.

295. With regard to system restoration, each generator, coordinated by the system operator, should develop and periodically update a logical plan to re-establish the system in a stable and orderly manner in the event of a partial or total collapse of the system. This plan should be coordinated with other control areas in the grid system to ensure a consistent grid system restoration plan. A reliable and adequate source of start-up power for generating units should also be provided. Where sources are remote from the generating unit, instructions should be issued to expedite availability. Generation restoration steps should be verified by actual testing whenever possible.[98] This section also covers communications for the grid system. The system operator is responsible for maintaining continuously available communication with all generators and distributors. Therefore, each generator, distributor and system operator is required to provide adequate and reliable telecommunication facilities to ensure the exchange of information necessary to maintain reliability. Procedures for operator-to-operator communication should be established by each

98. System restoration procedures should be verified by actual testing or by simulation.

generator or distributor working with the system operator so that communication between operating personnel is consistent, efficient and effective during normal and emergency conditions. Operating instructions and procedures should be established by each control area to enable communication in cases of loss of facilities.

296. Regulation 3(5)(4) provides the basic guidelines as to information which should be contained in the annual operations plan. This should include the adequacy and capability of generating units to meet forecast demand and energy for the next year to five years ahead, verification that generation and transmission outages are planned to maximize resource utilization, optimize placement of generation outages to produce a minimum running cost, ensure that the operational problems likely to be encountered are highlighted and alternative solutions considered and evaluated and verification that the actions taken and emergency procedures issued to deal with possible abnormal system conditions are adequate and satisfactory. The formal operations planning procedures to implement these major steps require the following: the dates by which relevant programmes should be issued, determination of the responsibility for the system operator and the generators and distributors to produce and provide data, definition of the work necessary for the system operator and the generators and distributors to contribute towards the annual operations plan and the lines of communication and interaction between the system operator and the generators and distributors. The annual operations plan should also show coordination of the outage requirements of the system operator, generators and distributors to ensure the security of the overall system. These procedures are to be prepared by the system operator and published in a document for reference by relevant parties.

297. The weekly operations plans are set out in Regulation 3(5)(5). The system operator should issue a preliminary weekly operations plan every Thursday. The weekly operations plan includes all generating units that are on stand-by duty as non-spinning reserves. By Saturday, the system operator should have prepared a weekly operations plan that takes into account the generating units' unavailability. It is the responsibility of the system operator to determine each week the allocation of reserve margin to each generator, with due consideration to start-up prices, response characteristics of the generating units on the grid system, system constraints, availability of generating units, hydro dam levels and the lake inflows rates in its weekly operations plan. The weekly operations plan should also state the amount of operating reserve to be utilized by the system operator in the scheduling and dispatching process. It may also include the possibility of shared spinning reserves with neighbouring systems. Under Regulation 3(5)(7), a list of response capability data required in connection with the spinning reserve for each generating unit should be submitted to the system operator before the unit comes into commercial operation. It should then be updated by the end of April each calendar year and should be within the parameters set out in the connection agreement between the system operator and the generator. The system operator should be informed promptly of any change in these parameters.

§8. Transmission Operations Planning

298. Regulation 3(6) provides that reliable operation of the grid system facilities requires coordination among all participants. A high level of reliability is achieved in the operation of a grid system when transmission equipment is operated within its normal rating, except for temporary conditions after a contingency has occurred; the capability of components of the grid system for both normal and emergency conditions has been established by technical studies and operating experience. In addition, a high level of reliability is achieved when the grid system operator can take immediate steps to relieve the conditions when line loading, equipment loading or voltage levels deviate from normal operating limits or are expected to exceed emergency limits,[99] and the system can be coordinated among systems and control areas.[100] Regulation 3(6)(2) deals with grid systems operations planning procedures.[101] The grid system coordinating studies should be undertaken in accordance with Regulation 3(6)(3).

299. This provides that the studies should determine the facilities on each system, which may affect the operation of the coordinated area, determine operating limitations for normal operation when all transmission components are in service and determine operating limitations of transmission facilities under abnormal or emergency conditions. In determining ratings of transmission facilities, consideration is given to thermal and stability limits, short and long-time loading limits and voltage limits. Periodic studies are made to determine the emergency transfer capability of transmission lines interconnecting control areas.[102] Studies are also made to develop operating voltage or reactive schedules for both normal and outage conditions.

300. Regulation 3(6)(4) covers emergency transfer capability. This is the total amount of power above the net contracted purchases and sales, which can be scheduled with the assurance of adequate system reliability for transfers over the transmission network for periods up to several days, based on the most limiting of the following constraints. First, all transmission loadings initially within long-term emergency ratings and voltages initially within acceptable limits, bulk power system capable of remaining stable after absorbing the initial power swings and upon the loss of any single transmission circuit, transformer, bus section, or generating

---

99. The steps which can be taken by the grid systems operator include notifying other systems, adjusting generation, changing schedules between control areas, initiating load relief measures and taking such other actions as may be required.

100. This includes coordination of equipment outages, voltage levels, MW and MVAR flow monitoring and switching that affects two or more systems of transmission components.

101. In order to accomplish the needed level of coordination, the system operator should perform studies to determine the grid system operating configurations, how the system is to be operated within emergency transfer limits, how protective relaying is to be coordinated and how maintenance outages are to be coordinated.

102. Studies shall be made annually or at such other time that changes are made to the bulk-system which may affect the emergency transfer capability.

unit and all transmission loadings within their respective short-time emergency ratings and voltages within emergency limits after the initial power swings following the disturbance but before system adjustments are made (and in the event of a permanent outage of a facility, transfer schedules may need to be reviewed).

301. Regulation 3(6)(5) covers protection coordination. The satisfactory operation of the grid system, especially under abnormal conditions, is greatly influenced by the relay equipment and relay schemes in effect. Relaying of tie points between the grid system is of primary concern to the respective systems, although internal systems often relaying directly affects the adjacent systems. Thus, individual generators and distributors have an obligation to implement relay application, operation, and preventive maintenance criteria according to the specifications of relays in the technical code. The application of the relay systems of the generators and distributors is coordinated by the system operator to enhance the system reliability and yet have the least adverse effect on the grid system.

§9. Maintenance Coordination

302. This is covered by Regulation 3(6) (6). The grid system and interconnections continually grow in size and complexity so that increasingly greater emphasis is placed on coordination of scheduled outages of equipment and facilities by the system operator that significantly affect performance and reliability of the grid system. Therefore, effective coordination of maintenance among systems and areas is essential in achieving the high degree of reliability required in the operation of the grid system. It is additionally essential that the length of maintenance outages is examined and minimized as required.

303. In order to achieve maintenance coordination, the following procedures should be followed. First, scheduled outages of generating capacity should be planned and updated and coordinated between the system operator and all generators as required within coordinated areas. Generating capacity maintenance schedules and revisions should be exchanged with adjacent areas as required.

304. Second, scheduled outages of transmission facilities which may affect grid system operation should be coordinated within and among adjacent coordinated areas and third, scheduled outages of system voltage-regulating equipment should be coordinated as required.[103] Finally, scheduled outages of telemetry and control equipment and associated communication channels should be coordinated between the affected areas.

103. The equipment includes automatic voltage regulators on generators, supplementary excitation control, synchronous condensers, shunt and series capacitors and reactors.

§10. EMERGENCY OPERATIONS

305. During the operations of the grid system, contingencies can occur that include equipment failure, system faults and interruption of service due to natural elements. To maintain continuity of supply to the maximum number of customers, procedures must be followed by the system operator, generators and distributors to perform emergency operations. The emergency operations set out in Regulation 3(7) include system disturbance monitoring, demand reduction procedures, load-shedding, sectionalizing and restoration procedures and black start procedures. Each of these emergency operations is covered in detail below.

306. Regulation 3(7) (2) provides for system disturbance monitoring. In the event of system disturbance, the primary requirement is to return the grid system to normal state as soon as possible. In so doing, the following are checked to determine abnormality, which can indicate serious abnormality: system frequency, external interconnected parties timeline flow, sequence of events to determine the cause and the condition of the remaining grid system, status of the connected generating units and system voltages, especially in strategic transmission substations. The system operator then determines what remains intact in the grid system and reconfigures the grid system to a safe and secure state, reconnects consumers in stages and ensures load or generation balance. Regulation 3(7)(3) provides for demand reduction procedures. In the event of insufficient generation, transfer of load breakdown or operational problems in the grid system, in order to keep system frequency within limits to prevent the loading of transmission lines or equipment beyond their thermal limits, a reduction in demand may be required. The procedures to reduce demand, prepared by the system operator and approved by ERA include issuance of various warnings, consumer demand reduction, emergency manual disconnection and automatic under-frequency demand disconnection.

When the estimates of the demand and plant availability for the following week indicate a potentially critical situation, warnings should be issued as soon as possible, bearing in mind that adequate notice must be given to consumers. During periods of protracted plant shortage exceeding several days, warnings should be issued. These should be based on the best information available at that time, indicating the amount of demand reduction anticipated. Confirmation or modification of the warning should also be issued as and when appropriate. It may be necessary for the system operator to issue a warning of possible demand reduction to cover a local situation where the risk of serious overloading of the generating and transmission equipment in a particular section of network is anticipated. The objective of the warnings is to obtain the necessary demand relief required with the least possible inconvenience to consumers and to ensure that response to requests for disconnection or reduction is both prompt and effective. Demand reduction is also required without warning if unusual and unforeseeable circumstances create severe operational problems. Warnings are also to enable distributors, big consumers and directly connected customers to assess their demand disconnection or reduction requirements.

307. There are different types of warnings. A colour-coded warning system is used in Uganda and is applicable during situations of serious supply shortages as follows. The yellow warning is issued by the system operator to generators and distributors when, for any reason, there is cause to believe that the risk of serious system disturbances is abnormally high. During the period of a yellow warning, generators and distributors affected are alerted and maintained in the condition in which they are best able to withstand system disturbances. An orange warning is issued during periods of protracted plant shortage to provide guidance to distributors in the most efficient utilization of their manpower resources in implementing disconnections or demand reductions as outlined in the load curtailment plan. A red warning is issued to indicate that demand reduction or disconnection under controlled conditions is imminent. Distributors are then required to take such preparatory action as is necessary to ensure that at any time during the specified period, disconnection or reduction of supply may be applied promptly and effectively. All warnings should state the hours and days of risk and, in the case of orange warnings and red warnings, the estimated amount of load reduction. If after the issue of a warning, it appears that system conditions have so changed that the risk of load reduction is reduced or removed entirely, the system operator should issue the appropriate modification. Different actions should be implemented in case of the above-mentioned conditions. First, whenever possible, an orange or red warning should be given to distributors as early as possible so that arrangements are made to import more power from the neighbouring systems. Second, except when protracted plant shortage is expected, load reduction should be implemented to prevent the system frequency from falling below 49.5 Hz.

308. The system operator is also required to instruct controlled demand reduction to directly connected consumers, instruct demand disconnection, which has been pre-arranged into groups, and when the system is normalized, the system operator should initiate demand restoration. In cases of protracted plant shortage or overloading of the main system, the following procedures should be followed in accordance with Regulation 3(7)(3)(5). First, the system operator should give warnings as early as possible to the distributors to enable them to assess their demand reduction or disconnection plan. Second, on the day during which demand disconnection is required, the system operator should confirm to distributors to initiate the demand disconnection stating the amount, time and duration when such disconnection is required. Distributors can rotate the demand disconnection to consumers as long as the amount of the demand curtailment remains the same; however, the system operator should be kept informed of the amount of the demand disconnected and the time of the disconnection. Finally, demand restoration should only be carried out with the agreement of the system operator. The system operator should be kept informed as the restoration is implemented.

309. However, in situations requiring rapid demand disconnection, the system operator may instruct block load. Regulation 3(7) (3) (7) makes provision for automatic under-frequency disconnection. Each distributor is required to make available up to a percentage, to be determined, of its peak demand for automatic under-frequency disconnection through the installation of under-frequency relays to limit the consequence of major loss of generation. The percentage is specified by ERA in consultation with the committee. Demand is split into discrete MW blocks. The number, size, location and associated under-frequency setting of these blocks are specified by the system operator as and when required in consultation with relevant distributors. Following the allotted load disconnections, should the system condition still be critical, the system operator can request distributors to implement additional demand disconnection and restore the equivalent amount that has been disconnected earlier. This is to prepare for subsequent fall in frequency due to other potential operational problems. Load disconnected by under-frequency relays may only be restored on instructions from the system operator, and when a restoration instruction is given, it is carried out systematically under the instructions of the system operator.

310. The system operator may include big consumers and consumers directly connected to the grid system in the under-frequency demand disconnection scheme. However, a generator can disconnect from the system either manually or automatically should the generating station itself be subjected to a frequency that may cause damage to its generating sets. Such a disconnection facility should be agreed upon by the system operator, and after automatic disconnection or manual reconnection, the system operator should be informed immediately, or as soon as it is practically possible, of such action. At all times, the system operator should be supplied with details of the actual load disconnected. Regulation 3(7)(3)(8) provides for equitable load-shedding. The system operator, in consultation with distributors, should endeavour, as far as practicable, to spread demand reduction equitably. In protracted plant shortage or overloading of the main system, large imbalances of generation and demand may cause excessive power transfers across the grid system. In cases where such transfers endanger the stability of the grid system or cause a risk of damaging transmission equipment, demand reductions should proceed, notwithstanding the inequalities of disconnection that may arise from such adjustments.

311. Regulation 3(7) (3)(9) sets out the preparation of demand reduction plans. The system operator, together with the distributors, is required to prepare a manual containing load-shedding guidelines. This manual should then be updated as and when required. In addition, they should prepare a load curtailment plan for appropriate levels of demand disconnection or reduction. This plan should also be revised as and when required. Regulation 3(7)(3)(10) makes provision for schedule and dispatch during demand reduction. During demand reduction, scheduling and dispatch in accordance with the merit order[104] can be suspended by the system operator. This can be done only if pieces of equipment of the security of the grid are being threatened by overloads or under-voltages or instability. However, the system operator is allowed to import as much power as possible from externally interconnected parties before implementing demand reduction. A major disturbance in the grid system may result in certain areas becoming isolated and experiencing abnormally low frequency and voltage levels. Any operation at low frequency causes a slowing down of electrically driven equipment and, in the case of generating plant auxiliaries, may

104. *See,* Clause 4(2).

make it impossible to increase or even maintain station generation. To provide emergency relief, general guidelines can be adopted and implemented by the various interconnected areas and regions in the application of under-frequency relays or other means for shedding load, sectionalizing systems and isolating generation in cases of major disturbances. Therefore, the importance of Regulation 3(7)(4), which provides for load-shedding, sectionalizing and restoration, is to lay down these guidelines.

312. Regulation 3(7)(4)(2) provides general guidelines. First, all spinning reserves and emergency generating capability should be utilized to the extent practicable before resorting to load-shedding. Second, the main objectives in the application of under-frequency relays are to shed load, to sectionalize a system, or to isolate generation to aid in the early restoration of service and to minimize the loss of generating capability as a result of a major disturbance. It is therefore preferable to shed load in an emergency for a short period of time to aid in maintaining or re-establishing the interconnection rather than risk operating for an extended period of time with low frequency and voltage. Third, a sufficient load should be shed, either by automatic or manual means, so that the remaining load in any isolated area does not exceed the available generating capability in that area, regardless of ownership. Automatic shedding of load whenever possible is preferred to manual shedding because of the speed with which loads can be shed. The amount and location of the load to be shed should be determined on the basis of studies relating to the specific area. The system operator is required to coordinate the system load-shedding programme and procedures. Regulation 3(7)(3) also provides for warnings of the possibility of load reduction. Warnings are issued by the system operator to generators, distributors, big consumers and directly connected consumers.

313. Restoration procedures are set out in Regulation 3(7) (4)(4). In order to expedite restoration in the event of an area shutdown of generating capability, the following steps are taken. First, each system sets up necessary operating instructions and procedures to cover emergency conditions, including loss of communication. Second, where an outside source of power is necessary for start-up, necessary switching procedures should be determined and periodically reviewed with dispatchers and the operating personnel. Third, as soon as system conditions, including frequency and voltage permit, any separated area should be synchronized with adjoining areas. When generating and transmission capability is available and frequency has been restored to normal, restoration of shed load should begin and at attended substations, any load-shedding by automatic or manual means should be restored only upon direct or pre-arranged order of the dispatcher. The system operator is again required to coordinate the rate at which the load is restored to prevent adding load faster than generating and transmission capability permits. In case a system experiences a total collapse or a partial collapse, a black start of the system may be required. Under Regulation 3(7) (4)(6), generators are required in consultation with the system operator to develop contingency plans to restart their own systems after a total or partial collapse in their area. All contingency plans should be reviewed and updated periodically to reflect changes in the system and to address any deficiency found.

§11. Operational Liaison

314. In order to maintain coordination of operation in the grid system, the system operator, generators and distributors are supposed to maintain communication and exchange information regarding the status of their respective systems and demand during normal operations and emergency situations. Therefore, Regulation 3(8) provides for operation liaison procedures. The system operator is required to inform a generator, distributor, or big consumer of an operation it intends to carry out that may have an effect on its system or demand. The intended time of operation should also be notified. A generator or distributor should also inform the system operator of an operation which may have an effect on the grid system. The system operator may pass such information to other relevant generators or distributors if, in the opinion of the system operator, such generators or distributors are likely to be affected by the reported operation.

315. A notification may be required when there is a planned outage of plant, apparatus or demand, operation of any circuit breaker, isolator or disconnect or voltage control and operation caused by any other event. The guidelines for notification include the following. First, it should have sufficient details to enable a recipient to assess the risk arising from such an operation or and the name of the information provider should be given, but the recipient has the right to clarify such information. Second, a generator or distributor cannot pass information it received from the system operator to persons other than another generator or distributor connected to the system or apparatus. However, such information, if the need arises, can be made available to ERA. Third, except during an emergency, notification, if orally received, should be written down and repeated back to the sender to confirm its accuracy. Finally, notification for a proposed operation should be given as far in advance as possible or as soon as possible after an event has occurred to enable the other party to assess the implications and risks. In the case of an event, reporting should be done immediately or as soon as it is practically possible. Regulation 3(8)(2)(5) provides for events on the grid system that may require notification. The systems operator is required to inform a generator, distributor or big consumer of any events that have an operational effect on their activities. In turn, they are also required to notify the system operator of any event that may have an operational effect on the grid system.

316. There are different situations where notification of events by the system operator is required. These are overloading of plant or apparatus that may be a hazard to personnel, activation of alarm or indication of abnormal operating conditions, adverse weather conditions, breakdown of or faults on, or temporary changes in capabilities of plant or apparatus, breakdown of, or faults on control, communication or metering equipment, increased risk of inadvertent protection operation and sudden extensive changes of demand. Regulation 3(8)(2)(7) sets out the notification of events guidelines. First, notification consists of a description of the event with sufficient details for a recipient to consider and assess the implication and risk and the full names and titles of the individual reporting. Second, a recipient may ask questions to clarify. In answering a question of the recipient, the second party should not pass anything further than what it has been told by the first party. Third, the system operator is required to make available fault reports of the relevant part of the grid system to ERA or any generator or distributor upon request. Regulation 3(8)(2)(8) provides for a significant incident report. If a generator, distributor or big consumer determines that an event under the Code is of significance, he or she may ask for a report of the event in writing from the party concerned. The significant incident report should contain as a minimum operation of plant or apparatus, either manually or automatically, voltage outside statutory limits, frequency outside statutory limits and system instability.

317. The procedures for significant incidents are also set out. First, a yellow warning should be issued by the system operator to all generators, distributors and big consumers who may be affected when the system operator knows there is a risk of widespread and serious disturbance to the grid network. This should contain such information as the system operator deems appropriate. For the duration of a yellow warning, each generator and distributor in receipt of the yellow warning is required to take the necessary steps to warn its operational staff and to maintain its plant or apparatus in the condition in which it is best able to withstand the anticipated disturbance. The scheduling and dispatch in accordance with the merit order may be affected during a yellow warning period.

§12. System Fault and Incident Reporting

318. Regulation 3(9) provides procedures to be adopted for reporting faults, breakdowns and significant incidents which may happen in the grid system or a generator, distributor or big consumer's system, which has an operational effect on the other's system. It also describes the procedure for setting up a joint investigation of a significant incident. Regulation 3(9)(2) provides for procedures for system fault and incident reporting. If the system operator determines an event to be significant or an event in its system is of significance, the system operator may request a generator distributor or big consumer to submit a detailed written report of the event. A written report of a fault should be sent within twenty-four hours of receiving an official request and should be in the form of a preliminary report. A full report should be submitted within one month. The author of the written report or the recipient may request a joint investigation of the significant incident if so warranted.

319. Regulation 3(9)(3) provides for exchange of information. Information should be transmitted to all parties associated with the operation of the system to provide them with the opportunity to correctly assess any situation and give the appropriate operating instructions. Meetings should be held to discuss long-range plans to develop strategies for inter-area operations. Interconnected systems should develop a reliable means of communication between system operators. System operators should notify their counterparts of changes in system status, such as system facilities operating near critical levels, abnormal voltage conditions or problems, changes or degradation of protective relays, changes in maintenance that may have an effect on interconnected operation, generation or transmission outages, new facilities, changes in communication media or routes and severe weather. In order to ensure that communication networks are working properly and that a timely exchange of information is taking place, specific procedures should be implemented between control centres of generators, distributors and the system operator. These procedures that are implemented should identify what information is to be exchanged within a schedule. In addition, there should be put in place, procedures for routine exchange of operating information. This should maximize the effectiveness of the communication system while providing essential information on the status of the system to be available to the operators, consequently enhancing the operators' ability to perform effectively during emergency situations.

§13. Testing and Monitoring

320. Regulation 3(10) makes provisions for testing and monitoring. It specifies the procedures for tests and requires the performance of tests on generating units to check if they have the capability to comply with the connection agreement and to ensure that they meet their generation scheduling and dispatch parameters. The tests on generating units are also undertaken to ensure that the generating units are available in accordance with their availability declaration. There are four objectives of these tests, namely: to establish that generating units can operate within their generation scheduling and dispatch parameters; to monitor the provision of ancillary services and the testing of reactive power and automatic frequency-sensitive operation; to establish whether each generation unit is available as declared and to establish, whether generators can provide those ancillary services which they are either required or have agreed to provide. The procedures for the tests are laid down in Regulation 3(10)(3). The system operator is required to monitor the performance of generating units against parameters registered and compliance by generators with the connection agreements. In the event that a generating unit, in the system operator's opinion, fails to meet in any material respect the parameters registered or fails persistently to comply with the connection agreement, the system operator is required to notify the relevant generator, giving details of the failure and of the monitoring that the system operator has performed.

321. The relevant generator will then provide an explanation of the reasons for the failure and the details of the action that it proposes to take within a reasonable period to enable the generating unit to meet the required parameters. The system operator and the generator should also discuss the action that the generator proposes to take and endeavour to reach an agreement as to the modified parameters which are to apply to the generating units. In the event that an agreement cannot be reached within ten days of notification of the failure, the generator should be required to perform a test to verify the results of the system operator's queries. Regulation 3(10)(4) sets out the procedure for testing the ability to comply with the connection agreement and to provide ancillary services. The first is the reactive power tests. The system operator may, at any time, based on reasonable grounds, issue an instruction requiring a generator to carry out a test to demonstrate that the generating unit meets the reactive power capability registered. This instruction is issued where the generator has declared the relevant generating unit as available in an availability declaration for the scheduled day. Such a test should be initiated by the issue of dispatch instructions in accordance with the parameters submitted and performed in conformity with the test procedures specified by the grid code committee. The second is automatic frequency-sensitive testing. Testing of this parameter should be carried out as part of the routine monitoring of generating units' compliance with dispatch instructions for frequency-sensitive operations. The system operator is required to notify a generator that it proposes to carry out such a test at least forty-eight hours prior to the time of the proposed test. The test should also be performed in conformity with the test procedures prescribed by the grid code committee.

322. The third is the fast start capability testing. The system operator can, at any time, based on reasonable grounds and whenever technically applicable, issue an instruction requiring a generator to synchronize and load up to its offered availability, any one or more of the generating units. The instruction can only be issued if the generator has declared that generating unit is available in any availability declaration for the scheduled day. This test should be initiated by the issue of dispatch instructions and performed in accordance with procedures prescribed by the grid code committee. In addition, there is the black start testing in which the system operator may require a generator with a black start system to carry out a 'black start test' on a generating unit in a black start station in order to demonstrate that a black start station has a black start capability. This test may be carried out once a year at a mutually agreed date between the system operator and the generator. The test should also be performed in conformity with the test procedures prescribed by the grid code committee.

323. The procedures for availability testing are provided for under Regulation 3(10)(4)(6). The system operator can carry out a test on the availability of a generating unit by scheduling and dispatching that generating unit. Accordingly, the generating unit should be scheduled and dispatched to its declared dependable availability. The generator whose generating unit is the subject of the dependable availability test should comply with instructions given by the system operator relating to the declared dependable availability test. The generating unit passes the test if it can maintain its load to the declared dependable availability for four hours continuously under normal system conditions. The dispatch accuracy testing, however, may be carried out to demonstrate that the relevant generating unit meets the relevant generator scheduling and dispatch parameters which have been monitored. The instruction to carry out the test can be issued if the relevant generator has submitted an availability declaration. The test should also be initiated by the issue of dispatch instructions and performed in conformity with the test procedures prescribed by the grid code committee.

324. Regulation 3(10)(4)(8) provides for instances where the generating units fail to pass a test. In case a generating unit fails to pass a test, the generator is required to provide the system operator with a written report specifying in reasonable detail the reasons for any failure of the test so far as they are known to the generator after due and careful inquiry. This report should be provided within three business days of the test. If a dispute arises relating to the failure, the system operator, with the agreement of the generator, may carry out a retest with a forty-eight-hour notice. If the generating unit concerned, in the system operator's view, fails to pass the retest and a dispute arises on that, either party can refer such dispute to ERA for a decision. If the generator has failed a test or a retest, it is required within fourteen days to submit in writing to the system operator for approval the date and time by which the generator will have brought the generating unit concerned to a condition where it complies with the relevant capability. Once a generating unit fails the test, the generator is required to amend the registered parameters of the generating unit relating to the capacity for which it has been tested for the period until the generating unit can achieve the parameters previously registered, as demonstrated in a retest. Once the generator has indicated to the system operator the date and time that the generating unit can achieve the parameters previously registered, the system operator should either accept the information or require the generator to demonstrate that the relevant capability of that generating unit concerned has been restored by means of a repetition of the test by a forty-eight hours' notice.

§14. Scheduling and Dispatch Code

325. Scheduling the operations of generating units is a major component of operations plans. Scheduling of the generating units depends upon the pattern of demand by the system, the order-of-merit operation of generating units, the availability of generating units, the flexibility of operation of generating units, constraints on the transmission system, security requirements and system losses. Regulation 4 of the Grid Code sets out in detail the scheduling and dispatch code. The generation scheduling procedures include the submission of an availability declaration by each generator to the system operator, the submission to the system operator of any revised generation scheduling and dispatch parameters by the generators, the submission of certain system data by each generator to the system operator and the issue to the system operator of a generation schedule the day before the scheduled day. In instances where an externally interconnected party outside the country is connected to the grid system for the purpose of system security enhancement and economic operation, the generation scheduling and, hence, power transaction should be governed by inter-utility joint operation agreements and other inter-utility agreements.

326. Generation scheduling requires generator data to enable the system operator to prepare a merit order to be used in scheduling and dispatch and the preparation and issue of a generation schedule. Based on these data, the system operator is required to ensure that there is sufficient generation to meet system demand at all times in the most economic manner, together with an appropriate margin of reserve, while maintaining the integrity of the grid system and security and quality of supply. The procedure for a generation schedule is set out in Regulation 4(1)(3). Its computation requires the following information: availability declaration, generation scheduling and generation dispatch parameters and other relevant generation data. Every day, each generator is required to submit to the system operator in writing all such information. Regulation 4(1)(4) makes provision for the availability declaration. It should be expressed in a whole number of MW per generator unit, in respect of any time period. A revised availability declaration for a generating unit refers to one where since the time at which the availability declaration for that generation unit was prepared, has either become available at a different wattage or, in the case of a generating unit declared to be not available for generation in an availability declaration, has become available for generation. A revised availability declaration submitted by a generator should state the time periods in the relevant availability declaration and, if such generating unit is available, at what wattage, expressed in a whole number of MW, for each given time period. Regulation 4(1)(5) provides for generation scheduling and dispatch parameters. The generation scheduling and dispatch parameters should reflect the true operating characteristics of generating units. A generation schedule should be compiled daily by the system operator as a statement of which units may be required for the next following scheduled day.

327. In compiling the generation schedule, the system operator should take account of and give due weight to the following factors. First, the grid system constraints from time to time, as determined by the system operator and as advised by the generator; second, for generating units, their parameters registered as generation scheduling and dispatch parameters and third, the requirements, as determined by the system operator and as advised by distributors, for voltage control and MVAR reserves. Other factors to take into consideration are the following: the need to provide operating margins as determined by the system operator and the requirements as determined by the system operator for maintaining frequency control. After the completion of the scheduling process, but before the issue of the generation schedule, the system operator can deem it necessary to make adjustments to the output of the scheduling process. Such adjustments can be made necessary by the following factors: first, changes in offered availability or generation scheduling of dispatched parameters of generating units, notified to the system operator after the commencement of the scheduling process; second, changes to system demand forecasts, changes to transmission constraints, emerging from the necessarily interactive process of scheduling and network security assessment, including either changes to the numerical values prescribed to existing constraint groups or identification of new constraint groups; third, changes to generating unit requirements within constrained groups, following notification to the grid system operator of the changes in capability.

328. A written record of the adjustments should be kept by the system operator for a period of at least twelve months in situations where adverse weather is anticipated; a yellow warning has been issued, a demand control has been instructed by the system operator or total or partial collapse exists. These factors may mean that a generating unit is chosen other than in accordance with the merit order. Any other deviations from the use of the merit order by dispatch should be reported by the system operator, including those responsible for the deviation. These reports should then be consolidated into a weekly report by the system operator to the generators, distributors and ERA. The generation schedule should contain the following information. First, it should indicate, for a generating unit or interconnection power transaction, the period for which it is scheduled during the following scheduled day. It should also include generating units or interconnection power transactions running as a result of non-system reasons and system requirements and generating units and externally interconnected parties assigned to a specific reserve role. The generation schedule can be followed by a list of special actions that the system operator requests a generator to take in respect of generating units or an externally interconnected party to take in respect of a generation power transaction in order to maintain the integrity of the grid system. For consumers directly connected to the grid system to which power stations or consumers are also connected, these special actions should generally involve load transfer between the grid supply points or arrangements for demand reduction by manual or automatic means. However, these special actions should be discussed and agreed upon with the generator, externally interconnected party, distributor or consumer concerned. If not agreed, generation may be restricted, or demand may be at risk to develop and implement plans for the construction, maintenance, operation, refurbishment and repair of its distribution system to economically meet reasonable consumer expectations of distribution services; comply with the laws and other performance obligations which apply to the provision of distribution services; and develop, test or stimulate and implement contingency plans to deal with events which have a low probability of occurring, but are realistic and would have a sustainable impact on consumers. ERA may review a licensee's practices if there is a substantial decline in the quality or reliability of supply or evidence of a significant risk that such a decline may occur in the future when compared to the licensee's historical performance and its performance targets.

§15. Consumer's Installation and Equipment

329. Under Regulation 6(3), a consumer should use its best endeavours to ensure that all electrical installation and any equipment within it complies with the Code, is maintained in a safe condition and protection equipment in the consumer's electrical installation is in compliance with safety regulations or requirements of the licensee within the framework of such standards. A consumer should use the best endeavours to ensure that the distribution system and the reliability and quality of supply to other consumers are not adversely affected by the consumer's actions or equipment and not to allow a supply of electricity to its electrical installation to be used other than at the consumer's premises nor supply electricity to any other person.

330. Under Regulation 6(4), a consumer should not interfere, or allow interference, with any licensee's equipment installed in or on the consumer's premises and allow its licensee to provide and maintain on the consumer's premises any reasonable or agreed facility required to protect any equipment of the licensee. If official identification is produced by the licensee's officers or agents on request, a consumer should provide the licensee's officers or agents at all times with safe, convenient and unhindered access to their equipment on the consumer's premises for any purposes associated with the supply, metering or billing of electricity or the inspection or testing of the consumer's electrical installation. Where necessary, the consumer should provide safety equipment and appropriate safety instructions to officers or agents of the licensee to ensure safe access to the consumer's premises. A licensee should, in cases other than emergencies, use its best endeavour to access a consumer's premises at a time which is reasonably convenient to both parties.

§16. Connection of Supply

331. Pursuant to Regulation 7(1), a licensee should, in accordance with the licensee's specifications approved by ERA, provide, install and maintain, in a manner which is sensitive to the environment and the amenity of the area, equipment for the supply of electricity up to the point of supply and provide, install and maintain standard metering and necessary ancillary equipment, at a suitable location to be provided by the consumer. A licensee should use its best endeavours to connect the consumer at a supply address previously supplied by the licensee as soon as it is practically possible. The consumer should make an application in writing and provide acceptable identification as required by the licensee, agree to pay the licensee's connection fee, the standing service fee and the electricity usage charges in accordance with the licensee's charge rates approved by ERA. In addition, the consumer should provide contact details for billing purposes if the request is made in respect of a rental property, provide contact details for the property owner or the owner's agent, satisfy the licensee that necessary safe, convenient and unhindered access to the supply address, the meter and the electrical installation is available, provide the licensee with estimated electrical load information for the consumer's proposed use of the supply address and provide a security deposit, or enter into a payment arrangement. The licensee should connect the consumer's supply address only if the consumer's electrical facilities are in compliance with the applicable requirements for wiring.

332. Regulation 7(3) also provides for new connections. A licensee should use its best endeavour to make supply available at a new supply address on the date agreed with the consumer or where no date is agreed upon with the consumer as soon as practically possible. A consumer should ensure that a completion of wiring certificate from an electrician has been provided to the licensee, satisfy the licensee that necessary safe, convenient and unhindered access to the supply address, the meter and the electrical installation is available, provide the licensee with estimated electrical load information for the consumer's proposed use of the supply address, agree to pay the licensee's connection fee, the standing service fee, and electricity usage charges and provide contact details for billing purposes.

§17. USE OF SUPPLY

333. Under Regulation 7(5), a consumer should not allow electricity supplied by a licensee to the consumer's supply address to be used at another supply address, take, at the consumer's supply address, electricity supplied to another supply address, supply electricity to any other person, except in accordance with a licence issued by ERA or an exemption granted under the Electricity Act. In addition, the consumer should not tamper with the meter or associated equipment, bypass or allow electricity supplied to the supply address to bypass the meter or allow electricity supplied under a specific purpose tariff to be used for another purpose. Under Regulation 7(6), where a consumer has obtained supply otherwise than as permitted by the Code, the licensee may estimate the usage for which the consumer has not paid, take debt recovery action for the unpaid amount, or take action to disconnect supply to the consumer's premises. Where a consumer's action in obtaining supply results in damage to the licensee's equipment, the consumer may be liable for repair or replacement costs, and the licensee may take action to recover such costs.

§18. QUALITY OF SUPPLY

334. According to Regulation 8, a licensee should use its best endeavours to provide electricity supply in accordance with the Code. The system operator is responsible for the frequency of each licensee's distribution system, having an obligation under the Code to use reasonable endeavours to maintain system frequency. A licensee has no obligation in respect of the frequency of its distribution system beyond complying with the system operator's instructions. Under Regulation 8(3), a licensee should maintain a nominal voltage level at the point of supply to the consumer's electrical installation in accordance with the specified standards. A licensee should use its best endeavours to minimize the frequency of allowable voltage variations. Under Regulation 8(4), a licensee may send, in accordance with the established standard, signals for the following ripple control systems, medium-frequency power line carrier systems, or radio-frequency power line carrier systems.

335. Regulation 8(5) requires a consumer to ensure that its demand for reactive power does not exceed the maximum level allowed by applying the power factor limits specified in the connection agreement to the consumer's maximum demand for apparent power or active power. If the consumer's network tariff includes a charge for the maximum demand for apparent or active power, the consumer's maximum demand for apparent or active power is to be taken to be the maximum demand for which it was most recently billed. A consumer is also required to use its best endeavours to keep the power factor of its electrical installation within the relevant range set out in the connection agreement when the consumer's demand for active or apparent power is more than 50% of its maximum demand. Regulation 8(6) provides that a licensee should ensure that the harmonic levels in the voltage at the point of common coupling nearest to a consumer's point of supply comply with the levels specified within the appropriate standard. A licensee should comply with the Institute of Electrical and Electronics Engineers (IEEE) Standard 519-1992 'Recommended Practices and Requirements for Harmonic Control in Electrical Power Systems' and keep harmonic currents below the limits specified and otherwise comply at its nearest point of common coupling with the IEEE Standard 519-1992. A licensee should also ensure that inductive interference caused by its distribution system is within acceptable limits of good utility practice. Any third-party constructing facilities in the vicinity of an existing right of way of the licensee should ensure that its facilities are not subject to excessive interference from the licensee and should itself be held responsible for any costs that might be incurred for rectifying such problems. Regulation 8(8) obliges a licensee to maintain the negative sequence voltage at the point of common coupling to a consumer's three-phase electrical installation or a level less than 1%.

336. Regulation 8(9) provides for load balance. A consumer should ensure that the current in each phase of a three-phase electrical installation does not deviate from the average of the three-phase currents by more than 5% for a standard nominal voltage up to 1 kV and by more than 2% for a standard nominal voltage above 1 kV. However, deviations are permissible for periods of less than two minutes up to 10% for a standard nominal voltage up to 1 kV and up to 4% for a standard nominal voltage above 1 kV. Section 8(10) stipulates that a licensee should maintain voltage fluctuations at the point of common coupling of a level which maintains the integrity of service to all affected consumers. A consumer should ensure that its equipment does not cause voltage fluctuations at the point of common coupling that creates unacceptable deviations from nominal service voltage for adjacent consumers. If two or more consumers' electrical installations are connected at the same point of common coupling, the maximum permissible contribution to voltage fluctuations allowable from each consumer should be in proportion to their respective maximum demand unless otherwise agreed. Under Regulation 8(11), each licensee should monitor quality of supply in accordance with good asset management principles. Regulation 8(12) guarantees the consumer's right to information. Where a consumer requests, the licensee should provide within ten business days an explanation for any change in the quality of its electricity supply outside the allowed limits.

§19. Reliability of Supply

337. Regulation 9(1) empowers ERA to determine requirements for reliability of supply in each licensee's license, and as a minimum, these targets may include the total time consumers may experience loss of supply, the frequency with which supply to consumers may be interrupted, including momentary interruptions and the duration of interruptions, excluding momentary interruptions, for consumers on average, and to a substantial majority of consumers. Where groups of consumers are expected to receive substantially different levels of service, separate requirements may be set. A licensee is to use its best endeavours to ensure that the duration of interruptions to the supply of electricity to consumers' electrical installations is held at a minimum, taking into account the relationship between costs and reliability of supply. Under Regulation 9(3), a licensee can interrupt supply at any time for the following reasons: planned maintenance repair, or augmentation of the distribution system, unplanned maintenance or repair of the distribution system in circumstances where, in the opinion of the licensee, the consumer's electrical installation or the distribution system poses an immediate threat of injury or material damage to any person, property or to the distribution system, the need to shed energy because the total demand for electricity at the relevant time exceeds the total supply available, as required by the system operator, the installation of a new supply to another consumer in the case of an emergency or to restore supply to a consumer.

338. Regulation 9(4) makes provision for unplanned interruptions. In the case of an unplanned interruption or an emergency, the licensee should, within thirty minutes of being advised of the interruption or emergency, or as soon as is practicable, provide by way of a twenty-four-hour telephone service, information on the nature of the interruption and an estimate of the time when supply will be restored or when reliable information on restoration of supply will be available. It should also provide options for consumers who call the service to be directly connected to a telephone operator if required and use its best endeavours to restore the consumer's supply as soon as possible, making allowance for reasonable priorities. Wherever reasonable and practicable, a licensee should provide prior information to consumers who may be interrupted by load-shedding. With respect to planned interruptions, Regulation 9(5) provides that a licensee should provide affected consumers with at least two or more business days' notice of the interruption. Such notice may be advertised in a paper of wide circulation in the area where the interruption is planned. The notice should specify the expected date, time and interruption duration and provide a twenty-four-hour telephone number for inquiries. The licensee should use its best endeavours to restore the consumer's supply as quickly as possible.

§20. Safety of Supply

339. Regulation 10 sets out the obligations of the licensees to ensure that the distribution system is safe and meets the requirements of any regulation made under the Electricity Act and applicable codes. On the one hand, at the request of a consumer, provide the consumer advice on the facilities required to protect the licensee's equipment and on the consumer's use of supply so that it does not interfere with the licensee's distribution system or with supply to any other electrical installation. On the other hand, the consumer's obligations include maintaining the electrical installation at the consumer's supply address in a safe condition, providing and maintaining at the consumer's supply address, a facility to protect the licensee's equipment which meets the licensee requirements prescribed by ERA, and ensuring that all the consumer's electrical installations and changes of such are made by certified electricians. The consumer is also required to provide safe, convenient and unhindered access to the supply address to enable work to be carried out, keep all vegetation at the supply address clear from all low-voltage service lines at the supply address and all vegetation on the supply address clear of any private electric line on neighbouring property and keep all structures and vehicles clear of all electric lines at or over the supply address. A consumer should however not allow a person other than a person who is an electrician in possession of a valid installation permit to perform any wiring work on an electrical installation, use the electricity supply in a manner that the consumer ought reasonably to be aware may interfere with the licensee's distribution system or with supply to any other electrical installation; or cause damage or interference to any third party; or interfere, or knowingly allow interference, with the licensee's distribution system or any metering equipment at the supply address, except as may be permitted by law.

§21. Embedded Generation

340. Regulation 11 requires a licensee to ensure that its distribution system is able to receive a supply of electricity from an embedded generating unit connected to its distribution system in accordance with an agreement with the embedded generator on the terms and conditions of dispatch, connection and disconnection. If such an agreement is sought by an embedded generator, the licensee and the embedded generator should negotiate in good faith. If two or more embedded generating units are connected in parallel, their obligations under the Code apply to the point of common coupling, and the maximum permissible contribution of each embedded generating unit should be in proportion to their capacity unless otherwise agreed. An embedded generator should ensure that the embedded generating unit is capable of continuous, uninterrupted operation at the system and permitted variations. An embedded generator should ensure that the embedded generating unit and any equipment within it that is connected to a distribution system complies with the Code, is maintained in a safe condition and protection equipment is at all times effectively coordinated with the electrical characteristics of the distribution system.

341. Regulation 11(4) states that an embedded generating unit that exports more than 1 MW to the licensee should have an excitation control system, including a voltage regulator; and a governor system responsive to system frequency changes. An embedded generator should ensure that each of its embedded generating units that exports more than 1 MW to the licensee complies with the Code's requirements with regard to response to disturbances, safe shutdown without external electricity supply, restart following loss of external electricity supply; and frequency responsiveness and governor stability. Under Regulation 11(5), an embedded generator should ensure that an embedded generating unit's contribution to the negative sequence voltage at the point of connection between the embedded generating unit and the distribution system is less than 1%.

342. Regulation 11(6) requires an embedded generator to ensure that an embedded generating unit's contribution to the harmonic distortion levels in the supply voltage at the point of connection between the embedded generating unit and the distribution system is within the limits specified. An embedded generator should comply with the recommended practices and requirements for harmonic control in electrical power systems and the current harmonic limits. Under Regulation 11(7), an embedded generator should ensure that inductive interference caused by its embedded generating unit is within acceptable limits of good utility practice. As regards fault levels, Regulation 11(8) is to the effect that an embedded generator should design and operate its embedded generating unit so that it does not cause fault levels in the distribution system to exceed the levels specified by the licensee.

§22. Billing and Payments

343. Regulation 12(1) deals with bills. It states that a licensee should issue a bill to a consumer at least every three months. A licensee should issue a bill to the consumer at the agreed address. Regulation 12(2) spells out the contents of a bill. The licensee should separately itemize the following charges on any bill issued the standing service fee; an electricity usage charge; the capacity charge, where applicable; and any other charges in connection with the supply of electricity, such as a reconnection fee or a charge for service provided, either at the request of the consumer or due to the failure of a consumer to perform an obligation. Where a licensee provides goods or services additional to those specified under Regulation 12(2), he or she may bill those goods or services separately. Where a licensee opts not to bill separately, the licensee should include the charges for such goods and services as separate items in its bills; apply payments received from a consumer as directed by the consumer; and where a consumer does not direct how the payment is to be allocated, apply the payment to the items referred to under Regulation 12(2) before applying any portion of it to the additional goods or services.

344. A licensee should include the following particulars on each bill in a consumer's billing cycle. The dates of the previous and current meter readings or estimates; the previous and the current meter readings or estimates; consumption, or estimated consumption; the relevant tariffs, the meter number, the amount due, the pay-by date, where and how the bill is to be paid, the telephone number for billing and payment inquiries, a twenty-four-hour contact telephone number for faults and emergencies, the consumer's supply address and any relevant mailing address, the consumer's name and account number; the amount of arrears or credit; the amount of any other charge and details of the service provided. Where a consumer requests and the data is available, a licensee should provide to the consumer free of charge the consumer's historical billing data for the previous three years. Regulation 12(3) gives the basis of a bill. A licensee should base a consumer's bill on a reading of the meter at the consumer's supply address and read the meter at a consumer's supply address at least once in any six months or for unmetered supply, based on a consumer's bill on tariffs as approved by ERA. Where a licensee is unable to base a bill on a reading of the meter at a consumer's supply address because access is denied as a result of action by the consumer, a third party, weather conditions or an industrial dispute, access is denied for safety reasons, the meter or ancillary equipment has recorded usage incorrectly, or the meter has been tampered with, the licensee may provide the consumer with an estimated bill based on the consumer's reading of the meter or the consumer's prior billing history or where the consumer does not have a prior billing history, either average usage of electricity at the relevant tariff or average usage at the supply address, whichever is the lower. Where a licensee has provided a consumer with an estimated bill and the licensee is subsequently able to read the meter, the licensee should adjust the estimated bill in accordance with the meter reading. Where a consumer denies access to a licensee for the purposes of reading a meter as the consumer's supply address and subsequently requests the licensee to replace an estimated bill with a bill based on a reading of the meter, provided the consumer allows access to the meter, the licensee should comply with the request and may impose a charge for doing so, determined by reference to its approved statement of charges.

345. Regulation 12(4) provides that where a licensee undercharges a consumer as a result of the licensee's error, the licensee may recover from the consumer the amount undercharged. Where a licensee proposes to exercise its right under Regulation 12(4) to recover an amount undercharged as a result of its error, the licensee should limit the amount to be recovered to the amount undercharged in the twelve months prior to the consumer's last bill, list the amount to be recovered as a separate item in a special bill or in the next bill in the consumer's billing cycle together with an explanation of the amount, not charge the consumer interest on the amount; and if the consumer requests it, allow the consumer time to pay the amount undercharged in agreed instalments, up to a period equal to the period in which the undercharging occurred, to a maximum period of twelve months. Where a licensee undercharges a consumer as a result of the consumer's fraud, the licensee may take action. According to Regulation 12(5), where a consumer is overcharged as a result of an error by a licensee, the licensee should rectify the anomaly at the next billing. No interest shall accrue to a credit or refund. Under Regulation 12(6), where a consumer's bill covers a period other than the consumer's usual billing cycle, the licensee should adjust the standing service fee and the kWh usage calculation for step tariffs on a pro-rata basis. In case a consumer's tariff is changed or a consumer's tariff rate changes during a billing period, the licensee should calculate the consumer's bill on the basis of the pro-rata application of each tariff to its respective period.

346. A consumer is required under Regulation 13 to pay a bill by the pay-by date specified in the bill. The payment methods include paying in person at a network of agencies or payment outlets providing an adequate level of consumer access or by any other payment arrangement as agreed. Payment difficulties are dealt with under Regulation 13(3) to the effect that where a residential consumer indicates to a licensee that the consumer is experiencing difficulties in paying a bill or requires assistance, the licensee may offer an instalment plan option. A licensee is empowered under Regulation 13(4) to review a consumer's bill at the consumer's request. Where a licensee is reviewing a bill, the consumer should pay that portion of the bill under review that the consumer and the licensee agree is not in dispute or an amount equal to the average amount of the consumer's bills in the previous twelve months and any future bills. Where, after conducting a review of the bill or check reading and examination of a meter, a licensee is satisfied that it is correct, the consumer may request the licensee to conduct a meter test. The consumer may require that the test be conducted by a third competent neutral party. If the meter is found to be accurate, the consumer should pay the cost of the test and the amount of the bill. If it is incorrect, the licensee should make a correction. With regard to shortened collection cycle, Regulation 13(5) provides that where a licensee issues a consumer who is on a monthly billing cycle with two disconnection warnings, the licensee may place the consumer on a shortened collection cycle.

347. Regulation 13(6) deals with the aspect of vacating a supply address. A consumer should give the licensee at least three business days' notice of the date on which the consumer intends to vacate the consumer's address and a forwarding address to which a final bill may be sent. Where a consumer gives such notice, the consumer should remain responsible for paying for electricity supplied to the supply address and otherwise remain responsible for fulfilling the consumer's obligations under the Code at the supply address to the date notified under Regulation 13(6). If a consumer does not give notice in accordance with Regulation 13(6), the consumer should remain responsible for paying for the electricity supplied to the supply address and otherwise remain responsible for fulfilling the consumer's obligations under the Code at the supply address until three business days after the licensee has received notice to discontinue supply at the supply address, or until a new consumer commences to take supply at the supply address, whichever occurs first.

348. A licensee may, under Regulation 14(1), require a consumer to provide a security deposit before connection to supply. The amount of a security deposit should be not greater than for a consumer who is on a quarterly billing cycle, 1.5 times the estimated quarterly bill, and for a consumer who is on a monthly billing cycle, 3 times the estimated monthly bill. The amount for security deposit should be calculated with reference to a schedule of type of consumer and type of business. A licensee may increase any consumer's security deposit when the existing deposit becomes insufficient to secure the consumer's current electricity usage. If agreed between the licensee and the consumer, a bank guarantee may be accepted as an alternative to the security deposit arrangement. Where a licensee receives a security deposit from a consumer, the licensee should pay the consumer interest on the deposit at a rate and on terms and conditions approved by ERA. Regulation 14(3) empowers a licensee to use a consumer's security deposit and interest which has accrued to it under the following conditions: to offset any amount owed by a consumer to the licensee if the consumer refuses to take supply after work at installations to provide that consumer supply has been conducted, if the consumer fails to pay a bill resulting in disconnection of the supply address, if the consumer defaults on a final bill or at the request of a consumer who is vacating the supply address or requesting disconnection of supply to the supply address. Where a licensee uses a security deposit, the licensee should provide the consumer with an account of its use of the security deposit and pay the balance of the security deposit to the consumer within the current billing cycle.

§23. Disconnections

349. According to Regulation 15(2), a licensee may disconnect supply to a consumer's supply address if a consumer has not paid or adhered to the consumer's obligation to make payments in accordance with an agreed payment plan. The licensee may also disconnect or interrupt supply to a consumer's supply address in the case of an emergency. Where a licensee exercises its disconnection right, the licensee should provide, by way of its twenty-four-hour emergency line, information on the nature of the emergency and an estimate of the time when supply should be reconnected and use its best endeavours to reconnect the consumer's supply address. Under Regulation 15(3), a licensee may disconnect or interrupt supply to a consumer's supply address for reasons of health or safety. Except in the case of an emergency or where there is a need to reduce the risk of fire or where relevant regulations require it, a licensee should not disconnect a consumer's supply address for a health or safety reason unless the licensee has given the consumer written notice of the problem, allowed the consumer five business days to rectify the problem and at the expiration of five business days the consumer, by way of a written disconnection warning, another five business days' notice of its intention to disconnect the consumer.

350. A licensee may, under Regulation 15(4), disconnect or interrupt supply to a consumer's supply address for the purposes of carrying out the licensee's planned maintenance on or augmentation to the licensee's system. A licensee's right to disconnect is subject to the licensee giving the consumer not less than two business days' written notice of its intention to disconnect. A licensee should use its best efforts to minimize interruptions to supply occasioned by the licensee's planned maintenance or augmentation and restore supply as soon as practicable. A licensee may disconnect supply to a consumer's supply address immediately where the consumer has obtained a supply of electricity at the supply address contrary to the provisions of the Code. Regulation 15(6) bars a licensee from disconnecting supply to a consumer's supply address where a consumer has made a complaint directly related to the reason for the prepared disconnection to ERA, the tribunal or the court or another external dispute resolution body, and the complaint remains unresolved. It also bars disconnection where the consumer has failed to pay an amount on a bill which does not relate to the standing service fee, the electricity usage charge, capacity charge or charges for other services rendered by the licensee after 3:00 p.m. on a weekday, or on a Friday, on a weekend, on a public holiday or on the day before a public holiday, except in the case of a planned interruption. A licensee should use its best endeavours to disconnect supply to a consumer's supply address and finalize the consumer's accounts in accordance with the consumer's request.

351. A licensee is under an obligation to reconnect a consumer. Under Regulation 16(1), where a licensee exercises its right to disconnect supply to a consumer's supply address for non-payment of a bill and the consumer pays or agrees to accept an offer of an instalment plan or other payment option, the customer provides access to the meter; the consumer has rectified the problem; the consumer ceases to so obtain supply and pays or makes an arrangement to pay for the supply so obtained the licensee should reconnect the consumer's supply. Where the consumer makes a request for reconnection, the licensee should make a reconnection as soon as possible and not later than two business days from the request and receipt of the reconnection charge as listed in the licensee's approved statement of charges. Repair of public lights should be handled in accordance with standing written agreements or contracts with the respective local authorities.

§24. Provision of Information and Confidentiality

352. A consumer is obliged under Regulation 18 to inform the licensee as soon as possible if there is any proposed change in responsibility for the payment of the licensee's bill; to the consumer's contact details; to the major electricity usage proposal of the consumer's supply; affecting access to metering equipment; or to wiring or plant or equipment which may affect the quality or safety of the supply of electricity to the consumer or to any other person. A consumer should, upon request from a licensee, generally or specifically provide details of loads connected or planned to be connected to the distribution system which are required for the purpose of the licensee's planning, including the location of loads in the distribution system; existing loads; existing load profile; changes in load schedule; planned outages; forecast on development of loads; anticipated new loads; and anticipated redundant loads. The licensee's obligation with regard to provision of information is spelt out under Regulation 18(3). A licensee is required to provide information to a consumer on the type and frequency of bills the consumer should receive; payment options available to the consumer; how to make a complaint to or inquiry of the licensee; how to contact consumer organizations; the licensee's guaranteed service level; the licensee's twenty-four hour seven days a week consumer contact line; and the licensee's quality of supply obligations and the expected reliability and quality of supply. When requested by a consumer, the licensee should provide the consumer with reasonable information on the licensee's tariffs, the licensee's requirements in relation to the consumer's proposed new electrical installation, or changes to the consumer's existing electrical installation, including advice about supply extensions. The licensee should provide this information free of charge within ten business days of the consumer's request; upon request, provide this information in writing; or advise the consumer where he or she may obtain a copy of the relevant standards.

353. Pursuant to Regulation 19(1), a licensee to whom confidential information is provided should not disclose or give access to that confidential information to any person except as permitted or obliged under the Code or any other law. The licensee should only use or reproduce the confidential information for the purpose for which it was provided, or a purpose consented to by the disclosure; should regard it as confidential information if it is information about any person's private conditions except for place of birth, date of birth, citizenship, civil status, occupation, place of residence and work; and information about technical arrangements and undertakings and conduct of business which for competitive reasons should be of importance to keep secret. However, Regulation 19(1) does not prevent the disclosure, use or reproduction of information if the current information is at that time generally and publicly available other than as a result of a breach of confidence by the licensee or a related business associate. The disclosure of information to an employee or officer of the licensee or a related business associate, or a legal or other professional adviser or other consultant of the licensee, which requires the information for the purpose of tasks of advising the licensee or for the purpose of planning or augmenting the distribution system the disclosure, use or reproduction of information with the consent of the person the information is relating to the disclosure, use or reproduction of information to the extent required by law of any government or government body, authority or agency, including ERA, having jurisdiction over a licensee or its related business associate; any stock exchange having jurisdiction over the licensee or its related business associate is also allowed.

354. The disclosure, use or reproduction of information if required in connection with legal proceedings, arbitration, expert determination or other dispute resolution mechanism, or for the purpose of advising a person in relation thereto; the disclosure, use or reproduction of information if required to protect the safety of personnel or property; or the disclosure, use or reproduction of information as an identifiable component of an aggregate sum. In the case of disclosure of information under Regulation 19(1), prior to making such disclosure, the licensee should inform the recipient of the information about confidentiality and should take appropriate precautions to ensure that the recipient keeps the information confidential and does not use the information for any other purposes other than those specified.

§25. Non-compliance

355. According to Regulation 20(1), if a licensee breaches the Code, such a licensee should remedy that breach as soon as possible. If a licensee becomes aware of its failure to comply with any obligation of the Code which can reasonably be expected to have a material adverse impact on a consumer, such licensee should notify each consumer likely to be adversely affected by the non-compliance within five business days; undertake an investigation of the non-compliance as soon as practicable but in any event within twenty business days; and advise the consumer of the steps it is taking to comply. If a licensee becomes aware of a breach of the Code by a consumer, which is not of a trivial nature, the licensee should notify the consumer in writing of the details of the non-compliance and its implications, including any impact on the licensee and other consumers; actions that the consumer must take to remedy the non-compliance; a reasonable time period in which compliance should be demonstrated; any consequences of non-compliance; and the licensee's procedure for handling complaints. A consumer should use its best endeavours to remedy any non-compliance with the Code within the time period specified in any notice of non-compliance sent by a licensee.

356. A licensee may, pursuant to Regulation 20(3), disconnect supply to a consumer's supply address if the consumer has not fulfilled an obligation to comply with the Code. Where the licensee has given the consumer a five days' written notice of disconnection and the consumer fails to comply with the notice or the consumer enters into an arrangement to comply but fails to comply with that arrangement, the licensee can disconnect supply. A licensee should however not disconnect supply to a consumer's supply address if there is a dispute between the consumer and the licensee, which has been notified by the consumer and is still being dealt with by the licensee or is the subject of proceedings before ERA, the tribunal, the court, or any kind of arbitration.

§26. Complaints and Dispute Resolution

357. Under Regulation 21, if a consumer or another licensee has a complaint regarding the licensee's obligation under the Electricity Act, the Code or any other relevant law, code or standard or a licensee's acts or omissions, the consumer may contact its licensee to settle the complaint. Where, after raising the complaint to the licensee, the consumer is not satisfied with the licensee's response to the complaint, the consumer may refer the complaint to ERA. ERA may delegate its competence relating to dispute resolution to local or centralized committees established pursuant to the Electricity Act, or ERA may decide to conduct the dispute resolution itself, depending on the gravity of the dispute. Disputes resolved by committees as provided under Regulation 21(1) are appealable according to section 21(2) to ERA. Disputes resolved by ERA are appealable to the electricity dispute tribunal established under the Electricity Act. ERA may determine that dispute resolution delegated to committees provided under Regulation 21(1) may not be appealed to ERA or the electricity dispute tribunal if the disputed amount of money is limited and the dispute is of a non-principal nature. All disputes may, notwithstanding the Code, be referred to Court. Regulation 22 requires a licensee to provide to a consumer on request and free of charge advice on how a consumer may reduce the consumer's electricity costs; advice on how and at what estimated cost a consumer may arrange for an energy audit of the consumer's supply address; and advice on the typical running costs of major domestic appliances.

358. A consumer has an obligation under Regulation 23 to allow a licensee and its equipment safe, convenient and unhindered access to the consumer's supply address for the following purposes: to read the meter at the consumer's supply address, to connect or disconnect supply, to inspect or test the electrical installation at the consumer's supply address, to undertake repairs, testing, or maintenance of the licensee's distribution system, and to prune or clear vegetation from electric lines at the consumer's supply address. The licensee's obligation is spelt out under Regulation 23(2) to the effect that except in the case of an emergency, where the consumer is the person responsible for maintaining vegetation under the power lines, a licensee intending to prune or clear vegetation from electric lines at a supply address, should give the consumer at that supply address at least five business days' notice of its intention. A licensee's representative seeking access to a consumer's supply address should carry or wear, in accordance with the licensee's requirements, official identification and show that identification upon request by the consumer. As regards hazards, Regulation 23(3) states that where a consumer's supply address contains a hazard, the consumer should provide the licensee seeking access to the supply address with protection against the hazard, including any necessary protective clothing. Maximum permissible contribution to voltage fluctuations allowable from each consumer should be in proportion to their respective maximum demand unless otherwise agreed. Under Regulation 8(11), each licensee should monitor quality of supply in accordance with good asset management principles. Regulation 8(12) guarantees the consumer's right to information. Where a consumer requests, the licensee should provide within ten business days an explanation for any change in the quality of its electricity supply outside the allowed limits.

§27. Metering and Settlement

359. All electricity delivered or sold by a licensee or retail seller should be charged for by meter measurements unless a fixed monthly amount for electricity supply is determined. A licensee should read the metres at least once every six months. Each licensee should provide, install, own and maintain all metres necessary for measurement of electricity delivered to its consumers. No licensee is allowed to put in and use any meter that is not reliable and does not conform to ERA's approved standards. A licensee is responsible for all metered values from the metering points existing in its network. A licensee is responsible for ensuring that energy consumption or energy flow at meeting points in its network is metered and read. All meter points should be read regularly. Regulation 24(2) requires each licensee to keep a record of all its metres, showing the consumer's address and the date of the last test. All meter tests should be properly referenced. The record of each test made should show the identifying number and constraints of the meter, the standard meter and other measuring devices used, the date and kind of test made, by whom made, the error or percentage of accuracy at each load tested, and sufficient data to permit verification of all calculations.

360. Each licensee may, under Regulation 24(3), where a reasonable need has been made for testing at the request of a consumer, arrange to test the accuracy of the meter serving that consumer. The licensee should inform the consumer of the time and place of the test and permit the consumer or his or her authorized representative to be present if the consumer so desires. The consumer should be properly informed of the results of any test on a meter that serves him or her. A licensee may charge the consumer for coverage of the costs for tests on metres. The fee may be charged in advance. If the meter is found to be more than nominally defective to the consumer's or the licensee's disadvantage, any fee charged for a meter test should be refunded to the consumer.

§28. Agreements

361. Regulation 25(1) makes provision for preparation and use of end-user agreements. A licensee should prepare and use model agreements in distribution and retail sale of electricity in relation to their consumers within the framework of the

Code. Such model agreements may vary between different types or classes of consumers and is subject to approval by ERA. Licensees should negotiate and enter into agreements for the connection between the distribution system and embedded generation and the transmission grid. Such agreement should be within the framework of the Code and subject to approval by ERA.

Chapter 7. The Electricity (Isolated Grid Systems) Regulations 2020

362. The Regulations apply to generating stations for commercial purposes with a generation capacity not exceeding 0.5 MW and to isolated grid systems where the generation capacity does not exceed 2 MW.

§1. Registration

363. Regulation 4 requires a developer or operator of a generating station not exceeding 0.5 MW for commercial purposes to apply to ERA for registration. ERA may approve or reject the application for registration after taking into account – (a) the impact of the proposed project on the social, cultural and recreational life of the community; (b) the need to protect the environment and conserve natural resources; (c) land use and siting or route of the project; (d) the ability of the applicant to operate in a manner designed to protect the health and safety of the consumers of electrical energy and other members of the public who would be affected by the operations of the applicant; (e) the technical, economic and financial capacity of the applicant to render the service for which the registration is required; and energy efficiency.

§2. Certificate of Exemption

364. Regulation 5(1) requires a person who intends to develop an isolated grid system with a generation capacity not exceeding 2 MW to undertake a feasibility study. Under Regulation 5 (2), such person shall obtain a confirmation of exclusivity over the proposed site from the REA. Regulation 6 application for certificate of exemption shall be made to the authority for an exemption from the requirement to hold a licence for the generation, distribution or sale of electricity using the form set out in Schedule 3 of these Regulations. Regulation 8 lists the obligations of holder of certificate of exemption that includes constructing, operating and maintaining the authorized isolated grid system in accordance with the applicable laws, regulations, terms and conditions of the certificate of exemption, directions of the authority, guidelines, standards and technical codes issued by the authority; comply with the environmental requirements prescribed under the NEA 2019; protect the safety of consumers and the public in operating the system; and comply with the customer service agreement approved authority.

§3. Technical Framework

365. Regulation 11 requires that the holder of a certificate of exemption shall adhere to the technical codes and standards for design, construction, operation and maintenance, including the Distribution Line Construction Guidelines, 2017. Regulation 12, a holder of a certificate of exemption shall comply with the Electricity

(Safety Code) Regulations 2020. Under Regulation 13, a holder of a certificate of exemption shall use calibrated energy meters or current limiting devices in order to measure the energy use of a consumer or to limit the current drawn. The energy meters shall comply with the metering requirements prescribed under the Electricity (Quality of Service Code) Regulations 2020 and the Weights and Measures (Electricity Meters) Rules 2015.

366. Regulation 17 requires the holder certificate of exemption to submit a sample consumer service agreement to the authority for approval. The holder shall connect new consumers within reach of the isolated grid distribution network within the time prescribed under the Electricity (Primary Grid Code) Regulations 2003 and the Electricity (Quality of Service Code) Regulations 2020.

§4. Tariffs

367. Regulation 19 requires a holder of a certificate of exemption to obtain approval of the retail tariffs from the authority. Regulation 20 regards the tariff structure. An applicant for a holder of certificate of exemption may propose different retail tariffs for different consumer categories taking into consideration – the place and time of supply; the quantity of electricity supplied; the load and power factor of the consumers; the purpose for which supply is taken; and the ability of the consumers to pay. For any tariff adjustment and review, the holder has the authority to use the form set out in Schedule 5 of the Regulations and in accordance with the terms and conditions of the certificate of exemption.

§5. Interconnection to the Main Grid

368. Regulation 23 provides for a holder of a certificate of exemption to have exclusive rights to undertake the authorized activity in the isolated grid service area approved by the authority, in accordance with the Act and terms and conditions of the certificate. The REA or the distribution licensee operating in the area shall give at least six months' notice to a holder of certificate of exemption before extension of the main grid into the isolated grid service area.

§6. Record Keeping and Reporting

369. Under Regulation 25, a holder of a certificate of exemption shall maintain records of the activity authorized under the certificate. The records shall describe the legal, technical, financial, hydrological or environmental issues and any other relevant information relating to the operation of the isolated grid system. A holder shall, on an annual basis, submit to the authority information in relation to the isolated grid system using the reporting format in Schedule 7 to these Regulations.

A holder shall immediately notify the authority of any event that affects the operation of the isolated grid system, in any event not later than fourteen days from the date the event occurs.

Chapter 8. The Electricity (Quality of Service Code) Regulations, SI No. 78 of 2020

370. Under Regulation 2, these regulations apply to a holder of a distribution licence under the Act and a consumer.

§1. Quality of Service

371. Regulation 4 sets guaranteed service standards for new service connections. A holder of a distribution licence shall connect a consumer for new service within ten working days where the connection requires a single-phase or no pole service, within fifteen working days where the connection requires one or more pole services, and within fifteen working days where the connection requires a three-phase service. Under Regulation 5, a person wishing to connect electricity supply to his or her premises shall make an application to the holder of a distribution licence. The application for new service connection shall be accompanied by an installation completion certificate. Regulation 6 provides that in case of complete demolition, reconstruction or substantial renovation of premises by an existing consumer, the consumer shall apply for a new connection in accordance with Regulation 5.

§2. Liability of Supply

372. Regulation 7 deals with Interruptions for scheduled maintenance. A holder of a distribution licence may disconnect or interrupt electricity supply to a locality or a consumer for the purpose of carrying out scheduled maintenance, including repair and installation of new equipment. The holder of a distribution licence shall not, except for an emergency, disconnect or interrupt electricity supply unless the holder informs the consumer of the intended disconnection or interruption, specifying the duration of the disconnection or interruption through a public notice of not less than fifteen days before the interruption of the electricity supply; or direct contact by telephone, electronic mail, or any other information technology system. Regulation 8 emphasizes that a holder of a distribution licence shall take reasonable steps to prevent interruption of supply of electricity. A holder of a distribution licence may, in an emergency situation, disconnect or interrupt the supply to a consumer without notice to the consumer but shall notify the consumer within two hours and take the appropriate measures to restore service.

§3. Consumer Relations

373. Under Regulation 10, a holder of a distribution licence shall enter into agreements regulating the terms and conditions for the connection between its installations and installations of another holder of a distribution licence, regulating business relations with another holder of a distribution licence, and defining its relationship with consumers. The agreements shall be submitted to the authority for review and approval prior to signing by the parties. Regulation 13 requires that a holder of a distribution licence to whom confidential information is provided shall, in accordance with the Access to Information Act 2005 and the Data Protection and Privacy Act 2019, not divulge or give access to the confidential information to any person except as permitted under these Regulations or any other relevant law, and only use or reproduce the confidential information for the purposes for which it was provided under these Regulations. Regulation 14 provides for consumer complaints and dispute resolution. Where a consumer has a complaint regarding the holder of a distribution licensee's obligations under the Act, these Regulations or any other relevant law, code, standard or licence, the consumer may lodge a verbal or written complaint with the holder of a distribution.

§4. Refusal and Discontinuation of Service

374. Regulation 15 lists the ground for discontinuation of service, and these include where the consumer fails to pay the bills for the electrical energy consumed for more than thirty days from the date of demand for payment; the consumer defaults on a payment arrangement agreed upon under these Regulations; the consumer tampers or interferes with a meter or a holder of a distribution licensee's equipment or permits any person to damage any of the holders of a distribution licensee's installation or equipment; the consumer illegally connects the service or allows the service to be used in such a manner as to interfere with the supply to other consumers; any part of the apparatus, installation or equipment connected with the supply of electricity to the premises of the consumer becomes defective or unsafe; or the consumer requests for disconnection of service. Under Regulation 16, except in the case of an emergency, a holder of a distribution licence shall not disconnect electricity service to a consumer without written notice to the consumer at least fourteen days before the date of disconnection of electricity service.

375. Regulation 17 gives special consideration to health facilities. Where a health facility fails to pay for the electricity service for more than sixty days from the date of demand of payment, the holder of a distribution licence shall contact the health facility and endeavour to agree on a payment arrangement. Where the payment arrangement cannot be made or where the payment arrangement agreed upon is dishonoured by the health facility, the holder of a distribution licence shall give the health facility a notice of intention to disconnect and shall continue to provide the electricity service for thirty days from the date of the notice before disconnecting service.

§5. Billing and Meters

376. Regulation 24 requires a holder of a distribution licence to issue an electricity bill every month to a consumer except a consumer on the prepaid metering system, indicating the electrical energy used in the month and other charges. The electricity bill shall be prepared by the holder of a distribution licence as promptly as possible following the reading of a consumer's meter or an estimated electricity bill based on the energy consumption of the previous month. Regulation 31 requires a holder of a distribution licence to provide, install and maintain a meter to measure and record the amount of electrical energy supplied to the consumer within the accuracy limits of the meter prescribed in the Weights and Measures (Electricity Meters) Rules 2015. Regulation 34 requires a holder of a distribution licence to conduct a periodic inspection and testing of electricity meters. Under Regulation 37, a holder of a distribution licence shall ensure that all prepaid meters are installed with the ability to upgrade to smart metering function. A holder of a distribution licence shall provide prepaid meters with a communication module hot plug-and-play functionality.

§6. New Construction

377. Under Regulation 41, a holder of a distribution licence shall construct, install, operate and maintain its plant, structure, equipment and lines in accordance with construction standards approved by the authority. Regulation 42 provides for network extension plans. A holder of a distribution licence shall, by the 30th day of August every year, prepare and submit to the authority a network extension plan for approval. Under Regulation 43, a holder of a distribution licence shall submit to the authority a notice for planned construction works sixty days prior to commencement; or for transfer of licensed installations or activities.

Chapter 9. The Electricity (Safety Code) Regulations, SI No. 22 of 2003

378. These regulations contain comprehensive safety provisions intended to apply to electrical systems and to associated plants and apparatus under their ownership or control. Under Regulation 4, each licensee is required to sufficiently inform and instruct its employees about the system, plant or apparatus affected by a particular operation or work and the rules, procedures or documents which apply to such operations. A licence should also furnish information to other persons not being its employees who are likely to be exposed to danger by the operations or work to such an extent as may be reasonably practicable. Under Regulation 6, all work on or testing of apparatus, conductors or plant should be carried out in accordance with the safety requirements.

Regulation 7 provides for objections. Any person who has an objection regarding carrying out instructions regarding the operation of or work upon a licensee's systems and associated plant and apparatus should lodge an objection with the person issuing the instructions. Where an objection has been raised, the licensee or other concerned entity should cause investigations to be conducted into the merits of the objection and, if necessary, refer the matter to a higher authority for a decision before proceeding with such an operation or work. In addition, under Regulation 8, every electrical accident and dangerous occurrence involving a licensee's high-voltage system should be reported immediately to the control engineer. Each accident and dangerous occurrence involving a low-voltage system or associated plant or apparatus should be reported immediately to the appropriate designated officer.

379. The regulations also emphasize the importance of ensuring that all persons engaged in the operations or work of electrical systems and associated plant and apparatus should comply with these Regulations and other related documents and legal procedures relevant to their duties. A person should not neglect his or her duties on the ground that he or she is ignorant of the relevant legal requirements and procedures. Thus, anyone who has any doubts as to any of these duties should report the matter to a higher authority for advice before proceeding with the work.

380. Under Regulation 9, every licensee should obtain and issue to its employee safety equipment and protective clothing approved by the ERA. In cases of employees working under the circumstances requiring safety precautions, they should wear appropriate protective clothing and footwear or such other protective clothing as may be necessary, having regard to the work such employees may be involved in. In addition, every licensee is required under Regulation 11 to train every person involved with the operation of or work upon the licensee's system and associated plant and apparatus in the treatment of electric shock.

381. Regulation 12 provides for safety provisions relating to access to and work in operational premises. First, no person should enter or have access to any operational premises like a control room, substation, switching station or underground chamber belonging to or under the control of a licence without authority. A barrier, door or gate restricting access to an underground chamber or other confined space, substation or tunnel should be kept locked, and the control of the keys should be in accordance with approved procedure. In addition, no one should enter or work in any indoor substation or confined space such as an underground chamber, tunnel, vessel, tank, pit, culvert or pipeline without the consent of a senior competent person. In cases where it becomes necessary for a person to enter and work in any of the places, adequate precautions should be taken against the danger arising from toxic and flammable or abnormal temperatures. Safety precautions should include the use of approved natural or forced ventilation or air conditioning, wearing approved breathing apparatus, testing the atmosphere using approved specialized equipment, prohibition of smoking and use of exposed flame and posting a person outside such place to keep in constant touch with the person engaged in the work with appropriate rescue equipment, ready and capable of assisting in an emergency. A person using the apparatus should be specially trained in its use. Before a person enters an area, he or she should be issued with a limitation of access, and the arrangements for access and work and the precautions to be taken should be in accordance with approved procedures.

382. Regulation 13 provides for safety requirements for vessels containing flammable substances. In such a case, no person should be allowed to smoke or expose a flame near an open vessel containing or has contained oil or any other flammable substance. In addition, no one should engage in work involving application of heat on a vessel unless such person has taken all practical precautions to prevent a fire or explosion. The prevention of fire or explosion should be by removal of the flammable substance and any fumes or by rendering them non-explosive and non-flammable. Finally, no person should enter a vessel that has recently been emptied of oil or other flammable or toxic substance unless a senior competent person is satisfied that all dangerous vapours have been expelled and a limitation of access has been issued.

383. The safety requirements for working in fire-protected areas are also provided in Regulation 14. The automatic control should be rendered inoperative and the equipment left on manual control, and a caution notice attached. The precautions taken to render the automatic control inoperative and the conditions under which it may be restored should be noted on a safety document or written instruction issued for such access or work or other activity, and the automatic control should be restored immediately after the persons engaged in the work have withdrawn from the enclosure. Only approved portable fire extinguishers should be made available and should be the only extinguishers to be used near live apparatus and conductors. Additionally, in the handling of fire extinguishers, safety distances should be maintained. After the discharge of a portable fire extinguisher in an enclosed space, personnel should leave the space until precautions have been taken. After an explosion, fire or discharge of a fire extinguisher in an enclosed space, the space should be adequately ventilated before any personnel enter it.

384. Regulation 15 provides for safety requirements when climbing, testing and working on poles, towers and high structures. No person should climb any pole unless such a pole has been tested in an approved manner. Second, no one should climb a pole which is impaired by decay or damage or whose stability is in doubt until such pole has been supported by approved means. Where a pole is supported, such pole should be climbed by one person at a time, or access to its top may be by other approved means independent of the pole. A person gaining access to work on a tower, pole or other high structure should use safety belts, harnesses or other safety equipment of an approved type. A person working on a tower, pole or other high structure should be in the visual range of another person who should be fully conversant with approved rescue procedures. Finally, every gate or device to prevent climbing of towers and gantries supporting high-voltage conductors should always be kept secured in an approved manner, and access should be controlled by a senior competent person or a competent person in receipt of an appropriate safety document.

385. Regulation 16 relates to access to high-voltage apparatus and conductors. Guards to an access ladder, barrier, door or gate on or in an outdoor compound preventing access to a live high-voltage conductor should be kept secured in an approved manner, and access to them should be according to approved procedure. Any barrier, door or gate preventing access to a totally enclosed chamber, cubicle or cell containing live high-voltage conductors should be kept locked, and the keys should be accessible only to a senior competent person. Any spout shutter not required for immediate work or operation should, if the spout is not otherwise made inaccessible, be locked and the key accessible only to a senior competent person.

386. Regulation 17 also relates to high-voltage switching. High-voltage switching should not be carried out by any person other than an authorized person, a senior competent person or remotely directed by a control engineer. A competent person may, for the purpose of training and acting under the personal supervision of an authorized person or senior competent person, carry out high-voltage switching. Except in cases of emergency, high-voltage switching should not be carried out without the authority of the appropriate control engineer. When a control engineer gives authority for high-voltage switching to be carried out, he or she should communicate directly with the person intending to carry out the switching, and where for special reasons, direct communication is not possible, an approved procedure should be followed.

387. In addition, before any high-voltage switching is carried out on any system that may affect another system, the control engineer authorizing the switching should communicate with the control engineer of the other system and the switching should be agreed upon between them and recorded in the respective control books of all control engineers concerned. Where high-voltage switching is to be carried out for issuing a safety document, and there are two or more control functions involved, in the absence of a standing agreement for such matter, the control engineers concerned should all agree on the person to be in control of the part of the system in the isolated state and to be responsible for giving consent to the issuing of a safety document, and such agreement between the control engineers should be recorded in the respective control log books by each control engineer. Where there are special requirements to be complied with before, during or after high-voltage switching operations, approved procedures should apply, and special provisions should be made to ensure that the control engineers, the operators and others affected are aware of their responsibilities.

388. High-voltage switching with the control engineer's authority should be carried out without undue delay, and all such switching or switching in an emergency should be reported to the control engineer as soon as possible. For emergency switching, the circumstances demanding such switching should be reported at the same time. If a switchgear shows any sign of distress, the operator should report its condition to the control engineer, who should, in turn, report to a higher authority in order to have it examined before taking a decision about further operation. An operator should, while operating a switching gear mounted on a pole or other structure from ground level where necessary, wear rubber gloves or use other approved equipment. Finally, no person should undertake to switch or work on high-voltage equipment by signal or pre-arranged understanding after an agreed interval of time.

389. Regulation 18 provides for records. Every message by telephone or otherwise relating to the operation of a high-voltage system should be recorded and should be repeated to the sender to ensure that it has been accurately received. A control engineer should ensure that a record is made of the time and particulars of all high-voltage switching, including that carried out by the control engineer by remote control. Under Regulation 19, in case of a failure of supply to or from any part of a high-voltage system for whatever cause, it should be immediately reported to the control engineer. During a failure of supply, all apparatus and conductors are regarded as live unless they are isolated and proved dead by approved means. Regulation 20 relates to voltage testing devices. Voltage testing devices should be of an approved type and should be used in accordance with approved procedures. Voltage testing devices should be tested in an approved manner immediately before and after use, and where this is not practically possible, in accordance with other approved procedures.

390. Safety Precautions for Work on or Near High-Voltage Systems are provided for under Regulation 21. Under Regulation 21, no person should undertake any repair, maintenance, cleaning, alteration or such work, on or within the safety distance of an exposed conductor, part of a high-voltage system distance of an exposed conductor or part of a high-voltage system unless such parts of the system are dead, isolated and all practicable steps taken up to lock off from all points of supply with caution notices fixed at all points of isolation, earthed by approved means at all points of disconnection of high-voltage supply from the system or between such points and the point of work, screened where necessary to prevent danger, and danger notices are attached to apparatus containing live conductors and attached near other live conductors, identified at the point of work by approved means and released for work by the issue of an appropriate safety document that should not be issued unless such person is fully conversant with the precise parts of the systems, apparatus and conductors to be worked upon, the nature and extent of the work to be done and the safety precautions to be taken. It is the duty of the person issuing the appropriate safety documents to ensure compliance.

391. Regulation 22 provides for the isolation of apparatus and conductors. Isolation or reconnection of high-voltage apparatus or conductors should not be initiated except with the sanction of the control engineer. Safety locks should be used to lock all switchgear at points where the circuit on which work is to be carried out is likely to be energized, and the keys for such locks should be kept in a key safe if provided or in some other safe place in possession of an authorized person. Safety locks should be fitted to the switch gear at all points of isolation immediately following the sectionalization of defective apparatus. Details of the isolation and the deposit of safety lock keys associated with the isolation should be recorded by the Control Centre. Where the circuit on which work is to be carried out is controlled only by fuses or links, the fuses or links (and carriers) should be removed and kept in a safe place, preferably in possession of the person responsible for issuing the safety documents. Finally, when the mechanical isolation of a voltage transformer involves physical difficulty in withdrawal to achieve total high-voltage isolation, the withdrawal of the voltage transformer secondary fuses or links may be accepted as isolation, and fuses or links so withdrawn should be kept in a safe place in possession of the person responsible for issuing the safety document, and caution notices should be fixed at all points of isolation.

392. Regulation 23 provides for the earthing procedure. Where high-voltage apparatus or conductors are to be discharged and earthed, it should be done when reasonably practicable by using a circuit breaker or earthing switch provided for the purpose of making the earthing connection. In cases a circuit breaker is used, the trip feature should be rendered inoperative before closing unless this is not practicable when it should be done afterwards. After closing, the circuit breaker or earthing switch should be locked in the earthed position so that it remains inoperative while it is the circuit main earth. Where a circuit breaker is used to make the earth connection, the operation of closing to earth should be carried out locally, and Supervisory Control and Data Acquisition (SCADA) should not be used. Where work is carried out on an overhead system to which a consumer remains connected, a circuit main earth should be provided and maintained between that consumer and the point of work. Due to the possibility of low-voltage and high-voltage inversions like from customers' generation, care should be taken when using earthing lead following a test with the indicator to verify that the circuit is not live, and one conductor should be earthed, and subsequent tests carried out to verify that the retaining conductors are not live before applying an earth to them.

393. Earthing leads and associated clamps should be of an approved type and of adequate capacity for the duty at the point of application and should be adequately maintained and always examined immediately before use. The general procedure to be followed when using earthing leads should be as follows. First, the circuit should be verified that it is not live and, where practicable, checked by means of an approved voltage testing device or other approved means. Second, the circuit should be verified that it is not live and, where practicable, checked by means of an approved earthing pole or other approved appliance, and care should be taken to ensure that good contact is made and that earthing leads are clearly visible, earthing leads should be connected to earth before being connected to the phase conductors.

They should only be connected to the phases by means of an approved earthing pole or other approved appliance. Care should be taken to ensure that good contact is made and that earthing leads are clearly visible. All phases should be earthed, even if work is to be carried out only on one phase. Earthing leads should not be applied in any cell or compartment in which there is any exposed metal live at high voltage that may be a source of danger and should be applied so that they remain clearly visible as far as it is reasonably practicable. When earthing leads are being removed, each should be disconnected from its phase conductor by means of an approved earthing appliance before it is removed from its earth connection, and finally, for earthing on spout contacts of metal-enclosed switchgear, only approved appliances should be used, and a person should not insert a hand or tool into contact with spouts.

394. A person should not operate a high-voltage earthing switch or circuit main earth connected or disconnected, except with the consent of the control engineer or under the terms of a sanction for test or by an authorized person or by a senior competent person acting under the personal supervision of an authorized person. Each operation of circuit main earths should be reported to the control engineer as soon as possible after completion, and when operating to an HV switching schedule, the application or removal of circuit main earths should be reported to the control engineer at the appropriate control break. The location of each circuit main earth should be recorded on the safety document. Additional earths applied after the issue of a permit to work or sanction for test may be attached or removed by a senior competent person. The safety requirements while approaching exposed live high-voltage conductors or insulators supporting them are set out in Regulation 24. The safety distances designated in the second schedule should be maintained at the respective system voltages between any part of a person or object and the nearest exposed live high-voltage conductor. A distance of 300 mm should be maintained at all system voltages from the portion of insulators supporting live high-voltage conductors, which is outside the appropriate safety distance from the conductors. No person should allow any part of his or her body or any other object not provided for within the approved procedures to approach exposed high-voltage conductors or insulators supporting such conductors within the safety distances. Where exposed high-voltage conductors are not isolated, the only objects that should be caused to approach them or insulators supporting them within the safety distances should be insulated devices approved for high-voltage live line work or approved voltage testing devices.

395. Where exposed conductors are isolated but not proved dead, the only objects that should be caused to approach them or insulators supporting them within the safety distances should be insulated devices approved for high-voltage live line work or approved voltage testing devices. Where exposed 132 KV conductors in a high-voltage substation compound have been isolated, a circuit main earth may be applied to the apparatus following a visual examination to confirm that adequate isolation has been achieved. Taking account of the nature and location of the work and the hazards and the presence of persons, an authorized person or the person in charge of the work should establish working and access clearances such as to ensure that the safety distances are maintained both in respect of those persons present and the objects being handled. Recommended working and access clearances for the guidance of authorized persons are specified in the third, fourth and fifth Schedules. Where work is to be carried out within a one-meter distance of the safety distance, the supervisor should ascertain if any of the following additional precautions have been taken before work commences: danger notices or red pennants are attached to the pole or structure at a distance, not less than is specified in paragraph 20, or a limitation of access has been issued defining the work to be carried out in the vicinity of live conductors and detailing any specified potential hazards to be avoided. Danger notices or red pennants should be attached by a senior competent person or engineer or by a competent person acting under the personal supervision of an authorized person or senior competent person.

396. Regulation 25 provides for precautions that can be taken regarding work in substations and switching stations containing live high-voltage conductors. Such precautions include identifying and defining such zones of work by an authorized person using approved barriers roping, yellow demarcation ribbons or other approved means and should be so arranged that the specified working and access clearances from the nearest exposed live conductor or supporting insulator to ground level or platform or access way which may be repaired to be used are established; the zone of work to be defined at ground level should be only that in which the work is to be carried out; if the work cannot be carried out without leaving the ground level or a platform or access way, the working and access clearances should be obtained from the nearest exposed live high-voltage conductor to the points from which work is actually carried out, and in such cases access should only be by means of an approved ladder or other approved means; a person should not climb any structure to gain access. In the case of terminal poles in substations, access should be in accordance with approved procedures; if the work is such that the specified working and access clearances are not sufficient to avoid danger, other suitable arrangements should be made; and the approved barriers or roping should be clearly visible, so far as it is reasonably practicable, and should not be supported by any structure carrying electrical apparatus or conductor and should not carry any notice; and at ground level the section so defined should be clearly distinguished by green flags by day or, if not otherwise satisfactorily illuminated by green lights at night, fixed on separate supports and suitably spaced within the safe boundary. Danger notices should be attached to adjoining apparatus containing live conductors or adjacent conductor supports at the limits of the zone of work.

397. Where necessary to prevent danger, the means of access to and from the zone of work should be defined in an approved manner. The following provisions apply to the use of portable ladders and long objects where there are exposed live conductors. The type of portable ladders should be approved and should be of no greater length than is required for the work involved, portable ladders and other long objects should not be used without the permission of an authorized person, who should define the conditions of use to the senior competent person in charge of the work, the movement and erection of such ladders and objects should then be carried out only under the personal supervision of the senior competent person in charge of the work, and when moved at ground level should be carried only in a horizontal position and as near the ground as reasonably practicable; portable ladders provided for giving access to fixed ladders which terminate above ground level, and to provide access in other approved cases, should be padlocked in position or otherwise secured by a senior competent person while work is being carried out; and all portable ladders within substations, or switching stations should be securely locked to a suitable anchorage when not in use. When using cranes, scaffolds and other equipment, the following provisions should apply. First, when cranes, scaffolds or other equipment and materials transported by vehicles or otherwise are taken into or out of a substation, the route to be followed should be agreed upon by an authorized person, and the cranes, scaffolds or other equipment should be connected to the substation earthing system as soon as reasonably practicable; the limits of operation of such equipment should be defined by an authorized person to a senior competent person who should be in charge of the work and thereafter the equipment should be erected or moved only within such limits under the personal supervision of the senior competent person. Danger notices, barriers and screens should be fixed or moved only by or under the personal supervision of an authorized person. In the event of a lightning storm, work on exposed conductors in outdoor substations or outdoor switching stations or on apparatus directly connected to exposed conductors should cease immediately, where necessary, to prevent danger, and the control engineer should be informed.

398. As regards permit to work, Regulation 26 states that it should be issued by an authorized person before any work is carried out on any apparatus or conductor, and it should only be issued with the knowledge of the control engineer, who should maintain a record of the issue and cancellation of each permit to work. When working on a high-voltage switching schedule, the issue and cancellation of a permit to work should be recorded by the control engineer as soon after its issue as is practicable. Where more than one working party is involved in work on apparatus or conductors associated with the same circuit main earths, the authorized person in charge of the high-voltage switching schedule should record the issue of all safety documents on his or her copy of the high-voltage switching schedule or danger envelope. If, after agreement with the control engineer, it is found necessary to move any point of isolation located between the zone of work and a live high-voltage system, every outstanding permit to work should be cancelled and new ones issued for any subsequent work on the apparatus. A permit to work should be explained and issued to the person in direct charge of the work, who, after reading its contents and confirming that he or she understands it and is conversant with the nature and extent of the work to be done, should sign its receipt and its duplicate. The recipient of a permit to work should be a competent person who should retain the permit to work in his or her possession or at all times while work is being carried out. Where more than one working party is involved, a permit to work should be issued to the competent persons in direct charge of each working party, and they may, where necessary, be cross-referenced with each other.

399. The circumstances under which a permit to work can be cleared and cancelled include when work on the apparatus or conductor for which it was issued has been completed, where it is necessary to issue a sanction for test, in which case all permits to work that are associated with the apparatus and conductors to be tested should be cancelled; where it is necessary to change the person in charge of the work detailed on the permit to work; at the discretion of an authorized person, when it is necessary to interrupt or suspend the work detailed on the permit to work. The recipient should sign the clearance and return the permit to work to an authorized person, who should cancel it and inform the control engineer, and in all cases, the recipient should indicate in the clearance section whether the work is complete or not, and all the gear and tools have been removed or not. Where more than one permit to work has been issued for work on high-voltage apparatus or conductors associated with the same circuit main earths, the control engineer should ensure that all such permits to work have been cancelled before the circuit main earths are removed. Where there is a requirement for a permit to work to be temporarily withdrawn or suspended, such withdrawal or suspension should be in accordance with an approved procedure.

400. Sanction for Test: According to Regulation 27, a sanction for test should be issued by the authorized person initiating the testing before any testing is carried out on any apparatus or conductor. A sanction for test should only be issued with the knowledge of the control engineer, who should maintain a record of the issue of each sanction for test or its cancellation. When working on a high-voltage switching schedule, the issue or cancellation of a sanction for test should be recorded by the control engineer as soon after its issue or cancellation as is practicable. A sanction for test should be explained and issued to a person in direct charge of the testing, who, after reading its contents and confirming that he or she understands it and is conversant with the nature and extent of the testing to be done, should sign its receipt and its duplicate. The recipient of a sanction for test should be a senior competent person who should retain the sanction or test in his or her possession at all times while tests are being done. When testing on apparatus for which a sanction for test has been issued is suspended or completed, the recipient should sign the clearance and return the sanction for test to an authorized person who should cancel it and inform the control engineer.

401. Where there is a requirement for a sanction for test to be temporarily withdrawn or suspended, such withdrawal or suspension should be in accordance with an approved procedure. Under Regulation 29, provision is made for limitation of access to the effect that a limitation of access should be issued by an authorized person or a senior competent person specially authorized to do so when it is considered necessary to have written instructions to avoid danger and when a permit to work or a sanction for test is not applicable. Where a limitation of access is required for work above ground level in a 132 kV compound, it should only be issued by an authorized person with the knowledge of the control engineer. A person issuing a limitation of access should determine from the nature of the work occasions when the control engineer should record its issue and cancellation. A limitation of access should, when there is danger, be issued for the following types of activity: work in proximity to, but outside the working and access clearance from exposed live high-voltage conductors when work is to proceed in the vicinity of an overhead line and the line is made dead in accordance with Regulation 21; access to and work in underground chambers and similar confined spaces; work on plant operated by or containing compressed air or other gases; or such other access or work as may be specified by a designated engineer.

402. A limitation of access should be explained and issued to the person in direct charge of the work, who, after reading its contents and confirming that he or she understands it and is conversant with the nature and extent of the work to be done, should sign its receipt and duplicate. The recipient of a limitation of access should be a competent person who should retain it in his or her possession at all times while work is being carried out. Where more than one working party is involved, a limitation of access should be issued to the competent persons severally having personal supervision of each working party. A limitation of access should be cancelled by the recipient signing the clearance and returning the limitation of access for cancellation to an authorized person or senior competent person specially authorized to do so.

403. Safety Precautions and Procedure Applicable to Low-Voltage Systems: Part V of these regulations makes provision for the procedure applicable to low-voltage systems. Under Regulation 30, it is provided that where work or testing is carried out on or near low-voltage apparatus and conductors, precautions should be taken to prevent danger from body injury due to electric arc or electric shock; the conductors should be covered with insulation and screening, and the adequacy of these materials to prevent danger should be assessed before work, or testing is carried out; and the precautions appropriate to work on or near exposed danger precautions appropriate to work on or near exposed conductors should be applied. The circumstances under which danger may arise include where a person confuses apparatus and conductors which have been made dead with those which remain live; dead apparatus and conductors are accidentally or inadvertently made live; if a person accidentally or inadvertently makes contact with adjacent live conductors; or if inadequate precautions are taken during live work or testing.

404. The term 'earthed' when applied to the low-voltage system comprises the bonding of the phase conductors to the neutral conductors by means of an approved device or leads. Control and operation of low-voltage systems should be in accordance with an approved procedure, and only persons appointed in accordance with an approved procedure should carry out activities such as switching and the live testing of low-voltage systems. Work or testing of low-voltage apparatus and conductors should be carried out by a competent person, and where working arrangements so require, approved procedures for the control of work, including the issue of a safety document, should apply. Where work or testing involves the initial connection or the re-arrangement of conductors to a consumer, the electricity supply should not be provided to the consumer until checks have been made at an appropriate point on the system to ensure correct polarity at the supply terminals and where necessary, in the case of a three-phase supply, the phase rotation should additionally be checked. A person should not erect or dismantle a low-voltage overhead line under a live high-voltage overhead line without the authority of an authorized person, who should ensure that, when necessary, because of insufficient clearance, the high-voltage line is made dead and a permit to work issued. When a low-voltage overhead line conductor is to be raised or lowered or otherwise held on temporary support or connections, approved procedures should be followed to ensure that no danger is caused at locations such as road or rail crossing where other persons may be present.

405. Under Regulation 31, the requirements for work on dead low-voltage apparatus and conductors are set out; they include isolating the conductors from all sources of supply from the system; applying safety locks where the isolating devices are lockable; removing components such as fuses and links, fixing caution notices at points of isolation and keys and removed components should be kept in a secure place in possession of the person in charge of the work. Conductors should be earthed using an earthing device or earthing leads approved for use on the conductors concerned. Except when work on a low-voltage system is being carried out as part of approved high-voltage live line work, the following requirements apply. If the work requires a point of isolation to be established on a high-voltage system, an appropriate safety document should be issued; if the work requires a high-voltage system to be made dead, isolated and earthed, a permit to work should be issued; and if the work is being done in conjunction with work on a high-voltage system which has been made dead, isolated and earthed, this work should be included on the permit to work issued for the high-voltage work.

406. Suitable precaution should be taken by approved screening or other approved means to avoid danger from inadvertent contact with adjacent live conductors, including, where necessary, the fixing of danger notices to apparatus containing live conductors adjacent to other live conductors and at the limits of the zone in which the work may be carried out. Where conductors are likely to become live due to the operation of a consumer's generator, the following precautions should be taken to prevent danger: the conductors should be isolated from the consumer's system, or the conductors should be earthed on an earth provided between the point of work and the consumer's system. Before work is connected, the apparatus and conductors should be identified and proved dead at the point of work by means of an approved voltage testing device, and while work is in progress, any live working method that can reasonably be applied to minimize the risk of danger from the conductors being accidentally or inadvertently made live should be used.

407. The precautions for work on deadly low-voltage cables are set out under Regulation 32 to include unless the point of work can be visually traced from a point where the conductors are accessible and have been proved dead at that point, it will be necessary to open the cable as if it is live and test each conductor with an approved voltage testing device; and if the cable has been damaged or is faulty, it should not be presumed dead, and consequently, the test should be made at a safe distance from the suspected point of damaged fault, and the cable should be visually traced from the point of test to the suspect point of damage or fault. Appropriate precautions should be taken to avoid danger from electric arcing until the point of damage or fault is located. Where work is to be carried out on an auxiliary cable which may be subject to induced voltage from a high-voltage circuit, additional precautions to prevent danger from these voltages should be taken in accordance with approved procedures. The following precautions under Regulation 33 are to be taken with regard to work on dead low-voltage overhead lines: bare open-wire low-voltage conductors should be earthed using approved earthing leads, and where insulated but unscreened conductors are present, the requirements for live working should be observed until the conductors have been proved dead. Any unearthed steelwork, such as an offset racket or the upper portion of a stay above the insulator, should be treated as live until it is or the conductors have been proved dead.

408. A person should not carry out low-voltage live work except in accordance with an approved procedure, which should ensure adequate protection from danger from electric shock and inadvertent short-circuiting of the conductors. Where low-voltage live work is to be carried out, the competent person in charge of the working party should make an assessment of the site conductors, and the work should only commence where site conditions enable work to be done safely. If the site conditions become unsafe, low-voltage live working should be suspended, and the following requirements should be assessed: the apparatus to be worked upon should be visually inspected to ascertain if it is in a satisfactory condition; there should be adequate working space and safe means of escape; the working space and the apparatus to be worked on should be adequately illuminated; and if the work is outdoors, the weather conditions should not be unduly adverse. Every person who carries out live work should be a competent person and should have received appropriate training in the particular low-voltage live working procedure and be adequately instructed by the competent person in charge of the working party. Tools and equipment approved for that purpose should be the only tools used for work on or the testing of low-voltage apparatus and conductors. A person should not carry out work which involves, or is equivalent to, manipulation of bare live conductors unless accompanied by another person who should be available to render or obtain assistance in an emergency.

409. Regulation 38 makes provision for testing and adjustment of low-voltage apparatus in the following terms. Testing and adjustment, including functional testing, may be made with low-voltage apparatus live if a person making such testing and adjustment uses approved insulated tools and instruments. If the testing or adjustment requires covers to be removed so that terminals or connections that are live or can be made live are exposed or temporarily disconnected, precautions should be taken to prevent unauthorized access to or interference with the apparatus. Such precautions should include, where necessary, personal supervision or erection of suitable barriers or screening and the display of danger notices. If the conductors are to be made dead in order to avoid danger, appropriate requirements under Regulations 31 and 32 should be applied. Regulation 39 deals with the general penalty, and it provides that: a person who contravenes the provisions of these regulations commits an offence and is liable on conviction to a fine not exceeding ten currency points or to imprisonment for a term not exceeding one year or both.

Chapter 10. The Weights and Measures (Electricity Meters) Rules 2015

410. The Rules provide unit measurements and standards of electrical energy. Rule 3 provides that the units of measurement for the sale of electrical energy shall be the watt-hour, the volt-ampere hour, or the volt-ampere reactive (VAR). Where the unit of measurement for the sale of electricity is the volt-ampere hour, vector addition shall be used to determine the total number of such units in a combination of polyphase circuits. The units of measurement for the sale of electricity shall include multiples and submultiples of such units. Rules 4 and 5 are instructive of the Director to procure and cause to be maintained suitable secondary standards to which all electrical energy testing meters shall be traceable and procure and keep records of working standards of electrical energy testing meters for the use of inspectors in the exercise of their duties.

411. Part III regards the metrological requirements of meters. Rule 7 regulates the accuracy requirements of meters. Rule 8 provides directions of energy flow. The polarity of energy flow shall be defined by the manufacturer's connection instructions for the meter and shall be capable of bi-directional energy flow. Rule 12 provides for timing requirements for interval and multi-tariff meters. An interval electrical energy meter shall be able to measure and store interval data for a minimum of thirty-five days of thirty-minute interval data. Rule 14 provides that the metrological properties of every meter shall be protected. Rule 15 regards software identification. The software of an electrical energy meter shall be clearly identified with the software version or another token. Rule 16, the legally relevant software of a meter shall be secured against any unauthorized modification, loading or change. Rule 18 provides for data quality. The measurement value stored or transmitted in a meter shall be accompanied by all relevant information necessary for future legally relevant use. Rule 19 provides for data storage. All measurement data in a meter shall be stored automatically as soon as the measurement is concluded. Part IV regulates the type, approval, documentation and importation of meters, Part V functions of the bureau, and Part VI verification of meters.

Chapter 11. The Electricity (Tariff Code) Regulations, SI No. 23 of 2003

412. The objectives of these regulations include providing consumers with fair and reasonable price structures consistent with the maintenance of a financially and operationally secure electricity supply system, structuring the costs reflected in the tariff in such a way as to encourage consumers to make efficient use of generating, transmission and distribution assets and providing all licensed participants in the public electricity industry with a fair and reasonable return for their service and production, including a reasonable profit. In implementing these regulations, regard should be given to the following underlying and guiding principles. Tariffs should be based on accurate cost information provided by operators and a transparent formulation and review process; tariffs should reflect short-term variations in costs to reflect the fact that electricity as a commodity cannot be stored; tariffs should be structured and developed in such a way as to reflect variations in costs imposed on the system by the time of use, seasonal factors, consumer load profile, voltage levels and similar factors and should also reflect the true cost of service and provide clear price signals to the consumers on the economic and efficient use of energy. The components of tariff computation for each licensee should be in accordance with the tariff methodology approved by ERA in respect of each particular licence and may include the following general categories of costs: power acquisition-related costs, operation and maintenance costs, investment-related costs, return on investment, adjustment factors, for system losses, inflation and foreign exchange and other costs as approved by the Authority. However, it is the licensee who is responsible for justifying that any costs or investments included in the formulation of tariffs are reasonable, and ERA may challenge such costs or investments.

Chapter 12. The Electricity (Uniform System of Accounts) Regulations 2020

413. Under Regulation 7, a licensee or a holder of a certificate of exemption shall prepare and submit to the authority the uniform system of accounts in electronic form every calendar year and, in any case, not later than 31 March of that calendar year. Under Regulation 9, a licensee or a holder of a certificate of exemption shall allocate costs in a manner that separates business units in relation to the way in which human and financial resources are assigned and with reference to the business unit or activity-giving rise to the cost. A licensee and a holder of a certificate of exemption shall maintain a cost allocation manual, setting out the cost allocation method, affiliate transactions and transfer pricing policies.

Chapter 13. The Electricity (Approval and Verification of Investments) Regulations 2020

414. These Regulations apply to the approval and verification of investments of licensees by the authority. The purpose of these Regulations is to prescribe the processes, principles and standards for the approval and verification of investments in the electricity supply industry, to prescribe the requirements for approval of investment plans and completed investments, and to prescribe the stages of the investment planning and verification process. Under Regulation 5, a licensee shall not undertake any investment without the approval of the authority. Regulation 6 requires every licensee to prepare and submit to the authority for approval a five-year investment plan in respect of the investments it proposes to undertake six months from the date of commencement of these Regulations. In addition, a licensee shall prepare and submit to the authority for approval an annual investment plan consistent with the five-year investment plan. The annual investment plan shall be submitted to the authority ninety days before the end of each calendar year. Under Regulation 6(11) and (12), an investment plan shall be accompanied by an environment and social impact assessment certificate issued in accordance with the NEA 2019 and a resettlement action plan, where applicable, respectively. Under Regulation 7, the authority shall, upon receipt of an application for approval of investment plan, under Regulation 6, invite interested parties to make representations within the time specified in the notice of invitation and shall determine the application for approval of an investment plan within sixty days from the date of receipt of the application. Under Regulation 8, where a licensee is dissatisfied with the decision of the authority, the licensee may apply to the authority to review the decision within twenty-one days from the date of receipt of the decision. Regulation 12 requires a licensee to submit to the authority a progress report on implementation of the approved investment plan within six months of the approval of the plan. Regulation 13 regards verification of completed investments. The authority shall verify completed investments undertaken by a licensee for inclusion in the rate base or retail tariff, as appropriate. Under Regulation 14, a licensee shall submit to the authority an application for verification of completed investments within sixty days after the end of the tariff year.

Chapter 14. The Electricity (Reporting and Record Keeping) Regulations 2019

415. Regulation 3 requires a licensee to keep reports and records relating to its operations in accordance with these regulations. The reports and records shall describe the legal, technical, financial, hydrological, environmental and any other relevant issues relating to the operations of the licensee. Under Regulation 5, a permit holder shall, within one month after the end of each quarter, prepare and submit to the authority a report of the studies and any other activities undertaken in the quarter, which shall contain the matters specified in Schedule 2 of the regulations. Regulation 6 specifically requires a holder of a generation licence to provide a report in respect of operations within one month after the end of each quarter during the construction phase of the project. Regulations 7 and 8 oblige a holder of transmission licence and distribution licence, respectively, to submit report in respect of operations. Regulation 9 requires a holder of transmission and distribution licences to provide report in respect of load-shedding and power outages.

416. Regulation 10 regards a report on revenue by holder of distribution licence: a holder of a distribution licence shall, by the 31 March of each calendar year, prepare and submit to the authority, for the preceding calendar year, a report on the consumers who contribute more than five % of the holder of a distribution licensee's annual distribution revenue. Under Regulation 11, a holder of a distribution licence shall keep records of each complaint made to it and the manner the complaint is dealt with. Regulation 12 provides for holders of transmission and distribution licences to provide reports in respect of the environment. Regulations 15, 16, and 17 provide for a report on assets, a report of affiliate arrangement and transactions, and a report of change in corporate structure, respectively.

Chapter 15. The Electricity (Licence Fees) (Amendment) Regulations SI No. 3 of 2014

417. These regulations revoked the Electricity (Licence Fees) (Amendment of Schedule) Instrument, 2011 and amended the Schedule to the Electricity (Licence Fees) Regulations 2003, SI. No. 20 of 2003. Table 12 presents the schedule of licence fees.

Table 12 Schedule of Licence Fees

CAT. I	Very large Generators 200 MW or above	USD 75,000 per 50 MW or part thereof.
CAT.II	Large Generators up to 200 MW 50 MW and above but less than 200 MW	USD 47,950 per 50 MW or part thereof.
CAT.III	Medium Generators up to 50 MW 10 MW and above but less than 50 MW	USD 12,000 fixed plus USD 6,000 per 25 MW or part thereof.
CAT.IV	Small Generators up to 10 MW 2 MW and above but less than 10 MW	USD 12,000
CAT.V	Very Small Generators up to 2 MW (a) 0.5 MW and above but less than 2 MW (b) Below 0.5 MW	USD 6,000 USD 2,500
	(a) Transmission (b) System operator (c) Bulk supply	USD 75,000 USD 75,000 USD 75,000
CAT.I	Very Large Distributors 200 MW or (1,600 GWh) & above (a) Distribution (b) Supply	USD 175,000 fixed USD 175,000 fixed plus USD 25,000 per 100 GWh or part thereof.
CAT.II	Large Distributors of 50 MW (500 GWh) or above 50 MW (500 GWh) but less than 200 MW (1,600 GWh) (a) Distribution (b) Supply	USD 125,000 fixed plus USD 25,000 per 100 GWh or part thereof

CAT.III	Medium Distributors 50 MW (400 GWh) 10 MW (10 GWh) and above but less than 50 MW (400 GWh)	USD 12,000 fixed plus USD 6,000 per 10 GWh or part thereof.
CAT.IV	Small Distributors up to 10 MW 2 MW (15 GWh) and above but less than 10 MW	USD 12,000
CAT.V	Very Small Distributors up to 2 MW (a) 0.5 MW but less than 2 MW (b) Less than 0.5 MW	USD 3,500 USD 1,500
CAT.V	Very Small Distributors up to 2 MW (a) 0.5 MW but less than 2 MW (b) Less than 0.5 MW	USD 3,500 USD 1,500
		FEE
CAT.I	Medium Generators up to 50 MW 10 MW and above but less than 50 MW	USD 12,000 fixed plus USD 6,000 per 25 MW or part thereof.
CAT.II	Small Generators up to 10 MW 2 MW and above but less than 10 MW	USD 12,000
CAT.III	Very Small Generators up to 2 MW (a) 0.5 MW and above but less than 2 MW (b) Less than 0.5 MW	Exempt
		FEE
CAT. I	At a Voltage above 33 kV Import & Export	USD 75,000
CAT.II	At a Voltage of 33 kV & below (a) Import (b) Export	USD 12,000 USD 12,000
1.	Permit for Feasibility Studies	USD 3,000
2.	Licence Application	USD 3,500
3.	Licence Transfer Application	USD 3,500
4.	Licence Amendment Application	USD 3,500
5.	Permit Extension Application	USD 1,000
6.	Application for licence exemption	USD 3,000

Chapter 16. Regulatory Framework Concerning Petroleum

§1. Policy Issues in the Petroleum Subsector

418. The petroleum subsector provides about 5% of the country's energy consumption requirements. Petroleum products are obtained entirely through imports. Although petroleum production in Uganda has not been established, the hydrocarbon-generating capacity of its rift basins is very evident. The main petroleum products consumed in Uganda are gasoline, aviation gas, kerosene, diesel, fuel oil and LPG. This consumption is somewhat sector-specific; for example, kerosene and LPG are mainly consumed by the residential and commercial sectors, while gasoline, diesel and aviation gas are largely consumed in the transport sector, while fuel oil in the industrial sector. The petroleum subsector covers both upstream and downstream industries. The upstream industry deals with exploration, development and eventual production of petroleum, while the downstream covers transportation (of both crude and refined products), refining, storage, distribution and marketing of petroleum products.

419. The Energy Policy of 2002 identifies the petroleum subsector as one of the important subsectors in the energy industry. As a result, it identifies several key issues for policy intervention. In the upstream industry, the policy identifies two key issues, which are limited public resources available for investment resulting in ineffective promotional campaigns and inability to acquire seismic data in the exploration areas which are not yet licensed to oil companies and low investment in the upstream subsector by oil companies. However, in the downstream industry, the major issues are inadequate institutional and legal framework to regulate the petroleum supply industry[105] resulting in lack of competition and transparency, significant smuggling of petroleum products along the borders; low storage private capacity compared to national requirements, lack of quality control of the oil products posing an increasing hazard to public health and the environment and high transport costs and high margins by oil companies. To this end, the objective of the energy policy with regard to the upstream industry is to establish the petroleum potential of the country and to promote its exploitation, while the objective of the policy with relation to the downstream industry is to ensure an adequate, reliable and affordable supply of quality petroleum products for all sectors of the economy at internationally competitive and fair prices within appropriate HSE standards.

420. The general strategies are to create conducive conditions for attracting more investors in both the upstream and downstream subsectors and develop a mitigation plan to reduce environmental hazards in all oil operations. The specific strategies for upstream are to facilitate the acquisition of geological and geophysical data for assessing the petroleum potential of the country, promote investment in petroleum exploration and production by packaging and disseminating preliminary

105. As a result of the policy, a new legal framework regulating petroleum supply has been put in place.

exploration data and build capacity and maintain an efficient institution to monitor and regulate petroleum exploration and development.

421. The specific strategies for downstream are to adopt and implement the new petroleum legal framework (Petroleum Act, regulations and antitrust laws) involving: the establishment of an appropriate institutional framework (Department of Petroleum Supplies and the Technical Petroleum Committee); the establishment of an open and competitive market; the implementation of a monitoring system for the petroleum industry; the establishment of a transparent and efficient system of issuing permits for construction and licences for operation of petroleum supply installations; the adoption and adaptation of international standards and codes of practice; and the institution of a general petroleum fee on petroleum sales for sustainability of the subsector activities. In addition, there is a commitment to ensure the security of supply of imported petroleum products by maintaining at least two supply routes and keeping appropriate levels of strategic stocks based on an assessment of the risk of supply disruption. Improve transportation and storage of products by: promoting the development of the Eldoret-Kampala pipeline extension project, improving management and safety measures of the national strategic reserves and implementing quality-monitoring systems, including equipped mobile inspection team.

§2. Petroleum Exploration and Production

422. In 2006, the GoU announced that there were commercial oil reserves in the Albertine Graben along the border between Uganda and the Democratic Republic of Congo. More discoveries have been made and preparations are underway to exploit these oil resources, and production is expected in FY 2025. The oil fields found so far are estimated to contain deposits of around 6.5 billion barrels of oil. In terms of potential capacity, the reserves are estimated at 1.4 billion barrels of oil equivalent. The oil found so far lies in the Albertine Graben area, about 500 kilometres long and up to 45 kilometres wide, forming Uganda's western border with the Democratic Republic of the Congo (DRC) and stretching from Lake Edward in the south to the border with South Sudan in the north. The 'graben', which means a depressed crust of the earth's surface lying between two geological fault lines, has been the most intensively surveyed and prospected of Uganda's sedimentary basins. Other basins that may have oil deposits are the Hoima basin (to the east of Lake Albert), the Lake Kyoga basin (further east, in the centre of the country), and the Kadam-Moroto basin, still further east, in the Karamoja sub-region.

423. Initially, the oil companies were licensed as follows: In 1997, Heritage Oil and Gas Limited was licensed for Exploration Area 3 (Semliki Basin); in 1998, Heritage acquired the first 2D seismic data (170 line km) in Uganda; in 2001, Heritage acquired an additional 228.39 line km of 2D seismic data in Semliki Basin with identified drillable prospects and confirmation of structures earlier mapped by gravity and magnetics; Hardman Resources and Energy Africa was also licensed for exploration Area 2 (Northern Lake Albert Basin); in 2004, Heritage and Energy.

424. Africa (Tullow Oil) was licensed for exploration area 1 and Exploration Area 3A (Semliki basin) was relicensed to Heritage and Energy Africa (Tullow Oil and in 2007, Dominion Petroleum was licensed for Exploration Area 4B (Lakes Edward and George Basin).

425. In December 2009, Heritage offered its 50% stake in Exploration Areas 1 and 3A to Italian oil company ENI for a cash consideration of USD 1.45 billion, but Tullow decided to exercise its pre-emptive right to buy the stake at the same price ENI had offered USD 1.5 billion. Tullow then needed to bring in an even bigger oil company partner with more financial resources to invest in production. Tullow chose the CNOOC, which each agreed to pay USD 1.45 billion in a deal that would give Tullow, Total and CNOOC an equal stake in the areas once jointly prospected by Tullow and Heritage.

426. The government has made efforts to attract investment in petroleum exploration and production by acquiring geological and geophysical data in the graben. Exploration Area 3 has been licensed to a consortium of Heritage Oil and Gas Limited of the United Kingdom and Energy Africa of South Africa. A Production-Sharing Agreement (PSA) has been signed with the companies. Exploratory drilling in this area is expected to commence during 2002. Exploration Area 2 (Northern Lake Albert) was recently licensed to Hardman Resources N.L. of Australia and Energy Africa of South Africa. The government continues to promote the other unlicensed areas. The principal prospective area for petroleum in Uganda is the Albertine Graben, which forms the northernmost part of the western arm of the East African Rift Valley. It stretches from the border with Sudan in the north to Lake Edward in the south, a distance of over 500 km. Although of variable width, the Graben is an average of 45 km wide and extends into the Democratic Republic of Congo in some parts. An agreement of cooperation for exploration and exploitation of any common fields between the two countries is in place. The GoU has defined five exploration areas (EAs) in the Albertine Graben. These comprise the following sizes:

- Exploration Area 1 – 4,285 sq km;
- Exploration Area 2 – 4,675 sq km;
- Exploration Area 3 – 4,630 sq km;
- Exploration Area 4 – 5,913 sq km;
- Exploration Area 5 – 6,040 sq km.

427. The PEPD under MEMD is the technical arm responsible for the initiation and supervision of exploration agreements and manages the data relevant to upstream petroleum activities in the country. The policy goal of the department is to establish the petroleum potential of the country and to promote its exploitation. The specific roles and functions of PEPD are to promote investment in petroleum exploration and production by packaging and disseminating preliminary exploration data, monitor and regulate petroleum exploration operations undertaken by oil companies in the upstream subsector, participate in the geophysical, geological and geochemical data acquisition, processing and interpretation in order to assess the petroleum potential of the country, initiate policy and legislation on petroleum exploration and development and build national Institutional capacity in the field of petroleum exploration and development.

§3. The Petroleum (Exploration, Development and Production) Act, No. 3, 2013

428. The Act is comprised of 191 sections, 17 parts and 3 schedules. It repeals the Petroleum Exploration and Production Act, cap 150 but reserves the instruments made under the repealed Act for as long as they are consistent with the Act.[106] Part I provides for the preliminary aspects, which include the purpose, interpretation of the Act and compliance with environmental principles; section 1 provides that the main purpose of the Act is to operationalize the National Oil and Gas Policy of Uganda of 2008 by ensuring transparency and accountability in petroleum activities. Part II deals with petroleum rights and introduces the public trust doctrine in accordance with Article 244 of the Constitution of the Republic of Uganda, where all property in the petroleum is vested in the GoU; it prohibits the conduction of petroleum activities within Uganda without authorization contravention of which is an offence.

429. Part III provides for the institutional framework, which includes the minister and his or her functions; it establishes the PAU, its functions and powers and the National Oil Company of Uganda. The Authority is a body corporate with perpetual succession and an official seal with capacity to acquire, hold and dispose of property. Among the many functions of the Authority is to monitor and regulate exploration, development and production of petroleum in Uganda and to consult and cooperate with ministries, departments and agencies of government having related duties and functions.[107] It is enjoined to perform its functions in an open, objective, fair, reasonable, and non-discriminatory manner and promote fair competition. The Authority shall be governed by the Board of Directors, consisting of seven members, of whom at least three shall be women. The term of office is four years, and this is subject to reappointment for only one more term. Such positions can be terminated by a member's thirty days notification of their resignation to the minister in writing. Also, the president has the power to remove a board member where information is brought to the President's attention that would have precluded him or her from appointment for incompetence or inability to perform their functions arising from infirmity of body or mind, among others.

430. The National Oil Company shall be wholly owned by the state to manage Uganda's commercial aspects of petroleum activities and the participating interests of the state in the petroleum agreements and shall be subject to the Companies Act 2012 though, in case of any conflict between the two Acts, the Act shall prevail. It

106. Petroleum (Exploration, Development and Production) Act, s. 189.
107. *Ibid.*, s. 10.

shall have a board of directors appointed by the President with the approval of Parliament that shall plan for the management of the company and inform the minister of matters which are to be submitted to the annual general meeting.

431. Part IV of the Act deals with licensing, as no person shall carry out any petroleum activity within Uganda without a valid licence for the same. The Act provides for petroleum exploration licences and petroleum production permits. Minister shall make a public announcement of areas to be opened up for petroleum activities which shall be made available to the public before a licence can be issued. The applications shall be through a public bidding process carried out in accordance with the Act. It however also provides for direct applications in exceptional circumstances like where invitations for bids have been sent out three times in vain, among others. It also provides for reconnaissance permits that are applied for by the minister. The licence so granted therefore shall, while still in force, confer on the licensee the exclusive right to explore petroleum and to carry on such activities and execute such works as may be necessary for that purpose in the exploration area. The licensee expires in accordance with its terms and duration provided therein, and upon expiration, the holder can apply for its renewal. The licences impose certain duties and obligations on the holders as espoused in this part of the Act.

432. Development and production of petroleum are catered for under part V of the Act, where the licensee is under a duty to submit to the Authority information pertaining to the volume of petroleum produced, including test production, the use, injection, gas venting and flaring and the volumes and other results of monitoring as well as the monitoring procedure.

433. Under Part VI, the Act deals with cessation of petroleum activities which include decommissioning plan, fund, notification of termination of use, disposal of decommissioned facilities, and liability for damages for disposal of decommissioned facilities, among others. Part VII covers supplies and pricing. It is unique in that it caters for supplies at the time of peace and at the time of war, threat of war or other crises in Uganda. The pricing of petroleum shall be done in accordance with the prescribed method under regulations.

434. Part VIII provides for state participation in petroleum activities and national content through a licence or contract granted under the Act; it provides for training and employment of Ugandans, training and technology transfer to the Ugandans. Part IX elevates the status of a licence to the level of security as part of the financing of the activities associated with the production licence in a manner prescribed by the regulations. Part X imposes liability for pollution which is strict liability without regard to fault save for where it is demonstrated that an inevitable event of nature, act of war, exercise of public authority or extent under circumstances which are beyond the control of the licensee. Any action for compensation for pollution shall be brought before a competent court in the area where the effluence of discharge of petroleum takes place or where the damage is caused.

435. The Act further provides for restrictions and surface rights under Part XI, where a land owner in an exploration and development area shall retain the right to graze stock upon or cultivate the surface of the land in so far as it does not interfere with the petroleum activities or safety zones in the area. The licensee shall be liable for compensation for the disturbance of the said rights. The Act provides for safety in the conduct of petroleum activities and in accordance with the Occupational Health and Safety Act 2006, under section 140. Provision is made for safety zones to surround every facility for the carrying out of petroleum activities under the Act and a requirement for possession of the necessary qualifications to perform the work under the licence in a prudent manner.

436. Part XIII deals with information and documentation where all petroleum data generated shall be owned by the state except data acquired under a reconnaissance permit or data not generated under a cost recovery regime provided for in the Act. The licensee is enjoined with keeping accurate records of petroleum activities. Provision is made for the availability of information to the public in accordance with the Access to Information Act 2005. Among the information to be availed to the public are the petroleum agreements, licences and any amendments to the same. The Act provides for confidentiality of all data submitted to the minister by a licensee subject to the Access to Information Act.

437. The Act addresses payments under Part XIV, among which is royalty which can be paid in monetary form or in-kind failure, which may lead to refusal of removal of any petroleum from any development area. The Act makes provision for the payment of annual fees by a holder of an exploration or production licence failure which leads to the cancellation of the licence. Late payments attract a surcharge of 5% of the amount in default for each default day.

Offences under the Act are catered for under Part XV, which include obstruction of an authorized officer, obstruction of a license, conflict of interest, commission of which an order for forfeiture of any funds, money instruments, facilities, vehicles, crafts, vessels or equipment used in the commission of the offence shall issue.

438. The miscellaneous is provided for under Part XVI of the Act, which makes provision for the use of the spare capacity of a facility which should be done on objective and non-discriminatory conditions. Regulatory supervision of petroleum activities, survey of wells, maintenance of property, agreements between affiliated parties, security for fulfilment of obligations, scientific investigations, service of documents, indemnity of the GoU against all claims, actions and demands that may be made against government by reason of anything done by the licensee in the exercise of the rights conferred by the license. Section 183 authorizes the minister to make regulations to give effect to the provisions of this Act. Subject to the Constitution, the NEA, and the Access to Information Act 2005, this Act shall take precedence over all existing Acts relating to petroleum activities in Uganda.

439. The last part XVII of the Act deals with transitional provisions that include the continuation of a licence that was issued under the repealed Act but before the coming into force of this Act and the continuation of the office of commissioner and other officers that were in existence before the coming into force of the Act. The first schedule to the Act provides for the currency point to be UGX 20,000; the second provides for board meetings to be convened by the chairperson at times and places as the board may determine subject to a fourteen days' notice to each member in writing. The quorum of such a meeting is four, and members are required to declare any interests in anything to be decided upon by the board at the board meeting. The board has the power to regulate its procedure. The third schedule deals with the graticulation of the surface of the earth where the Minister shall cause to be prepared a reference map showing the geographical area of land in Uganda, divided into blocks constituted as provided in this Schedule, such map to be kept and used as evidence.

440. The Petroleum (Exploration, Development and Production) Act is the major legislation on Petroleum Exploration and Production and has the following statutory instruments made under:

- The Petroleum (Exploration, Development and Production) Regulations 2016
- The Petroleum (Exploration, Development and Production) (HSE) Regulations 2016
- The Petroleum (Exploration, Development and Production) (Metering) Regulations 2016
- The Petroleum (Waste Management) Regulations 2019.

§4. The Petroleum (Exploration, Development and Production) Regulations 2016

441. Under regulations, a licensee is under the obligation to operate in accordance with the Act and the regulations. They enjoin the minister to carry out impact assessments prior to the opening of new areas for petroleum activities. The Minister shall consequently make a public announcement of areas to be opened up for petroleum activities. Under part three, the regulations provide for licensing. Among others, provision is made for: application for a reconnaissance permit to the Minister, notification and grant of reconnaissance permit, grounds for grant or rejection of an application for reconnaissance permit, announcement of areas for petroleum exploration licence, bidding process for licensing rounds, application for petroleum exploration licence, notification and grant of petroleum exploration licence, application for renewal of petroleum exploration licence, relinquishment of areas, disposal of petroleum during exploration and announcement of areas for petroleum production licence.

442. The regulations further provide for: application for a petroleum production licence, notification and grant of a petroleum production licence, renewal of petroleum production licence, field development plan, variations or alterations in the approved field development plan, petroleum reservoir report, application for licence for the placement and operation of facility, criteria for the grant of a facility licence, duration of facility licence which shall be as specified in the licence, approval to alter facility, circumstances under which the Minister may change an operator, licensing of natural resources other than petroleum, duties on termination of licence, approval of work programmes and budgets, revision of approved work programmes and budgets and approval of costs. Part four of the regulations provides for geological surveys, geophysical surveys, other geoscientific surveys and other studies. They provide for programmes for geological, geophysical and other geoscientific surveys, seismic surveys, submission of study proposals, and notice of intention to commence operations.

443. Under part five, provision is made for drilling operations where drilling of a well must be with the written approval of the Authority. They provide for the casing programme, cementing programme, deviation survey programme, formation evaluation plan, coring programme, well test programme, well completion programme, certification of drilling rig, designation of wells, suspension of a well, abandonment of a well, approval to re-enter a well, daily drilling and operations reports, well completion reports, end of well test report, general well reports, well barriers, well control, shallow gas and shallow formation fluids, safety of suspended wells and specific requirements for testing of blowout preventer and other pressure control equipment. The regulations under part six provide for development and production of petroleum. A licensee shall use approved methods and practices acceptable to the Authority for the production of petroleum from a reservoir. It, among others, regulates economic practicability of a reservoir, test production, production permit, production of petroleum and monitoring of reservoir during production process, coordination of activities across licence boundaries, unit development, pricing of crude oil, pricing of natural gas and the use of currency exchange rates.

444. Part seven provides for onshore operations, facilities design and construction. They regulate, among others: consent for construction of onshore facilities, general requirements for the design of facilities, submission of final designs for approval, pipeline systems, valves and actuators, rotating machinery, consideration of materials during design, corrosion and decay of materials, protection against low and high external temperatures, additional requirement for process and auxiliary facilities, pneumatic facilities, heating facilities, inert gas facilities, hazard and operability review, leakage control, monitoring and reporting requirements, test methods and procedures, piping arrangements, pipes and vessels handling high-pressure petroleum, loading and unloading facilities and operations, handling of samples, laboratories and pilot plants, disruption to continuous operation of facility, installation of pressure equipment or a pressure system and approval for the construction of accommodation facility or material bases. In part eight, the regulations provide for offshore operations. They regulate general requirements for design of offshore facilities, applications for consent to construct fixed platforms, mobile platforms, location of mobile platforms, raising or lowering of mobile platforms, person-in-charge of platform, public address and telephone system on platform, marking of platform and a record of arrival and departure from platforms.

445. Part IX provides for third-party access to facilities. They regulate the application for third-party access, grant third-party access, setting and approval of tariffs.

Part X provides for payments, and a licensee shall pay acreage rental, surface rental or area fees calculated per square kilometre for the acreage held under a petroleum exploration licence or petroleum production licence on the grant of a licence and thereafter annually on the anniversary of the grant until the termination of the licence. In Part XI, the regulations provide for reports, data, samples, records and information. The licensee shall submit to the Authority copies of all reports of petroleum activities undertaken under the Act and the Regulations. They provide daily, weekly, monthly, quarterly and annual progress reports. They further provide for final geophysical and geological reports, well test interpretation reports, submission of final cost reports, duty to report petroleum reserves and resources, classification system required to be used, reporting of contingent resources, reporting of prospective resources, reporting unconventional resources, requirement for qualified petroleum resources evaluator, auditing of reserves and resources, reporting of resources and reserves to third parties, reporting of production, reporting of annual petroleum production, responsibility of licensee to report and submit data, review of existing data, general reporting requirements, reporting of well-log data, reporting of core data, submission of geochemical data and reports, reporting of wellbore seismic data, reporting pressure test data, reporting of well test surface and bottom-hole data, submission of processed well data among others.

446. Part XII provides for procurement and contracts. They provide for bidding procedure, submission, opening and evaluation, the award stage, notification of awards and regrets, complaints, submission after contract award, audit by the authority. Under Part XIII, provision is made for inspection and enforcement by authorized officers. In Part XIV, the regulations provide for offences and penalties, and Part XV provides for the miscellaneous. These regulations therefore operationalize the Petroleum (Exploration, Development and Production) Act 2013.

§5. The Petroleum (Exploration, Development and Production) (Health, Safety and Environment) Regulations 2016

447. The regulations impose an obligation on the licensee to conduct its operations in accordance with the Act and the Regulations. Part two provides for general health, safety and working environment requirements. It, among others, provides for general duties of a licensee, which are to prevent incidents, hazards and accidents and limit their consequences to human health and the environment and to ensure that occupational safety and health in all petroleum activities are satisfactory for the health and safety of employees and the environment. It provides for risk assessment, planning and implementation, major accident prevention policy, safety concept, risk-reducing measures, community health and safety where a licensee shall take measures to protect the community where the facility is located or where a petroleum activity is taking place from impacts of a facility or petroleum activity during the construction, operation and decommissioning of facilities.

448. Part III provides for occupational hazards where among other things, handling and storage of hazardous materials and substances is addressed. Part IV addresses electrical installations, and a licensee shall implement the necessary measures to prevent injury to persons and minimize hazards, incidents and accidents during work near live installations, in or near earthed and short-circuited installations, and during operation of low and high-voltage installations. It provides for safety procedures in electrical installations, isolation of electrical equipment, and defective electrical equipment, among others. Under Part V, the regulations provide for regulation of working environment in facilities and during petroleum activities where among others, they impose a duty on a licensee to ensure a safe and healthy environment, provision of adequate sanitary conveniences, hot work operations in confined spaces and ventilation equipment in confined spaces. Part VI regulates safety appliances, equipment, materials devices and clothing. They provide head, eye, face, and respiratory protection, protective foot and hand wear, fall protection systems, emergency escape device, and protection against drowning and extreme temperatures, among others.

449. Part VII provides regulations for fire and explosion protection in facilities and during petroleum activities. Regulation is made for fire-fighting equipment and systems for fire-fighting, technical requirements for the fire divisions, fire safety, fire and explosions, active smoke control, fire and evacuation alarm, fire and gas detection systems and escape exits, among others. In Part VIII, the regulations provide for emergency preparedness which, among others, provides for emergency plans, alerts and notifications, rescue measures and evacuation. Under Part IX, the regulations provide for safety requirements for plants and equipment. They provide for training of inexperienced employees in the use of machinery, operation of mobile equipment, safety requirements relating to plants, tools and equipment, arrangements for incidents and emergencies for pipeline systems, pipeline warning signs, identification of pipeline installations, safe operating practices for pipeline systems, and prohibition of smoking and use of naked light. Part X provides for medical facilities and first aid services where they provide for special requirements for health care and health services, medical examinations for employees, medical facilities and first aid services, ambulance stations and training of rescue teams and persons in first aid.

450. Part XI regulates handling, investigation, recording and reporting of incidents, hazards and accidents. They provide for reporting by employees, recording of incidents, hazards and accidents and inquiry into accidents and incidents, among others. Part XII provides for the miscellaneous, where it provides for spillage at the facility during petroleum activity, effluent and drainage disposal at facility or during petroleum activity, establishment of safety committees and offences and penalties. These regulations generally regulate occupational health and safety during petroleum exploration, development and production and also that such activities are conducted in an environmentally friendly manner and according to best petroleum industry practices. They are intended to ensure that petroleum activities are carried out in such a way as not to affect life and the environment as a whole.

Chapter 17. Petroleum (Exploration, Development and Production) (Metering) Regulations 2016

451. The Metering regulations were made pursuant to section 183 of the Petroleum (Exploration, Development and Production) Act of 2013. Regulation 5 requires every licensee to establish a management control system for metering and measurement of petroleum which shall include organization, processes, procedures and resources necessary to ensure compliance with the Act and these Regulations. Regulation 7 requires metering activities to be carried out in accordance with the requirements prescribed under these Regulations, standards approved by PAU and best petroleum industry practices. This part of the Regulations provides for general requirements relating to metering and metering systems, including the allowable metering uncertainty, units of metering in oil fields and requirements for design of metering systems. Part III regulates the start-up of metering system. A licensee shall obtain approval from PAU prior to start-up of the metering system. Part IV deals with operation and maintenance of metering systems. Metering systems shall be operated and maintained to the standard to which it is designed, standards approved by PAU and best petroleum industry practices; Part V deals with documentation requirements for metering system at all stages.

Chapter 18. The Petroleum (Waste Management) Regulations 2019

452. These regulations apply to a person involved in the production, importation, exportation, transportation, storage, treatment or disposal of petroleum waste; and the construction and operation of petroleum waste management facilities.

Part II of the regulations regards general provisions relating to petroleum waste management. Part III regulates licence for petroleum waste management. Part IV deals with the classification and characterization of petroleum waste. Part V regulates handling, labelling and storage of petroleum waste. Part VI regulates transportation, treatment and Disposal of Petroleum waste. Part VII regulates decommissioning of petroleum waste management facilities and handling of petroleum waste during decommissioning. Part XI deals with transboundary movement of petroleum waste.

Chapter 19. The Petroleum (Refining, Conversion, Transmission and Midstream Storage) Act 2013 Act No 4, 2013

453. An Act to give effect to Article 244 of the Constitution; to regulate, manage, coordinate and monitor midstream operations; to enable the construction, placement and ownership of facilities; to provide for third-party access to facilities; to regulate tariffs for facilities; to provide for an open, transparent and competitive process for licensing by the Minister; to provide for additional and particular HSE regulations not sufficiently regulated in other laws; to provide for cessation of midstream operations under this Act and decommissioning of facilities; and to regulate any other matters related to midstream operations.

454. This is a thirteen parts Act with one hundred sections and one schedule that is intended to operationalize the National Oil and Gas Policy of Uganda. The Act to give effect to Article 244 of the Constitution; to regulate, manage, coordinate and monitor midstream operations; to enable the construction, placement and ownership of facilities; to provide for third-party access to facilities; to regulate tariffs for facilities; to provide for an open, transparent and competitive process for licensing by the Minister; to provide for additional and particular HSE regulations not sufficiently regulated in other laws; to provide for cessation of midstream operations under this Act and decommissioning of facilities; and to regulate any other matters related to midstream operations. Section 3 enjoins a licensee to comply with environmental principles and safeguards prescribed by the NEA and any other laws applicable in Uganda. Part II makes provision for institutional arrangements, which include the minister who is responsible for, among others, issuing and revoking licences, the Petroleum authority, whose functions in section 6 are to monitor and regulate midstream operations and activities and to ensure the implementation of the Act and the regulations there under. The National Oil Company is provided for under section 7, where it shall participate in midstream activities in the Country.

455. Part III deals with licensing, where it prohibits the conduct of certain activities without a licence and makes it an offence therefore if a person contravenes this provision. Such licences shall be applied to the minister under section 10 in a manner prescribed by the regulations. The Act goes ahead and provides for operations that do not require a licence to include where the pipeline is located entirely within an industrial site for which the required licence has been granted or where the storage capacity does not exceed fifty metric cubic meters of any one product. A person carrying out such operation is only required to register with the Authority. The Act makes it mandatory for the minister to publish a notice of the application for such licence in the gazette. This makes it possible for the community in which such operations are to be carried out to object to the grant of the permit upon giving their reasons for the objection. Section 18 provides for conditions that may be set by the minister to be fulfilled for the grant of a license. A licence for the midstream operations shall be valid for a period of five years.

456. The Act under section 21 provides for the payment of an annual fee in respect of the licensed facility, and operation failure of which may lead to the cancellation of the license. The licence under the Act is renewable upon application for renewal by the licensee. Section 25 provides for the transfer or lease of a licence upon the minister's written approval. The Act prohibits the refining, conversion, transmission or midstream storage of any other substance other than the substance authorized by the licence, contravention of which is an offence whereupon conviction such person shall be liable to a fine not exceeding one hundred thousand currency points or imprisonment not exceeding ten years or both. A licence may be suspended or cancelled where a licensee is in default. However, this shall follow the minister's consultation with the Authority and approval of the Cabinet and a notice served in writing to the licensee. It is apposite to note that under section 31, the revocation of a licence, surrender of rights or lapse of rights for other reasons does not discharge the licensee from the financial obligations under this Act, regulations issued under this Act or any other law in Uganda or specific conditions attached to the license. All licences issued under this Act shall be registered in the midstream operations register in accordance with the regulations.

457. Cessation of midstream operations is provided for under the sixth part of the Act, where the licensee is required to submit a decommissioning plan to the Authority before the licence to install or operate a midstream facility expires or is surrendered. Provision is made for a decommissioning fund to be established by the minister through regulations. Notification should be given to the Authority before the expiry of the licence of a facility if the termination is going to be permanent. Section 49 imposes liability on the licensee for the damage or inconvenience caused in connection with the disposal of the facility or other implementation of the direction. The liability accrues for even abandoned facilities by the licensee.

458. Section 50 vitiates any lien, charge or encumbrance on a facility that requires removal by the government. The government may also take over a facility of the licensee when the licence expires, is surrendered or cancelled or when the use of a facility has been terminated permanently. State participation and national content are ensured under Part VII, where the government may participate in midstream operations under the Act in the form and manner specified by the minister and the cabinet. The Act imposes an obligation on the licensee to submit for approval a detailed programme for recruitment and training of Ugandans in midstream operations. A licensee shall include a clearly defined training programme for the local employees of the licensee, which may be carried out in or outside Uganda.

459. The Act caters for liability for damage due to pollution in Part IX where under section 58, the licensee is liable for such pollution damage from midstream activities without regard to fault save for where it is demonstrated that an inevitable event of nature, act of war, exercise of public authority or a similar force majeure event has contributed to a considerable degree to the damage or its extent under circumstances which are beyond the control of the licensee, the liability may be reduced to the extent it is reasonable with particular consideration to the scope of activity, the situation of the party that has sustained the damage and the opportunity for taking out insurance on both sides.

460. Part X deals with health and safety. Under section 63, midstream operations shall be conducted in such a manner as to enable a high level of safety to be maintained and further developed in accordance with technological developments and laws relating to health and safety. Operators are therefore under a duty to take precautions as are necessary to ensure the safety of any employee or otherwise present or in the vicinity of any facility and protect the facilities, the environment and natural resources, including taking precautions to prevent pollution and ensure that the persons referred to are duly informed of these precautions. Section 65 imposes an obligation on the licensee and any other participant in midstream operations to maintain efficient emergency preparedness with a view to dealing with accidents and emergencies which may lead to loss of lives or personal injury, pollution or major damage to property. The licensee, under section 69, is required to prepare a health and safety plan to be submitted to the minister as part of the regulatory health and safety supervision. The minister may appoint a commission of inquiry under section 71 where an accident occurs, and the minister considers it to be serious in connection with midstream operations to inquire into such accident, and the findings shall be made public within six months upon completion of inquiry. The report shall be laid before parliament.

461. Section 72 requires a licensee to notify the Authority of complete and accurate developments regarding midstream operations, failure of which is an offence under the Act. Upon termination, revocation or expiration of a licence, the person who was the licensee shall immediately deliver to the Authority in a format acceptable all records, plans, maps, data which they maintained and technical designs of facilities which were prepared by or on the instruction of the licensee. In the bid to promote transparency and accountability, section 74 makes provision for availability of information on the details of all agreements, licences and any amendments thereto to the public in accordance with the access to information Act. However, the Act also provides for confidentiality of data submitted to the minister that shall not be released to third parties.

462. The Act in Part XII caters for offences. Section 76 prohibits the disclosure to any person who is not a minister or an officer in the public service of any information furnished or in a report submitted under this Act without the licensee's consent. It is an offence under the Act for any person who, without reasonable excuse, obstructs, molests or hinders an authorized officer in the exercise of their powers under the Act. The Act gives inspectors the power to enter any area, place or premises that they believe is used for the purpose of or in connection with midstream operations and whoever obstructs an inspector shall have committed an offence under the Act. This part provides for obstruction of a licensee, offences committed by a body corporate, orders for forfeiture and contravention of decisions and orders issued under the Act that constitute offences under the Act.

463. The last part of the Act provides for the miscellaneous. Section 84 deals with the complaints mechanism where a person may submit a written or oral complaint to the Authority in respect of any midstream activity, which the authority shall examine, determine and take appropriate action within a period not exceeding forty days from the date of receipt of the complaint. The Act provides for the settlement of disputes where the licensee is enjoined to negotiate in good faith and reach an amicable settlement of a dispute concerning a contractual matter and any matter designated by the authority. Where the minister has reason to believe that a person is in possession of any information or data relating to midstream operations, they may, by notice in writing, require that person to avail such information to the minister. Under section 91, the Act provides for the powers of the Authority and authorized officers to include issuing directions to and impose restrictions on the licensee or any person so employed by instrument in writing in respect to the health and safety of persons employed by the licensee.

464. Like the Petroleum (Exploration, Development and Production) Act, the Act in section 93 provides for the indemnity of the Republic of Uganda against all actions, claims and demands that may be brought against the government in respect of anything done by the licensee in the exercise or purported exercise of the rights of the licensee under the Act. The part provides for codes of practice, regulations, amendment of the schedule, application of the Act and compliance with the conditions of the licence, among other things. The Act has one schedule that provides for the currency point to be UGX 20,000. The Petroleum (Refining, Conversion, Transmission and Midstream Storage) Act 2013 has two regulations made under, namely:

- The Petroleum (Refining, Conversion, Transmission and Midstream Storage) Regulations 2016;
- The Petroleum (Refining, Conversion, Transmission and Midstream Storage) (National Content) Regulations 2016.

Chapter 20. The Petroleum (Refining, Conversion, Transmission and Midstream Storage) Regulations 2016

465. These regulations prohibit the construction of a refinery, conversion plant or any other petroleum process plant without a licence issued by the Minister in accordance with the Act and the Regulations. They regulate the process of issuance of licences by laying down the requirements to be met before a licence can be issued. They enjoin the licensee to operate within the environmental parameters provided under the NEA. Under Regulation 6, the licensee shall ensure that process and auxiliary facilities are designed to ensure that equipment upstream and downstream of the process facility is not affected in terms of HSE. The regulations are therefore intended to ensure that the licensee carries out its operations and designs in accordance with standards approved by the Authority and best petroleum industry practices. Under Regulation 11, a refinery, conversion plant or other petroleum process plant designs shall be subjected to structured and systematic techniques for plant examination and risk management hazard as well as operability review to identify different ways in which parameters can deviate from the intended design conditions and create hazards or operability problems at all stages.

466. A refinery, conversion plant or other petroleum process plant shall be subjected to Safety Analysis Function Evaluation (SAFE) relating to all sensing devices, shutdown valves and emergency support systems to their functions and the outcome documented in a SAFE Chart. Any work related to the construction, operation or decommissioning of a refinery, conversion plant or other petroleum process plant shall be conducted under the direction and supervision of a refinery, conversion plant or other petroleum process plant manager in charge of all operations authorized by the licence under which he or she is operating. Upon completion of construction of a refinery, conversion plant or other petroleum process plant or substantial modification of a refinery, conversion plant or other petroleum process plant to the satisfaction of the Authority, the licensee shall apply to the Minister in writing for a licence to operate the facility. The regulations impose a duty on the licensee to prevent and minimise pollution by putting in place measures approved by the Authority.

467. Under part three, provision is made for licensing, design, construction and operation of a pipeline, and no person shall construct a pipeline without a licence issued by the Minister in accordance with the Act and the Regulations. The design of pipeline systems must meet standards approved by the Authority and best petroleum industry practices. The licensee shall ensure that the design of a pipeline system or any substantial modification to the pipeline system takes into account the operating conditions for the pipeline, the conditions under which petroleum commodities or petroleum products are to be transmitted and the environment to which the pipeline system will be subjected. Part four provides for transmission of petroleum commodities and products in bulk by road, rail or water. The regulations prohibit a person's transmission of petroleum commodities or petroleum products by road, rail or water without a licence issued by the Minister in accordance with the

Act and the Regulations. They provide for the requirements to be met for the transmission of bulk petroleum commodities. They provide for the condition of tank vehicles, and each tank vehicle must bear the words 'highly flammable', and they should be operated by a competent person.

468. Part V of the regulations provides for a licence for midstream storage where specific provision is made for the design and specifications for aboveground field constructed midstream storage tanks. They prohibit the installation of underground steel storage tanks unless they are designed and installed in accordance with the manufacturer's instructions, standards approved by the Authority and best petroleum industry practices.

469. They enjoin the licensee to ensure that emergency drains for floating roof tanks are provided on the roof of a midstream storage tank to take care of disposal of water in case of choking or multi-functioning of the primary roof drain. The licensee shall ensure that midstream storage tanks for storage of bulk petroleum commodities or petroleum products are grouped in a dedicated bund wall according to their respective classification of petroleum commodities or petroleum products. The regulations provide for inspection and enforcement under part six. Under Regulation 159, an authorized officer may, at all times prior to giving the licensee notice, enter into any part of the licence area or any other location, facility, premises, structure or business place where a midstream operation is being undertaken by the licensee, contractors or subcontractors to check or examine anything authorized to be done under the licence in that area.

470. The last part, which is Part VII, provides for the miscellaneous, such as the procedure to be followed in considering licence applications, renewal of licences for midstream facilities, application to transfer interest in licence, use of licence as security, register of licences and charges, submission of designs, consideration of materials during designs, suspension of operation of facility, performance bonds, other forms of security and insurance, safety principles for the design and operation of facilities among others. The regulations, in a nutshell, provide for the regulation of petroleum refining, conversion, transmission, and midstream storage in accordance with standards approved by the Authority and best petroleum industry practices. They regulate the process of application for and issuance of licences and permits before any activities are carried out under the Petroleum (Refining, Conversion, Transmission and Midstream Storage) Act 2013.

Chapter 21. The Petroleum (Refining, Conversion, Transmission and Midstream Storage) (National Content) Regulations 2016

471. These regulations were made pursuant to section 95 of the Petroleum (Refining, Conversion, Transmission and Midstream Storage) Act 2013, Act 4 of 2013. The regulations are intended under Regulation 3 to promote the training and employment of Ugandans, transfer of knowledge and technology and the provision of goods and services by Ugandan companies, registered entities and Ugandan citizens in midstream operations; to require every licensee, contractor and subcontractor to give priority to the sourcing of goods and services from Ugandan companies; to require the provision of goods and services not available in Uganda to be provided by a company that has entered into a joint venture with a Ugandan company; to ensure enterprise development through provision of support to Ugandan companies, registered entities and Ugandan citizens.

472. Regulation 5 provides for the management and implementation of the National Content. This is intended to be achieved through the supervision, coordination and monitoring of the development of national content in midstream operations; appraising and evaluating national content programmes and reports submitted to the Authority; developing and operating the national content evaluation system for licensees, operators, contractors and subcontractors; developing guidelines for the implementation of national content; conducting studies and research that may further the development of national content in midstream operations among others. Upon the grant of a licence, the licensee under Regulation 7 is required after twelve months to submit a national content programme proposal that provides for, among others: the employment and training of Ugandans; the transfer of technology, knowledge and skills to Ugandan companies, Ugandan citizens and registered entities; procurement of goods and services obtainable in Uganda; local supplier development; the succession of expatriates by Ugandans; services to be provided by Ugandan companies, Ugandan citizens and registered entities.

473. The National Content programme shall contain a detailed plan on how the licensee shall give preference to goods that are locally manufactured or available in Uganda, where the goods meet the required quality and timeline for delivery. The regulations provide for prioritization of Ugandan goods and services during procurement wherein licensees, contractors and subcontractors shall give preference to goods and services which are produced and are available in Uganda and services which are rendered by Ugandan companies, registered entities and Ugandan citizens. Regulation 11 provides for contracts, goods and services to be provided by Ugandan companies, registered entities and Ugandan citizens where a licensee, contractor and subcontractor shall reserve contracts for goods and services specified in the Schedule. Under Regulation 12, every licensee, contractor and subcontractor shall ensure that the bidding process includes national content as one of the requirements for qualification. National content shall form part of the bid evaluation criteria, and in all circumstances, national content shall be allocated at least 10% of the total evaluation score.

474. The regulations provide for all contracts whose total budget exceeds USD 1,000,000 and which are to be executed in Uganda to contain a labour Regulation mandating the use of a minimum percentage of Ugandan labour in specific categories as may be stipulated under the national content programme approved by the Authority. The licensee is enjoined to develop and submit to the Authority for approval a policy and plan for employment of Ugandans, specifying the required minimum qualifications. The licensee shall, within twelve months after the grant of a licence and on each subsequent anniversary of that grant, submit to the Authority for approval, a detailed plan for recruitment and training of Ugandans in midstream operations. Under the Regulations the licensee, contractor and subcontractor shall apply for recommendation from the Authority prior to making any application for work permits for expatriates to the Government ministry, department or agency responsible for immigration under Regulation 21. They prohibit employment of a person whom the licensee, contractor or subcontractor knows to be unlawfully present in Uganda, contravention of which is an offence. A licensee is enjoined to submit to the Authority for approval an annual plan satisfactory to the Authority, setting out details and initiatives aimed at promoting the effective transfer of technology, technical knowhow and skills relating to midstream operations from the licensee to Ugandan companies, registered entities and Ugandan citizens.

475. Part III provides for information and reporting requirements which include the National Content performance report, which must be submitted quarterly, access to facilities by authorized officers, communication of national content policies to contractors and subcontractors, reporting by contractors and subcontractors whereby contractors and subcontractors are contractually bound to report national content information to the licensee and, upon request by the Authority, directly to the Authority. Under the miscellaneous, the Authority is enjoined to develop a national supplier database where companies to provide goods, works and services for midstream operations in Uganda shall be included. Under Regulation 31, the Authority shall, in consultation with industry stakeholders, establish, maintain and operate a national human capacity register which shall be administered in accordance with these Regulations and guidelines issued by the Authority.

476. The regulations under the schedule give a list of goods and services to be provided by Ugandan companies, and Ugandan citizens registered entities, including transportation, security, food and beverages, hotel accommodation and catering, human resource management, office supplies, fuel supply, land surveying, clearing and forwarding, crane hire, locally available construction materials, civil works, environmental studies and impact assessments, communications and information technology services and waste management, where possible. Conclusively, therefore, the regulations are intended to open up avenues for Ugandan citizens and registered entities to provide goods and services and boost local investment. The regulations are intended to minimize as far as possible reliance on foreign labour by encouraging the training of Ugandan citizens to be able to acquire the skills and replace the expatriates in the area of petroleum refining, conversion, transmission and midstream storage in the country.

§1. Petroleum Supply and Distribution

I. The Petroleum Supply Act 2003

477. This is an Act to provide for the supervision and monitoring, importation, exportation, transportation, processing, supply, storage, distribution and marketing of petroleum products. Section 4 provides for the application of this Act. It applies to the import, export, re-export, transport, processing, supply, storage, distribution, wholesale and retail sales and sales to industrial consumers of petroleum products and related activities and installations in Uganda and natural gas, whether imported or produced in Uganda, including CNG and LNG. Under section 5, 'petroleum' is defined to mean any naturally occurring hydrocarbon or a mixture of naturally occurring hydrocarbons, whether in the gaseous, liquid or solid state. The objectives of the Act are outlined in section 3, which include ensuring that petroleum supply in Uganda is adequate, reliable, efficient and economical for the country and the consumers according to the prevailing conditions at any given time, strengthening the institutional capacity of the government in order to better formulate and implement petroleum supply policies, improving petroleum governance by clarifying the functions of the institutions responsible for petroleum supply and making the operations of those institutions more accountable and transparent and ensuring public safety and protection of public health and the environment in all petroleum supply operations and installations.

478. Other objectives of the Act include ensuring effective delivery of petroleum products and services to consumers and ensuring equal access to petroleum products of adequate quality at competitive prices for all consumers, encouraging and promoting fair competition within the petroleum supply market to eliminate discrimination or preferential treatment of any participant and to prevent monopolistic control of any segment of the supply chain, creating favourable conditions for operators and investors for increasing the diversification of the sources of supply, improving services and expanding the infrastructure of the supply chain and ensuring a ready supply of petroleum products by the development and maintenance of national strategic stocks.

A. *Administration of Petroleum Supply*

479. Under section 6(1), the minister is responsible for the implementation of the Act. The specific functions of the minister are laid down in subsection 2 and include the following: initiation of legislation and making necessary regulations in order to support and promote continuous, secure and adequate supply of petroleum products at competitive cost for all consumers and to create favourable conditions for the availability of adequate import, transport, storage and distribution facilities within or, if necessary outside Uganda, promote the increase of opportunities for regional petroleum trade and encourage a diversity of supply sources, routes and means of transportation, approving by order the emergency petroleum supply plan prepared by the Commissioner, appointing members of the committee; and performing any other functions given to the Minister. In order to facilitate the carrying out of the functions of the Minister under the Act, there should be established Department of Petroleum Supply in the Ministry headed by a Commissioner.[108] Under section 7, the commissioner should supervise, control and ensure the effectual and impartial enforcement of the Act. The specific functions of the Commissioner include the following; providing technical advice to the Minister in all legislative and regulatory matters concerning the petroleum supply operations, establishing, implementing and administering an effective and equitable licensing system for petroleum supply operations and installations; receiving, evaluating and processing all applications for and approving the granting, renewal, assignment, suspension or revocation.

480. Of all permits and licences, the Commissioner is also responsible for ensuring the establishment, maintenance and periodic updates of the National Petroleum Information System (NPIS) and the evaluation and dissemination of the information derived from the petroleum information system, organizing, implementing and coordinating with other government agencies the monitoring process of the operations, installations and participants in the supply chain, including domestic and international market prices, in accordance with this Act, encouraging, monitoring and enforcing the implementation of, and the observance of the principles of the free market and fair competition in coordination with other government agencies in accordance with this Act. The Commissioner is also required to create and implement effective and adequate procedures to receive and resolve, without undue delay, all enquiries and complaints by other government agencies, consumers, recognized consumer organizations or participants in the supply chain concerning the safety of petroleum supply operations and installations or the quality, quantity or prices of petroleum products distributed or sold in Uganda, develop and maintain national strategic petroleum stock, and may also perform other functions as may be conferred from time to time.

B. Technical Petroleum Committee

481. This is established under section 8 and consists of representatives from the responsible ministry, UNBS, MoF, associations of licensees of petroleum import, re-export, wholesale or storage operations and a member of the association of licensees of petroleum transporters. The functions of the committee include advising the Minister on proposed legislation, technical standards and specifications relating

108. Petroleum Supply Act, s. 6(3).

to petroleum products and the supply chain, developing and submitting to the Minister proposals for the improvement of the petroleum supply policies, systems, regulations, technical standards and codes of practice, coordinating the preparation of the Emergency Petroleum Supply Plan and reviewing its final draft and any updates before the submission to the Minister for approval, advising and supporting the Minister and the Commissioner in the Commissioner in the implementation of the Act and other applicable laws advising the Minister on matters concerning taxes or levies on petroleum products and other petroleum supply operations and related matters, and serving as a mediating body in disputes between the participants in the supply chain and between the participants and the commissioner.

C. Petroleum Construction Permits and Petroleum Operating Licences

482. This is regulated under Part IV of the Act. Section 17 provides that no person should carry out the construction or major modification of installations or facilities of the supply chain without having obtained a Petroleum Supply Permit. It further prohibits any person from performing any supply operations without having obtained a petroleum operating license. Section 18 provides for a detailed procedure for obtaining a permit or a licence for one or more activities in the supply chain or for a renewal or assignment of a permit or license.

483. The applicant is required to submit an application in the prescribed format to the commissioner. The procedure for the submission of applications and for evaluating, processing and approving or rejecting the applications is provided in the regulations.

484. However, during the processing of an application, evaluation, approval or rejection, all applicants are to be treated equally without any discrimination or preferences. In addition, any approval by the Commissioner required cannot be unreasonably withheld. The applicant is however required to pay the requisite application fees. The commissioner may, with the agreement and at the expense of the applicant, employ local or international experts to review the application for permits or licences, and the amount and the terms of payment of the fees and the reimbursement of expenses for experts may be agreed with the applicant. However, where an agreement is not reached, the commissioner may reject the application. At the end of each month, the commissioner is required to forward to the Committee a list of all applications for permits and licences submitted during that month and the action taken by the Commissioner on the applications and, if requested, may provide further information. Information and particulars furnished with the application and classified as confidential by the applicant cannot be published or otherwise disclosed by the Commissioner without the prior consent of the applicant.

485. A permit can only be valid for five years or upon completion of the work in question and the acceptance of the work by the commissioner according to the prescribed procedure. However, it may be extended for five more years but cannot be valid for more than twenty-five years, depending on the type of activity to which it relates and may be renewable in accordance with the regulations. No permit or licence may be assigned or transferred without the prior consent of the commissioner and payment of any required fees. A permit or licence under this Act may be suspended by the Commissioner where there is a contravention of any provision of this Act or any other enactment concerning the protection of occupational health, public safety and the environment. Such a permit may be revoked if the holder fails to remedy or repeats such contravention that caused the suspension.

D. Obligations of the Holders of Permits and Licences

486. Every holder of a permit or a licence is required to keep and maintain records and should furnish all such reports and information as may be required by the commissioner.[109] The holder of a permit or a licence should maintain an address in Uganda to which communications may be sent and should notify the Commissioner of such address. The Commissioner or any person authorized by the Commissioner enter upon the premises of a licence or permit holder and carry out inspections in any area or premises where petroleum operations or construction works for facilities of the supply chain are being performed.

487. Such officer, however, should be accompanied by a representative of the holder during the inspections. The inspector may inspect the works, facilities and records, including the books of account connected with the operations. He or she may also, within any reasonable time, stop and search any vehicle or vessel belonging to the holder of a permit or license.

488. In order to ensure the continuity of the petroleum supply of Uganda, every licensee should, at his or her expense, maintain prescribed minimum working stocks of petroleum products. The level of the stocks should not be less than ten days of the average amount of any product handled or consumed by the respective licensee within Uganda during the period of three months preceding the effective date of determination. The minimum working stock should include all petroleum products held in storage depots in Uganda and should exclude petroleum products – in transit within Uganda or to and from any other country, held in retail service or filling stations and held in consumer storage locations. Where changes occur in the levels of minimum stocks for any licensee of petroleum products by the amendment of any regulations made by virtue of subsection (2), those changes should only apply to new licences or the renewal of existing licences. The level of minimum working stock for new licensees is determined at the start of operations, based on the information furnished with the application, for an initial period of one year, at the end of which the final determination is made in accordance with the Act. Any person who fails, without lawful excuse, to comply with subsection (1) commits an offence and is liable on conviction to a fine not exceeding twenty-four currency points.

109. *Ibid.*, s. 24(1).

E. The NPIS

489. Section 27 establishes the NPIS. This should be organized and maintained by the Commissioner. It should consist of an integrated and centralized database and information system covering all petroleum supply operations and installations, the principal market activities and statistics of Uganda, as well as international reference data.[110] In this regard, all licensees are required to submit to the Commissioner periodic reports and all required information. The Commissioner should publish data contained in the NPIS in aggregate form with the exception of information which is classified as confidential by the licensee in order to protect proprietary market data.[111] The Central Petroleum Registry (CPR) should form part of the NPIS and should include a record of all applications, grants, variations, assignments, other transfers, suspensions and revocations of permits and licences and all relevant information about the holders and their operations and installations.[112]

F. Market Competition and Assurance of Supply

490. Any person, whether Ugandan or foreign, may participate in all activities of the supply chain. Participants in the supply chain should not form cartels or attempt to control prices or create artificial shortages of products or services, or engage in any other restrictive trade practices or any other acts or omissions which are contrary to the principles of fair competition or are intended to impede the functioning of a free market for petroleum products in Uganda.[113] Participants in the supply chain should sell their products and offer their services to all interested persons without undue delay and without any form of deliberate discrimination by means of quality, quantity or price or other conditions and restrictions which cannot be justified under legitimate commercial or operational grounds.[114] Except where a petroleum supply emergency has been declared, the prices for petroleum products throughout the supply chain should be governed solely by the rule of supply and demand in a free and competitive market. The commissioner is required to monitor the conditions of the market and the trade practices of the participants in the supply chain. The reference prices used for monitoring prices should be calculated by the commissioner according to a formula established by order of the Minister after consultation with the committee.[115] The reference prices should be updated from time to time.

491. Where the minister is satisfied that there is existence of any restrictive trade practice or any other act or omission, the minister may intervene in public interest.

---

110. *Ibid.*, s. 25(4).
111. *Ibid.*, s. 27(3).
112. *Ibid.*, s. 28(2).
113. *Ibid.*, s. 30(1).
114. *Ibid.*, s. 30(2).
115. Section 30(10) the Petroleum Supply Act defines a 'reference price' to mean the price used by the commissioner to establish whether the price of a petroleum product is excessive or not.

In order to promote the creation of a competitive petroleum product market for participants in the supply chain, the following conditions are established for access to essential components of the infrastructure of the supply chain, such as depots, pipelines and other facilities. A licensee who owns or operates a facility which has unused capacity may negotiate in good faith with any qualified person interested in the use of that capacity in order to establish the tariff and other reasonable terms and conditions for using the facility, and the interested person must be a person who holds or has applied for the licence required for the operation in question and provides proof of his or her capacity to pay the tariff and fulfil other reasonable financial and technical conditions as agreed upon with the owner or operator or both, of the facility.

G. *Protection of Public Safety and the Environment*

492. The Commissioner is required to develop and implement or cause the implementation of a programme of gradual adoption and adaptation of the prevailing international standards, technical specifications and codes of practice in relation to the petroleum supply industry in cooperation with the National Bureau of Standards and the Committee.[116]

493. It further provides that the standards, specifications and codes of practice as established by the standards developing organizations which are recognized by the international petroleum industry in matters of quality, industrial safety and environmental protection should be adopted by the UNBS by reference and declared as national standards in accordance with the UNBS Act after being adapted as necessary taking into account the socioeconomic realities of the petroleum products market in Uganda.

494. In the meantime, before the adoption of the relevant international standards, the Minister is required to approve the temporary application of standards specifications and codes of practice by reference to any international standard proposed by the commissioner, which such adaptations as the Commissioner may recommend.[117] The commissioner acts as the 'lead agency' within the meaning of the NEA in the process of conducting ESIAs and audits and implementing other requirements for environmental protection in the supply chain. The Commissioner should prepare a classification of petroleum operations and projects and, in consultation with NEMA, prepare guidelines for ESIA and audits. However, in undertaking these functions, the Commissioner is required to periodically inform the committee and seek its opinion about the guidelines.

---

116. Petroleum Supply Act, s. 32(1).
117. *Ibid.*, s. 32(3).

H. Emergency Petroleum Supply Plan

495. Section 34 provides that in order to respond to interruptions in or serious distortions of the petroleum supply occasioned by accidents, political disturbances, natural disasters or similar events or by negligence of any person, the Commissioner, in cooperation with other government departments and agencies, the Committee and participants in the supply chain, prepare an emergency petroleum supply plan. This plan is approved by the Minister. In addition, where the minister is satisfied that the events stipulated above have occurred may, by statutory order, declare that a petroleum supply emergency has occurred, and the commissioner may, with the approval of the Minister, temporarily intervene in the supply chain and implement such measures as are provided in the emergency petroleum supply plan.

I. Mediation and Reviews

496. Section 40 provides that any dispute between the holders of permits or licences, or between such holders and the Commissioner concerning the implementation of the Act or regulations made under the Act, may be submitted by the parties involved to the Committee for non-binding mediation. In pursuance of such, the Committee may request the parties to appear before it, request any information, documents or testimony by the witnesses or experts which it considers necessary and conduct other investigations. Thereafter, the Committee is required to submit a written opinion about the dispute to the parties involved within sixty days of the receipt of the request for mediation.

497. This is unless the Committee extends the period by written notice to the parties. Unless otherwise agreed, the mediation proceedings should not be held in public, and the opinions submitted should not be published. The procedure for mediation is established by the Committee by resolution, and the Committee should, with the approval of the Minister, prescribe the fees and expenses to be paid by the parties to the mediation. Such fees are then paid to the Consolidated Fund.

498. Section 41 provides for administrative review by the minister. Any person who is aggrieved by the decision of the Commissioner may, within twenty-one days after being notified of the decision, request in writing an administrative review of the decision by the Minister. The Minister may, within forty-five days after receipt for administrative review, confirm, set aside or vary the decision complained of. The Minister should give reasons for his or her decision on a review. Under section 42, any person aggrieved by the rejection by the Minister of a request for administrative review or any direction or order by the Minister may within thirty days after receipt of notification of the act or omission complained of or if the Minister fails to decide on an administrative review, within thirty days after the expiration of the period prescribed in section 41 apply to the court for judicial review.

II. Petroleum Supply (General) Regulations 2009

499. These Regulations operationalise the Petroleum Supply Act. They provide detailed application procedures for petroleum construction permits, obligations of a holder of a permit or licence, and quality control of petroleum products. Part II of the regulations deals with applications for construction permits or petroleum operation licences. The application has to be made to the Commissioner in the form stipulated in Schedule 3 of these regulations. A summary of each application for a permit for a project has to be published by the applicant in a newspaper of national circulation for public comment or objection. The Petroleum operating licence shall be applied for by body corporates only and should also apply to the Commissioner as prescribed in Schedule 4 of these Regulations. Under Regulation 14, a licence or permit shall be valid for the following terms and may be renewed for equal periods: (a) importation and exportation – ten years, (b) pipeline transportation – twenty years, (c) other surface transport on land or water – five years, (d) storage, including industrial consumers – ten years, (e) wholesale and retail distribution and sales – five years, (f) processing or transformation or other operations involving the construction of physical plants – fifteen years.

500. Part III provides for general obligations of a holder of a permit or licence. The commissioner may direct to have inspected any books, accounts, documents or records of any kind concerning the petroleum supply operations and premises, and the holder shall comply with the direction. Part IV requires periodic reporting to the commissioner by the licence or permit holders regarding their operations. Part V regards quality control of petroleum products. The Commissioner, with the approval of the Minister, shall establish product grades, technical specifications and quality control practices for all petroleum products imported for distribution and sale in Uganda; exports and re-exports, where a National standard for a product is not established under another law. This provision specifically is subject to the provisions of the Uganda National Bureau of Standards Act Cap 327. Uganda National Bureau of Standards (UNBS) and the MEMD developed standards for the entire petroleum value chain.[118]

III. Guidelines for Licensing of Petroleum Facilities and Operators

501. In January 2003, the MEMD wrote to the Kampala City Council (KCC) to stop issuing new licences for construction of petroleum retail stations. Suspension of licences was for the purpose of ensuring that development of new petrol stations in Kampala is in accordance with the new guidelines to be issued by the Ministry. These guidelines are intended to serve that purpose.[119] In 1994, the government adopted a policy of a free market economy driven by the private sector. Price control and bureaucratic resource allocations were abolished. The government also

118. UBOS 2017, Oil and Gas catalogues as at December 2017.
119. General Notice issued under s. 6 of the Petroleum Supply Act 2003.

privatized its interests in the three oil-marketing companies, which were nationalized in the 1970s. The Energy Policy for Uganda was adopted in 2002. The policy covers, *inter alia*, the downstream petroleum subsector. After adoption of the Policy, the Ministry formulated a new legal framework to regulate the subsector on the principles of a free market with open access and fair competition. Industry regulation is therefore focused mainly on HSE standards unless there are elements of unfair competition in the market. The main goal of the energy policy is to meet energy needs of the population in an environmentally sustainable manner.

502. The broad policy objectives with respect to the downstream petroleum subsector are to: establish demand for the resource; increase access to modern affordable and reliable energy services; improve energy governance and administration; stimulate economic development; and manage energy-related environmental impacts. The strategy for achieving the above broad policy objectives is: to prepare a database on petroleum resources and build local capacity to acquire, access and evaluate the resource; to attract private capital and management in the provision of petroleum services; to promote and encourage competition; to create a transparent legal and regulatory framework; to ensure energy supply security and reliability; to promote petroleum trade within the region; and to strengthen environmental monitoring in the sector.

The guidelines are intended to implement the Energy Policy in the above context. The Petroleum Supply Act 2003 was enacted and came into force in November 2003. The Act repealed the Petroleum Act, Cap 97 of the 1964 Laws of Uganda and the Uganda Oil Board Statute of 1991.

503. The Act also revoked the Petroleum Filling Stations Rules, SI 27–29, issued under the Urban Authorities Act, Cap 27 of the 1964 Laws of Uganda. The Act provides for anyone intending to enter the petroleum supply chain to apply to the Commissioner of Petroleum Supply (the Commissioner) for grant of a petroleum construction (Permit) and/or grant of a petroleum operating license. For purposes of these guidelines, the petroleum supply chain covers petroleum import, export, re-export, storage, distribution and sale both at bulk consumer and retail outlets/stations.

504. The objective of the guidelines is to provide for a transparent, orderly and non-discrimination treatment of all applications to enter the petroleum supply chain. Existing facilities that currently do not meet the requirements of these guidelines will be required, within a given time frame, to realign their facilities accordingly or closedown. The procedure for application is also provided. The application for a permit and/or a licence is made in writing to the Commissioner. The application contains minimum information, but applicants are advised to include any other information they consider will support their application. The information required includes the name and address of applicant, corporate status of applicant, whether sole proprietorship, partnership, unincorporated business, incorporated private/ public company, association or a cooperative. If registered, a copy of the registration certificate, memorandum and articles of association or constitution, list of directors or of the executive of the company or organization, as the case may be, should be enclosed.

505. Location and ownership of sites where facilities are to be built: For each site, the applicant should indicate whether local authority approval to construct facilities has been granted. Where property is (to be) leased or rented from third parties, copy of agreement/contracts should be availed including the following: intended source/supplier of petroleum products; description of the project's overall design and layout, type(s) of pumps, product tanks, piping, forecourt, office block, availability and source of power, water supply and communication, sanitation and drainage, and fencing of the facility; project cost estimates including operating capital to be employed; indication of financial and technical resources available to the applicant including proof of necessary capital; organization structure and qualifications and experience of personnel to be employed to operate the system; undertaking to secure insurance protection against third-party liability during both construction and operational phases; a project brief giving likely and potential environmental impact of the project; description of surrounding area of the site for petroleum installation; description of safety programmes, equipment and plans for protection of occupational health, industrial safety and the environment during construction and operations of the facility.

The Commissioner is required to evaluate the application for suitability of the location, standards of design and safety as a petroleum facility, competence or experience of operator, adequacy of investment resources, and general financial/ economic viability. The Commissioner, acting as the lead agency and in consultation with the NEMA, will evaluate the environmental impact of the project and advise on mitigation measures to be undertaken. The evaluation process will include inspection of the site(s). Application fees are necessary to facilitate evaluation of the applications for permits and licences.

506. The modern principles of oil management are contained in the Oil and Gas Policy 2008. It recognizes transparency and accountability as the guiding policy principles. Openness and access to information are recognized as fundamental rights. It further stresses the importance of disclosing information 'that will enable stakeholders to assess how their interests are being affected'.

507. The Policy states that openness and access to information are fundamental rights in activities that may positively impact individuals, communities and states. It further adds that all information that can enable stakeholders to assess how their interests are being affected be disclosed. The policy aims at promoting high standards of transparency and accountability in licensing, procurement, exploration and development operations as well as management of revenues from oil and gas. The policy supports disclosure of payments and revenues from oil and gas using simple and easily understood principles in line with accepted national and international financial reporting standards. However, the policy does not clarify the role of local communities: how, for example, their relationship with oil companies would be structured or what benefits they would derive from oil exploitation or production in their area. The policy does not lay the foundations for future financial arrangements for the collection, sharing and reinvestment of oil revenues. At present, it only states that revenues should be used in an equitable, fair and transparent manner. 'The interests of local communities … shall be taken into account by, among other things, sharing of royalties in line with the Constitution and any relevant laws passed by Parliament.' (*See* section 5.1.6-spirit of cooperation.)

508. The policy's future action points include the adoption of a new law regulating the payment, use and management of petroleum revenues and participation in the processes of the EITI, which supports improved governance through the verification and full publication of company payments and government revenues from oil, gas and mining.

509. The policy supports the use of indigenous oil and gas resources to meet domestic and regional demand and export the surplus. This is aimed at facilitating value addition to these resources, import substitution of petroleum products, and subsequently, generation of additional revenues for the country.

Part IV. Interaction Between Energy Law and Environmental Law

510. For a long time, the people of Uganda have attached significance to and have had a special reverence for rivers, mountains, trees, etc., which reflects the general concern for the preservation of nature and the understanding of its importance. However, this enlightened attitude did not develop into a modern movement for the protection of the environment, barring a few exceptions, because being a developing country after independence, Uganda had no choice but to exploit its natural resources so that the basic necessities of the people were met. In this process, problems of pollution were bound to arise. Therefore, the policy of Uganda at that time gave priority to development over the environment.

511. The legislative and judicial activism triggered thereby have brought greater public awareness and resulted in the evolution of NGOs, which continuously take up the cause of the environment in various fora, including courts. Environmental concerns are now at the top of the world agenda, and the impact of pollution emanating from different energy sources has emerged as a major and significant issue and concern for the debate. These concerns are highlighted by and evident from the ongoing debate about the effects of pollution on health, environmental damage due to destruction and/or acidification of forests and lakes as a result of setting up hydropower stations, concern about the safety of nuclear power plants, radioactive waste management; and the potential risk of global climate change induced by the increasing atmospheric concentration of carbon dioxide and other greenhouse gases being produced by vehicular and other modes of transport. A flurry of legislation on the environment has thus emerged, which greatly impacts the energy sector.

Chapter 1. Legislation on the Environment

§1. The Uganda Constitution 1995, as Amended

512. The Uganda Constitution of 1995[120] provides that everyone has a duty to maintain a sound environment. Article 39 of the Constitution indicates that every person in Uganda has the right to a healthy and clean environment and, as such, can bring legal action for any pollution or disposal of waste. Chapter 3, section 245 stipulates that Parliament should, by law, provide measures intended to protect and preserve the environment from abuse, pollution and degradation. For acquisition of land for development and other purposes, Article 237(1) of the Constitution vests all land in Uganda in her citizens. However, under Article 237(1)(a), the government or local government may acquire land in the public interest. Such acquisition is subject to the provisions of Article 26 of the same Constitution, which gives every person in Uganda a right to own property. It provides procedures to follow during the acquisition of land for public interest, including energy development, and provides for the 'prompt payment of fair and adequate compensation prior to taking possession of land. The Constitution, however, does not make resettlement a right.

§2. The National Environment Act (NEA) No. 5 of 2019

513. This Act emanated from the NEAP, which ended in 1995 and aimed at providing for the sustainable management of the environment and natural resources. It is the framework legislation for environmental law in Uganda that repealed the NEA Cap 153. Under the Act, the NEMA was created with the responsibility of supervising, coordinating and monitoring activities related to the management of the environment.

514. The NEA brings together all sectoral agencies involved in environmental management. Under section 5, the principles of Environmental management include assuring all people of Uganda of the fundamental right of adequate for their health and well-being and encouraging the maximum participation by the people of Uganda in the development of policies, plans and processes for environmental management and to use and conserving the environment and natural resources of Uganda equitably for the present and future use. Under the Act, NEMA, in collaboration with relevant lead agencies, is empowered to issue guidelines and measures relating to management and conservation of lakes and rivers, lakeshores and riverbanks, wetlands, hilltops, hill-sides and mountainous areas, biological resources, forests, woodlots, ozone layer, waste, toxic and hazardous chemicals, rangelands, land use planning and protection of natural heritage sites.

515. In order to operationalize the broad measures above, NEMA issued regulations and standards to guide the sustainable use of environmental resources. These

120. Articles 31 and 41 of the Constitution of the Republic of Uganda as of 15 Jun. 2006.

were developed under the repealed Act, but they are maintained until they are revoked by the responsible Minister. The environmental regulations and Standards that have been developed include: Environmental Impact Assessment Regulations, Standards for Discharge of Effluent into Water or on land, waste Management Regulations among others, The National Environment (Hilly and Mountainous Area Management) Regulations, The National Environment (Wetlands, River banks and Lake Shores Management Regulations), The National Environment (Minimum Standards for the Management of Soil Quality Regulations).

516. An important element for the NEA is the integration of environmental planning at the national and district levels of economic planning. The latter is coordinated with the LGA and includes establishment of Environment Committees at the district, sub-county and local levels.

§3. The Local Government Act Cap 243

517. This Act consolidates and streamlines the existing law on Mini in line with the Constitution to give effect to the decentralization and devolution of functions, powers and services. The Act also provides for revenue, the political and administrative set-up of local governments, and to provide for election of LCs and any other matters that relate to local governments. Subsequent to the decentralization policy, the LGA provides that it is the responsibility of the Local Government to protect and preserve the resources from abuse, pollution and degradation and to manage the resources for sustainable development within the district.

518. The DC is the highest political authority in the district. It has both legislative and executive powers to be exercised in accordance with the Constitution and LGA. Under the district, there are lower local government councils, which consist of: a sub-county council, city division council, municipal council, municipal division and town council. These councils have legislative powers. The DCs have the power to enact district laws (Ordinances), while urban, sub-county division or village councils may, in relation to their specified powers and functions, make by-laws not inconsistent with national statutes or the constitution. Through this method, the district and other lower LCs are to effectively control and manage their natural resources and environment within their local areas and jurisdiction. However, no district has enacted ordinances or by-laws.

519. The Act further provides for the functions and powers of Local Government Councils. Accordingly, District Environment Committees (DECs) are in place, and District Environment Officers (DEOs) have been recruited by the local governments and are members of the District Technical Planning Committee to ensure that environmental concerns are integrated into development programmes. The local governments are responsible for the protection of the environment at the district level. This, therefore, implies that local governments should be consulted on projects to be located within their jurisdiction and on matters that affect their environment. The Electricity Act 1999 further authorizes the ERA to delegate some of its licensing functions to local governments and to be paid royalties by developers.

§4. The National Forestry and Tree Planting Act 2003

520. Uganda's forests consist of officially gazetted forest reserves at the central and local levels. They are found in wildlife-protected areas, private land, cultural land, communal land and public land. The Act provides for the conservation, sustainable management and development of forests for the benefit of the people of Uganda. The Act establishes the National Forestry Authority (NFA), whose functions are to manage all the Central Forest Reserves. Under section 6, the Minister may declare a central Forest Reserve to be: a site of specific scientific interest for purposes of protecting nature and scenic areas of national or international importance, enhancing biological and genetic resources, maintaining animal and plant indicators species or preserving rare, endangered or vulnerable species or high biological diversity; a strict nature reserve for the purposes of protecting streams, lakes, rivers, lakeshores, riverbanks or wetlands, soils, slopes and environment protection, the ecosystem; a joint management forest reserve; a recreation forest for purposes of eco-tourism.

521. Under section 13, a forest reserve should be managed to conserve biological diversity, ecosystems and habitats and sustain the potential yield of their economic, social, health and environmental benefits. Under section 14 and section 32, the Act restricts activities in the Forest Reserves and Community forests. Thus, no person can take or remove or disturb, damage, burn or destroy any forest produce or receive produce or clear, use or occupy any land for grazing, camping, livestock farming, planting or cultivation of crops or erecting of a building or enclosure or recreational, commercial, residential, industrial or hunting purposes except according to a license. It also provides for collaborative management. NFA or a responsible body may enter into a collaborative forest management with a forest user group for the purpose of managing a central forest or a local forest.

522. The Act also provides an aspect of private forestry. A private individual can own and manage a private forest. An owner can be able to transfer and mortgage a private forest so long as it is registered and is managed under a management plan approved by the authorities. This is an incentive for people who would like to invest in forestry.

523. The Act also requires the preparation of a management plan in a forest reserve or community forest. The management plan includes the following contents: a description of all matters relating to the forest, the forest produces and the use currently being made of the forest produce; the type of activities to be carried out in the forest; the management objectives of the forest; the measures to be taken for the sustainable management of forest and the resources likely to be available to enable the management plan to be executed. Under section 31, the Minister may declare a particular tree or group of trees on the land to be: preserving scenic beauty or attraction, conserving a distinctive specimen of any tree species, preventing soil erosion and conserving biological diversity or species diversity.

524. In 2016, the Minister responsible for the environment made the National Forestry and Tree Planting Regulations S.I No. 57 of 2016. The regulations are made pursuant to section 92 of the National Forestry and Tree Planting Act No. 8 of 2003. They apply to all types of forests or a part of a forest provided for under the Act, owners, producers and users of forest products provided for under the Act, and all matters relating to sustainable forest management as prescribed under the Act and the Regulations. Regulation 4 embodies the principles of sustainable forest management, which, among others, is conservation of ecosystems, habitats and biological diversity and their health and vitality and conservation of natural heritage of forest resources and their aesthetic, cultural and spiritual values. The minister is enjoined under the regulations to set standards, criteria and indicators for sustainable forest management. The Authority is under a duty to prepare a forest management plan for each central forest reserve.

525. Under Part X, provision is made for trade in carbon sequestration credits. Under Regulation 106, the regulations provide for the buying and selling of carbon in an open and transparent manner in support of sustainable forest management and poverty reduction, outline the elements and key players of carbon sequestration, provide for the buyer, seller and the verification process, and increase the sequestration of carbon from forests among others.

526. They impose obligations on the responsible body to ensure that the boundary of the land for afforestation or reforestation for purposes of carbon sequestration is clearly defined, development of a management plan for the area involved, the programme is managed in an open, transparent and responsive manner, the ownership of property rights to carbon services, from the trees and land shall be clearly defined in the agreement between the person and the owner of the land, provision for updated legislation establishing a framework for carbon credits, carbon accounting or emissions trading, an up-to-date database of the forests area under the programme and the rates of carbon sequestration is maintained, the local community provides alternative land for a carbon buffer stock to be developed in case the afforestation or reforestation fails.[121]

527. The regulations impose several obligations on the advisory body, key of which include to: develop and propose to the minister estimates of the rates of carbon sequestration for various plants, agricultural commodities and agricultural practices for the purposes of determining the acceptability of the agreement, ensure the maintenance of a national register of carbon service providers, prepare an annual report to the Minister that includes carbon sink enhancement made, carbon sink

121. Regulation 108.

practices and compliance with agreements or similar arrangements entered into and proposals for attracting private investment for carbon purchases.[122]

528. Generally, the regulations besides regulation of tree planting, harvest and use of forest products provide for carbon trade which is a source of energy in Uganda. The regulations, as discussed above, impose certain obligations to ensure the promotion and regulation of carbon trade in the country.

§5. The Water Act Cap 152

529. This Act provides for the use, protection and management of water resources and supply, the constitution of water and sewage authorities, and the devolution of water supply and sewerage undertakings. The objectives of the Act include promoting the rational management and use of the waters of Uganda through progressive introduction and application of appropriate standards and techniques for the investigation, use, control, protection, management and administration of water resources; coordinating all public and private activities which may influence the quality, quantity, distribution, use or management of water resources; and allocating and delegating responsibilities among ministers and public authorities for the investigation, use, control, protection, management or administration of water resources.

530. Under section 5 of the Act, all rights to investigate, control, protect and manage water are vested in the GoU, which is accordingly better placed to ensure that water resources are used sustainably.

531. The Act under section 9 establishes the water policy committee, an intersectoral body whose function, among others, is to coordinate the preparation, revision and keeping to date the comprehensive action plan for the investigation, control, protection, management and administration of water for the nation. Such planning may specify types of activities, development of works, which may not be done without the prior approval of the policy committee. The Act, under sections 18, 19, 20 and 21, provides for the user permits to use and supply water. A person who has to construct or operate any works or engage in the business of constructing boreholes needs construction and drilling permits, respectively, as provided in the Water Resources Regulations 1998.

532. A person who wishes to discharge waste into a water body has to acquire a waste discharge permit under the Water Discharge Regulations of 1998 and the National Environment (Standards for Discharge of Effluent into Water or Land) Regulations 2020. The permit system ensures that the use of water is environmentally friendly and promotes sustainable development. These controls also ensure that water is not treated as a free good but as a good with a value to be paid for. This economic valuation of water is an important incentive for its conservation.

122. Regulation 110.

533. Under section 36 of the Water Act, an easement may enable a holder of a water abstraction permit to bring water to or drain water from his or her land over land owned or occupied by another person. In the same way, an easement may enable a holder of a waste discharge permit to drain waste from his or her land over the land owned or occupied by another person. The works for which an easement is granted have to be maintained and repaired so as to comply with development, which is sustainable. The Act also promotes the provision of a clean, safe and sufficient supply of water for domestic purposes to all persons. The major gap in the Act is that it does not promote an ecosystem approach to the conservation of water resources and, therefore, does not cover all aspects of water use. Additionally, it does not provide for wetlands management, conservation of aquatic biodiversity and the management of cross-border water bodies.

§6. The Land Act, Cap 227

534. The Land Act provides for the ownership and management of land under four different types of land tenures (customary, leasehold, mailo and free-hold) and the procedure for applying for grant of any of the tenures. The Act states that non-citizens of Uganda may only be granted leases not exceeding ninety-nine years. The Act inter alia provides that the construction of electricity transmission and distribution lines, construction of dams and hydropower plants are public works, and any person authorized to execute public works on any land may enter into mutual agreement with an occupier or owner of the land in accordance with the Act. The developer of an energy project should seek to enter into mutual agreement with the occupier or owner of the land. The Act creates a series of land administration institutions consisting of ULC, District Land Boards (DLB), Parish Land Committees (PLC) and land tribunals. Section 78 of the Act gives valuation principles for compensation. Section 40 requires written consent from the spouse(s) and children before the household head transfers, sells or enters into a contract of land where the household derives its livelihood. The district land tribunals have the power to determine any disputes arising out of compensation for land. Under the Land Fund, there is a provision for resettling persons who have been rendered landless by government action. For energy development projects in general, the developer will have to source funds for resettlement or compensation.

§7. The Land Acquisition Act, Cap 226

535. This Act provides for the procedure and method of compulsory acquisition of land for public purposes, whether for temporary or permanent use. The minister responsible for land may authorize any person(s) to enter upon the land and survey it, dig or bore the subsoil or any other thing necessary for ascertaining whether the land is suitable for a public purpose. The government is expected to compensate any person who suffers damage as a result of any action. Any dispute as to the compensation payable can be referred by the Attorney General to court for decision.

§8. THE PHYSICAL PLANNING ACT 2010

536. The Act repeals the Town and Country Planning Act Cap 246 and provides for the establishment of the National Physical board, the composition, functions and procedure of the Board, the establishment of district and urban physical planning committees for the making and approval of physical development plans and for the applications for development permission and related matters. It defines building operations to include electrical operations. Any placing of new poles for the transmission and distribution of electricity and construction of substations must comply with the provisions of this Act.

§9. THE ROADS ACT 2019

537. The Roads Act is a critical piece of legislation with respect to the construction of access roads to energy provision facilities. It defines a road reserve as that declared by the minister on any land acquired by a road authority for purposes of road construction. The Act under section 15 (2) permits a road authority to, in writing, authorize any person or authority to use a road reserve for any approved activity, including the placing of public lighting, advertisements, pipelines, telephone lines, electric supplies, optic fibre cables and posts, drains, sewers, mains and other utilities. Further, under section 15(7), a person authorized to use a road reserve whose activity causes or is likely to cause damage to the road, road furniture or the surrounding environment of the road reserve shall restore the environment to its previous state and condition in accordance with the NEA, No. 5 of 2019.

§10. THE PUBLIC HEALTH ACT, CAP 281

538. The main objective of the Public Health Act is to safeguard and promote public health. Section 7 of the Act provides local authorities with administrative powers to take all lawful, necessary and reasonable measures for preventing the occurrence of, or for dealing with, any outbreak or prevalence of any infectious communicable or preventable diseases. Local Authorities are mandated to exercise powers and perform the duties in respect of public health conferred or imposed by this act or any other law. Section 105 of the Act imposes a duty on the Local Authority to take measures to prevent any pollution dangerous to the health of any water supply that the public has a right to use for drinking or domestic purposes. The Act also details the siting of waste disposal facilities, such as solid waste skips in relation to settlements and food points.

§11. THE OCCUPATIONAL SAFETY AND HEALTH ACT 2006

539. This Act consolidates, harmonizes and updates the law relating to occupational safety and health; and repeals the Factories Act Cap 220. The Act imposes a duty on an employer to take all measures for the protection of his/her workers and the general public from the dangerous aspects of the employer's undertaking at his or her own cost and to ensure that the working environment is kept free from any hazard to pollution by employing technical measures applied to new plants or processes and employing supplementary organizational measures.

Chapter 2. Environmental and Social Impact Assessment (ESIA) Guidelines for the Energy Sector 2004

§1. ESIA as a Tool for Environmental Management

540. The critical need to integrate environmental and socioeconomic concerns into the development process has been fully realized at both national and international levels. Efforts in this direction can be traced from several international declarations, notably the Rio Declaration, Earth Summit (1992). In Uganda, the NEA provides the legal basis for sound environmental management in the country. This Act emphasizes the usefulness of ESIA as a tool for ensuring sound environmental management and also spells out the responsibilities and mandates of different institutions in managing the country's environmental resources. The donor community, especially both the bilateral and multilateral agencies, stress the need to harmonize development actions with environmental concerns in development cooperation. One of the fundamental objectives of donor assistance where they are involved is to promote sustainable use of natural resources and protection of the environment. Following the development and adoption of the Guidelines on Environment and Aid, most donor agencies have developed guidelines for ESIA process, and these apply to all forms of development assistance where they are involved.

541. The ESIA is a universally accepted concept that can allow the effective integration of key project concerns into the policy and project planning process at the earliest possible planning and design stages. But it is also a proactive planning tool, an aid to the decision-making process and an instrument for attaining sustainable development. It is against this background that the NEMA developed ESIA Guidelines (1997) for the purpose of guiding development actions that are likely to impact Uganda's environment. Annex 3 of the NEMA guidelines lists energy projects/activities among those that should be subjected to an ESIA before they can be granted approval for implementation. These guidelines, however, are not specific to energy development projects but target all development actions that are likely to have significant adverse impacts on the environment. In view of this, ESIA sectoral guidelines have been developed specifically for energy development projects and for the energy sector in general.

542. In developing the sectoral guidelines, a holistic interpretation of the energy sector has been adopted, and the guidelines apply to the projects listed in Annex A. These can be new development projects or major modifications to existing infrastructure or facilities. The ESIA sectoral guidelines have been purposely developed to facilitate the easy implementation of new or planned developments in the energy sector by providing practical guidance to all the key players involved in managing different aspects of the ESIA process. The key players in the sector include the MEMD, which is also the lead agency. Others are NEMA, developers, ESIA practitioners, statutory and other consultees, and the general public. A reasonable degree of flexibility has been allowed so that the guidelines can be updated as and when new environmental conditions and realities demand so.

§2. Environment Management

543. Under the NEA, NEMA is the principal agency for the management of the environment and should coordinate, monitor and supervise all activities in the field of the environment. The NEA provides tools for environmental management, including ESIAs. The Act imposes a mandatory duty on a project developer to have an ESIA conducted and approved before embarking on a project. The NEA, under schedule 5, provides projects for which ESIA is mandatory, including energy projects.

§3. Water Resources Management

544. The Water Act provides for the use, protection and management of water resources and supply. The management framework for water resources in Uganda is spelt out in the Water Act and the National Water Policy. The NEA requires a developer to obtain a permit from the Department of Water Development (DWD) before the developer can undertake any construction on water resources, and an ESIA carried out before the DWD will issue a permit to construct a hydropower project.

§4. Wildlife Management

545. The Uganda Wildlife Policy formed the basis for the enactment of the Uganda Wildlife Act and the establishment of the Uganda Wild Authority (UWA). The purpose of the Act is to promote the conservation and sustainable utilization of wildlife throughout Uganda so that the abundance and diversity of their species are maintained at optimum levels commensurate with other forms of land use. The Act also emphasizes the importance of public participation in wildlife management. The Act requires an ESIA to be carried out for any project that has got potential to cause a significant impact on any wildlife species or community.

§5. Guidelines for Use by the MEMD in the ESIA Process

546. The Ministry for Energy is the lead agency for the energy sector in Uganda. It is mandated to promote the development, strategically manage and safeguard the national and sustainable exploitation and utilization of energy resources for socio-economic development in the country. The Energy Ministry is also charged with the role of inspecting, regulating, monitoring and evaluating activities of private companies engaged in the energy sector so that the resources are developed, exploited and used in a rational and sustainable manner. Further, MEMD provides policy guidance on all issues relating to the development, exploitation and management of energy resources. The MEMD should monitor compliance and implementation of activities to ensure that the design criteria, mitigation measures and monitoring requirements are implemented.

I. The Role of the MEMD in the ESIA Process

A. *Environmental Screening of Projects*

547. The developer prepares the project brief and provides ten copies to the NEMA. If NEMA deems the project brief to be complete, one copy is forwarded to MEMD. All projects are assessed according to their specific design and environmental components that are likely to be affected. NEMA, in consultation with MEMD, should decide on the project within two weeks after submission of the project brief by the developer, irrespective of whether conditional or unconditional approval for the project should be granted. A further assessment of environmental impact should be required. The developer and other interested/concerned parties should be notified of the decision taken, and such a decision should be contained in a Certificate of Approval of the ESIA issued by NEMA. If further assessment is required, the Terms of Reference (ToR) will be developed for the purpose of conducting the EIS.

B. *Environmental Impact Review*

548. If an EIR is required, the developer prepares an EIR report which is submitted to NEMA. NEMA and MEMD can rely on their expertise to assess the nature and level of likely environmental impacts. Depending on their assessment, the project can be approved, or it may be decided that a detailed ESIA is necessary. If the screening exercise determines that the project has significant environmental impacts and identifies appropriate mitigation measures, NEMA should recommend that the developer make necessary changes to eliminate the potential significant impacts. If the developer makes a commitment to fulfil the NEMA conditions to eliminate or reduce the effects of potential significant impacts, the project should be approved, and NEMA then issues a Certificate of Approval of ESIA. On the other hand, if potential significant impacts cannot be eliminated easily, the project should not be approved, and the screening decision will require that the project be subjected to a detailed EIS.

C. *Scoping Report and ToR for the EIS*

549. The developer, in consultation with NEMA, MEMD and other key stakeholders, should undertake to prepare the ToR for Environmental Impact Study (EIS). For this purpose, all relevant documents should be made available to the stakeholders. The scoping report, including the ToR, should be reviewed by MEMD.

D. *Review of Environmental Impact Statements*

550. The developer submits ten copies of the EIS to NEMA. NEMA, in consultation with MEMD, reviews the EIS to determine if it is complete and whether it addresses the potential significant environmental impacts as identified during scoping and as stipulated in the ToR for the study. NEMA should then circulate the EIS to other stakeholders and interested parties for review and comments; it then, in close consultation with MEMD, holds a public hearing to review the EIS.

E. Review Parameters

551. The main objective of the review exercise is to critically examine whether the EIS adequately addresses the significant environmental issues identified during scoping and in the ToR for the EIS; whether the results and findings presented are scientifically and technically sound and coherent enough to be understood by decision-makers and the public in general, and whether reasonable alternatives have been suggested to the proposed action. The MEMD should finally conduct an independent assessment of the EIS to determine its adequacy in informing a correct decision to be taken on the environmental aspects of the project before finally forwarding the comments on the EIS to NEMA so as to guide the latter in taking a final decision on the project.

1. Guidelines for Use by Project Developers in the Energy Sector

552. Developers of energy projects can be private investors, NGOs or MEMD. If MEMD is the developer, its responsibilities as a lead agency are taken over by NEMA. Developers ought to understand their ESIA obligations right from the planning and design stages and the associated screening activities by the time they submit a project brief or the EIS to NEMA. The ESIA should be part and parcel of the project owner's planning cycle.

2. Application of the ESIA as Part of the Project Cycle

553. The ESIA should be conducted as an integral part of the overall project cycle from project identification to pre-feasibility study, feasibility study, project design and other phases, and should therefore form the basis for environmentally sound project implementation and monitoring. The ESIA conducted at the early planning stage will serve as a tool that assists and guides developers through providing environmental information and raising environmental concerns at key stages in the project cycle leading to projects designed with in-built mitigation measures. Design proposals with potentially adverse environmental impacts can therefore be mitigated, while those found to be incapable of mitigation could be changed appropriately. The ESIA applied at this critical stage permits early indication of practical design changes aimed at either avoiding or minimizing identified negative environmental impacts or enhanced environmental benefits.

3. The Role of the Developer in the ESIA Process

554. The developer is responsible for undertaking an ESIA and should meet all the costs associated with it. Such costs should include, among others, the cost for conducting the EIS, preparation, production and distribution of EIS for comment and review by agencies, interested parties and other stakeholders. The developer must further ensure that the ESIA is carried out before projects can be licensed or approved by the responsible Agencies. This requirement is also demanded by all financing institutions, such as World Bank and other donors.

4. Steps a Developer Takes to Conduct ESIA

555. The developer is expected to go through the following steps from the design stage to the time their project is issued a Certificate of Approval.

5. Step 1: Initial Screening

556. Developers need to undertake their own screening to identify environmental issues of major concern at an early stage of the project. For screening energy projects, the following questions can offer guidance to the developer. On the nature of the project: will the project cause a significant environmental impact? Will the project lead to increased or decreased discharge of fossil carbon dioxide, methane or other greenhouse gases? On the siting of the project: is the project located within or near environmentally sensitive areas such as sources of public water supply, areas of unique historic, cultural, archaeological, scientific or geological interest and ecologically fragile ecosystems such as wetlands? On the natural resources affected: will the proposed project result in direct or indirect negative or positive impacts on the natural resources in the surroundings? Will the project develop systems which permit sludge-nutritive salts, building waste, excavated materials or other waste products to be taken care of or brought back into eco-cycles? Will the project improve or impair the living conditions of the settled population or nomadic groups?

6. Step 2: Assessment of Project Alternatives

557. At the early project stage, a thorough assessment of all the possible project alternatives should be conducted with a view to determining the most optimal in terms of environmental and social considerations. This assessment should begin early in the planning process before the siting, type and scale of an energy project are decided upon. For an energy project, the following alternatives should be considered: site/location alternatives; project scale or size alternatives; source of energy alternatives; construction, operation, decommissioning design alternatives; and 'no-project' alternatives.

7. Step 3: Project Planning and Designing

558. Once the developer has identified the potential environmental impacts, he or she will identify appropriate mitigation measures, which will be incorporated into the project design. This will minimize the time and costs associated with conducting ESIAs, and in any case, ESIA must be considered as part and parcel of the planning and design for all energy projects. Good practice demands that costs for mitigation are incorporated in the total project budget.

8. Step 4: Preparation and Submission of the Project Brief

559. The developer prepares a project brief which he or she submits to NEMA. The purpose of the brief is to provide sufficient and relevant information on the proposed project that can allow NEMA and MEMD to establish whether or not the project is likely to have a significant impact on the environment and determine the level of ESIA required. If adequate mitigation measures are identified in the project brief, this may eliminate the need for further assessment, and the project may be approved, subject to any other conditions that may be set to ensure implementation of the proposed mitigation plan. The developer is required to submit ten copies of the project brief to NEMA, which in turn sends a copy to MEMD.

9. Step 5: Screening of Projects

560. After submitting a project brief to NEMA, it is screened by NEMA in consultation with MEMD. The screening process is aimed at the identification of major environmental issues at a very early stage and the better utilization of financial and human resources by focusing on major environmental issues of the project. After this screening, NEMA is then in a position to determine whether a detailed EIS is required or an EIR is necessary, or the project is exempted.

10. Step 6: Environmental Impact Review

561. The objective of an EIR is to determine the environmental impacts an energy project may have and to define adequate mitigation measures for the significant impacts. The findings of the EIR are presented in the EIR report. This report should be brief and precise. Depending on the decision taken on the EIR by NEMA, the project will be subjected to an EIS, and a Certificate of Approval will be issued.

11. Step 7: Scoping

562. Scoping is then conducted to determine the most critical issues that need to be addressed during the EIS. The developer, in consultation with NEMA, MEMD and other interested parties, undertakes scoping. Good practice demands that there should be full participation of the public during scoping.

12. Step 8: Preparation of the ToR and Conducting an EIS

563. The ToRs for the EIS are developed based on the scoping results. The developer, in close consultation with NEMA, MEMD and other key stakeholders, should prepare the ToR for the study. The scoping results, including the ToR, should be submitted to NEMA in order for it to determine their completeness and adequacy. At this point, the developer needs to source and hire experienced experts to undertake the different tasks specified in the ToR. Most likely, this support is already acquired during earlier stages of the ESIA process. The EIS report should contain the following but not be limited to the following. The background and objectives of the project proposal; description of the project and the project components; description of the affected environment; a list of the potential significant environmental impacts of the project; identification of adequate mitigation measures to address the environmental impacts; a list of agencies, organizations and individuals consulted; a list of the technical team that conducted the EIR.

13. Step 9: Submission of the EIS to NEMA

564. The outcome of the ESIA is an environmental impact statement (EIS). Upon completion of the study, the developer should submit ten copies of the EIS to NEMA. NEMA will, in turn, send copies to MEMD and other key stakeholders for review and comments. The EIS should be a public document which will be made available to any person requesting it. Any comments made should be forwarded to NEMA so that these should be taken into consideration in approving or disapproving the contents of the EIS. A Certificate of Approval of the EIS should be issued by NEMA to the developer and should indicate whether or not the environmental aspects of the EIS have been approved. The developer should then present this certificate to MEMD, REA, ERA or any other licensing authorities that should take appropriate decisions on the project.

14. Developer's Role in Monitoring

565. The developer of an energy project that has obtained a Certificate of Approval on the basis of proposed mitigation measures should ensure that the mitigation measures and actions proposed to protect the environment are adopted and implemented. The developer should conduct self-monitoring, self-record-keeping and self-reporting. The information gathered through monitoring should be stored and made available during inspection. The developer should also undertake all reasonable measures to mitigate undesirable environmental impacts not contemplated in the EIS and should accordingly report on these measures to MEMD and NEMA.

15. Guidelines for Practitioners

566. An ESIA practitioner refers either to a team of individual consultants assembled for the purpose of conducting an ESIA or a firm of consulting specialists contracted to carry out a feasibility study and detailed engineering designs for a proposed project and to also plan and conduct the ESIA for the project. ESIA practitioners play a key role in the ESIA process. The major aim of these guidelines is to guide practitioners on procedures and steps for conducting ESIA, the EIS and preparing EIS for energy projects. After screening an energy project, NEMA, in consultation with MEMD, might decide that the project will lead to significant impacts on the environment. The developer will then be required to conduct a full ESIA.

16. Scoping

567. The project brief contains a good deal of baseline data about a given energy project. However, more often than not, it does not provide all the required information. The information gaps should be identified and more information collected to facilitate the identification of impacts. During the scoping of projects, roles and responsibilities of practitioners include: conducting an EIR, conducting and managing an ESIA for a proposed project, conducting the EIS and communicating and reporting on the findings of the EIS, also known as preparation of the EIS.

568. The scoping exercise is aimed at identifying all the key and significant impacts and issues pertaining to a development project. It is vital for defining the focus and scope of the EIS. Scoping of energy projects must involve the local community, independent experts, NGOs, government departments and international partners in development. Extensive consultations have to be made, especially for big hydro projects, so that they are accepted both locally and internationally. The scoping team should visit the project site to acquaint themselves with and obtain first-hand information on the local environment at the location of the project. The main output of the scoping exercise is to define the ToR of the EIS.

17. Preparation of the ToR for the EIS

569. The ToR for the EIS is developed based on the scoping results. This should be done in consultation with NEMA, MEMD and other key stakeholders. The scoping results, including the ToR, should be submitted to NEMA, which will review the scoping report and ToR with a view to ensuring their completeness and adequacy. The technical team to undertake the EIS is identified, and their names and qualifications are forwarded to NEMA for approval.

18. Environmental Impact Study

570. The detailed content of the EIS and the procedures for conducting the EIS and preparing the EIS will vary from project to project. The major tasks of the EIS are to: specify which issues and impacts the EIS should focus on and the methodologies to be used; formulate project alternatives to be assessed during the study; identify stakeholders and the methodology for their participation in the ESIA process; determine the type and quality of information and data required for the study and determine the type of specialists to constitute the study team.

19. Environmental Baseline Study

571. This involves the collection of relevant data and information on physical, ecological, economic, socio-cultural and demographic conditions in the project area. These data form the basis for determining the existing environment and the expected changes in the environment by implementing the project. The project brief and the baseline data for scoping might contain useful baseline data about a given energy project. However, most energy projects are relatively complex, and the information available from the project brief and the scoping exercise might not be adequate. The practitioner should be able to identify any information gaps and plan to collect more relevant data. Some of the required data might already be available in the research, academic and government departments, respectively. In Uganda, a wealth of information does exist in district environment profile reports, the census and other reports, and in several government departments such as meteorology, forestry, water development and others. The collected data should be comprehensive enough to address the specific issues identified in the EIS.

20. Description and Quantification of Impacts

572. The identification of most of the significant impacts, both positive and negative, is usually accomplished during the scoping exercise. More in-depth studies may be required to identify other impacts. After the identification of all the possible significant impacts, an attempt should be made to describe the precise nature of the impact on its receiving environment. The significance of impacts has to be judged upon their magnitude, extent, severity, duration and likelihood. Quantitative assessment methods may be useful in comparing different impacts. The quantification of significant impacts can be based on the use of various indicators and weighing the impacts against threshold values where these exist. Such threshold values may be in the form of standards for various environmental parameters to be assessed during the study. Where environmental standards do exist, the environmental parameters under investigation should be compared with the national standards to determine their acceptability and conformity with the regulations. It is worth noting that environmental standards are not well-developed in Uganda, and very few environmental parameters have such standards. It is, therefore, desirable that the importance or significance of such impacts is based on sound and scientific principles, that is, by-laws, World Bank standards, World Health Organization (WHO) and United Nations (UN) standards.

21. Environmental Economic Analysis

573. Whenever possible, environmental economic analysis should be made as part of ESIAs. This is important for several reasons. Economic analysis and valuation in monetary terms of the environmental impacts and of the proposals for necessary measures make it possible to integrate the conclusions of the ESIA into the economic and financial analysis of the project assessment. It is then possible to weigh up the project's costs and benefits and the advantages and disadvantages of different possible alternatives and scenarios. Environmental economic analysis can also be used to find the most effective instruments to solve environmental problems that may arise as a result of the project. Environmental economic analysis should be included in the ESIA if the cost of making this analysis is reasonable and if it is not too difficult or time-consuming. If a socioeconomic analysis is made of the project proposal, the environmental impact should always be included in it.

22. Project Alternatives

574. The EIS must include a thorough assessment of all the possible project alternatives with a view to determining the most optimal in terms of environmental and social considerations. This assessment should begin early in the planning process before the siting, type and scale of an energy project are decided upon. For an energy project, the following alternatives should be considered: site/location alternatives, project scale or size alternatives; source of energy alternatives; construction, operation, decommissioning design alternatives and 'no-project' alternatives.

23. Impact Mitigation

575. One of the main objectives of ESIA is to predict and prevent unacceptable adverse environmental effects by recommending the implementation of appropriate project modifications or actions that reduce, avoid or offset the potential adverse consequences of a project. Impact mitigation can only be possible when the full extent of the anticipated environmental and social problems is understood. Impact mitigation therefore has to affect the sources of impacts. Common sources include location, construction practices, operation and implementation of projects, maintenance and cumulative impacts. Mitigation should not be treated as an isolated activity but rather as being inherent in all aspects of the ESIA process right from the project design stage. The successful implementation of the prescribed mitigation measures is a good indication of the success of the project as a whole. This demands that mitigation costs are integrated into the contract dossier and bills of quantities as distinctive cost items so that both the contractor and the developer cannot overlook them.

24. Monitoring Programme

576. Identifying impacts and related mitigation measures without ensuring their compliance makes little sense. Therefore, a detailed monitoring and evaluation programme has to be part of the EIS. It should contain a schedule for inspecting and reporting upon the implementation of the project and associated mitigation measures. The monitoring programme should also identify the key indicators of environmental and social impact and their respective threshold level above which the impact is significant. The programme should provide a schedule for monitoring each indicator and for reporting the monitoring results to MEMD and NEMA.

25. Preparation of EIS

577. After conducting the EIS, the findings have to be presented in the EIS. The EIS should provide a description of the following: the project and the activities it is likely to generate; the proposed site and reasons for rejecting alternative sites; a description of the potentially affected environment, including specific information necessary for identifying and assessing the environmental effects of the project; the material inputs into the project and their potential environmental effects; economic analysis of the project; the products and by-products of the project; the environmental effects of the project including the direct, indirect, cumulative, short-term and long-term effects and possible alternatives; the measures proposed for eliminating, minimizing or mitigating adverse impacts; an identification of gaps in knowledge and uncertainties, which were encountered in compiling the required information; and an indication of whether the environment of any other state is likely to be affected and available alternatives and mitigating measures.

26. Guidelines for Mitigation of Social Impacts

578. An ESIA must also address the human or social environment, which includes the social and socioeconomic impacts due to the implementation of an energy project. One of the main objectives of social-ESIAs is to predict and prevent or moderate unacceptable adverse social effects on the proposed actions or projects. This is done by involving the community and all other stakeholders so that changes can be recommended at the planning, design and implementation stages. Social impact analysis should be carried out at every stage of the project cycle.

27. Project Planning

579. At the planning and design stage of all energy projects, it must be ensured in the design that people are an integral part of the environment and are going to be active participants in the overall project environment. The following guidelines apply. First, the developer identifies the social impacts focusing on preventing social impact. During the design, the consulting engineer/EIS team must describe the main phases of the project; vis-à-vis the project cycle to ensure that the stakeholders fully understand what the project is all about. The consulting engineer/EIS team should further take note of the significant social-cultural issues in the project area and formulate a plan to prevent undesirable social impacts, if possible, at the design/planning stage.

28. The Project Brief

580. For the purpose of addressing socioeconomic impacts in the project brief, the developer has to ensure the following: key socioeconomic activities and cultural issues within the project area are highlighted in brief, the methodology for addressing gender concerns during recruitment of personnel and distribution of socioeconomic benefits to the local community is clearly detailed and where possible the requirements of the LGA are fulfilled (Affirmative Action on Women). The ESIA expert who prepares the project brief should consult a competent sociologist/anthropologist.

a. Assessment and Mitigation of Social Impacts During the EIS

581. Although every project is unique, in most cases, there is a series of more or less standard steps through which the analysis must proceed in order to achieve good results. These steps include the following.

i. Step 1: Develop an Effective Public Involvement Plan

582. The level of public participation needed varies with the nature of the action under review. For a complex project, like a large-scale hydropower project, a social assessment may be useful at the outset to establish the general character of the community, define the potentially affected groups and determine the best mechanisms for their involvement. In a simpler case, like a wind farm, merely consulting with local leaders and experts may be sufficient to obtain the critical data on which to build a public involvement programme.

ii. Step 2: Identify and Characterize Alternatives

583. Alternatives are developed based on the purpose and need for the action, but the analyst needs to consider what they are and obtain sufficient data on each to frame the analysis.

iii. Step 3: Define Baseline Conditions

584. Having established a means of working with the public and obtaining basic data on each alternative, the analyst now tries to define the pertinent existing conditions in each potentially affected area. The analyst seeks answers to questions like: what populations may be affected? Are they concentrated or dispersed? How does each population relate to the natural or built environment? What is the historical background of each population? What are the political and social resources, power structure and networks of relationships in each group? Is there low-income or minority populations or other disadvantaged groups involved? Do they have special needs? What kind of cultural and attitudinal attributes characterize each group? How do they feel about political and social institutions? How do they relate to the environment? To change? What are the relevant demographic and economic characteristics? Is there significant unemployment or underemployment? Is housing available? Access to utilities? Education? Transportation? Are there seasonal or other patterns of in-migration and out-migration?

585. At a minimum, this kind of information should be developed based on existing literature, government documents and consultation with experts and the community. For a more complicated project, formal studies may be needed. Indicators should be used to describe the social structure. These indicators should facilitate the identification, especially of disadvantaged groups, and describe and measure the social impacts analysed in the sequel. These indicators could include social indicators like: registered crimes/disputes (per 1,000 population); crimes/disputes involving women (per 1,000 population); crimes/disputes involving vulnerable groups (per 1,000 population); primary school attendance male; primary school attendance female; number of households; number of female-headed households; number of community-based organizations. Economic indicators like: average land holding per household (hectares); percentage of households owning land; percentage of households owning domicile; percentage of households renting land; percentage of households renting domicile; agricultural production; maize (tonnes per ha. per annum); rice (tonnes per ha. per annum); millet (tonnes per ha. per annum); cassava (tonnes per ha. per annum); fish catch (tonnes per household/per annum); banana (tonnes per ha/annum); employment; number of male wage earners; number of female wage earners; average household income (per annum); average household expenditure (per annum); energy consumption (average per household); wood fuel (tonnes per annum); kerosene (litres per annum); electricity (kWh per annum).

iv. Step 4: Define the Scope of the Effort

586. The assessment of social impacts must be scoped to make sure it is focused on the right things and that the right methods are employed. The scope has to be included in the ToR for the EIS. Scoping must be carried out in consultation with the affected groups and through the public participation process. Factors to consider in establishing the scope include probability that an event will occur, the number of people potentially affected, duration of potential impacts, values of benefits and costs to affected groups, potential for reversibility or mitigation, likelihood of subsequent impacts, relevance to decisions, uncertainties over probable effects and controversy.

v. Step 5: Project Probable Impacts

587. Analysis of potential social impacts involves the study of data provided by the agencies involved, records of previous experience with similar actions or similar populations, census data and other vital statistics, documents and secondary sources, and field research involving interviews, meetings, surveys and observation. Social impacts are generally manifested in one or more of the following changes: people's way of life – how they live, work, play and interact with one another on a day-to-day basis; their culture-shared beliefs, customs and values; their community – its cohesion, stability, character, services and facilities; their environment – the quality of the air and water people use, the availability and quality of the food they eat, the level of dust and noise to which they are exposed, the adequacy of sanitation, their safety and fears about their security, and most importantly, their access to and control over resources. The ESIA expert should endeavour to analyse all these broad areas of impact so that no major types of social impacts are overlooked.

588. There are a number of methods of projecting impacts. These methods depend on factors like the scope of the action, the area where it occurs and the availability of pertinent data. Projection methods include: comparative project, comparing similar actions and their effects; straight-line trend projection: taking an existing trend and projecting it into the future; population multiplier: for actions involving increase or decrease in given populations; each unit of change in a given population implies a change in other variables such as housing and use of natural resources; scenarios: generate logical or data-based models and play them out; expert advice: obtain the thoughts of experts about likely scenarios or changes; calculation of 'futures forgone': for example, the future of small minority-owned businesses in a community if the proposed action does not take place; and computer modelling which is very suitable for quantitative impacts.

vi. Step 6: Predict Responses to Impacts

589. The following questions are important in predicting responses to impacts: Will a group be highly influenced by what its leaders think, and will the leaders be positive or negative about the project? Are there ways for the population to adapt to the project, or is it likely to relocate? Can a group continue to carry out its valued ways of life, or will they be irrevocably lost?

vii. Step 7: Consider Indirect and Cumulative Impacts

590. This is an important aspect that must be considered because most social impacts are not direct; they may occur well after the action is taken and possibly in areas distant from the project. Many populations, especially local communities, are severely at risk of cultural extinction due to a variety of pressures, and a given project may lead to their extinction.

viii. Step 8: Recommend New Alternatives as Needed and Feasible

591. As serious impacts are identified, consider what alternatives might alleviate the problems and work with the project managers and affected groups to determine whether these are feasible and implementable.

ix. Step 9: Develop a Mitigation Plan

592. Work with project managers and affected groups to establish ways to mitigate social effects and put this plan forward in the EIS. Establish monitoring programmes to make sure that mitigation actually occurs.

29. Guidelines for Public Consultations

593. Energy developments usually have different impacts or effects in areas where they are located. Such impacts may directly or indirectly affect different categories of social groups, agencies, communities and individuals. These are collectively referred to as project stakeholders or the 'public'. It is, therefore, very crucial that during the ESIA process, appropriate mechanisms for ensuring the fullest participation and involvement of the public are taken by MEMD or/and the developer in order to minimize social and environmental impacts and enhance stakeholder acceptance.

30. Energy Projects for Which the Public Must Be Consulted

594. The consultation and involvement of the public are very desirable throughout the ESIA process. However, it is very critical at the following stages: project design, scoping, and EIS review. It should also be noted that the need and degree of public consultation and involvement vary according to the nature and characteristics of the project. For example, very intensive and extensive consultations are required for a large hydropower project. This also generally applies to any other energy project characterized by the following: substantial land-take, displacement of families or communities, disruption of the means of livelihood of families and communities, destruction of communal assets and property, need for resettlement and compensation, and inundation of land and property.

31. Methodology for Involvement of the Public Selection of Stakeholders

595. An energy project has got a wide range of stakeholders. These generally include individuals, organized groups, MEMD, local and international NGOs or institutions with specific interest in a project. Sometimes, it might be useful to involve individuals such as academics and research scientists who may have special local knowledge about the project environment. It should be recognized that different stakeholders have different interests in a project, thus the need to carefully identify and appropriately categorize them. This should preferably be initiated as early as possible in the project cycle, preferably at the project planning stage. Special care should be taken to ensure that the concerns and views of the directly affected, the poor, minority and other highly vulnerable groups are not overshadowed by the more influential groups. The interests of women as a special group should also be captured.

32. Consultations with Stakeholders

596. Once the stakeholders have been identified and properly categorized, the process of involving them in the ESIA process should begin. For an energy project, consultations involve an exchange of vital information or facts and key issues between the developer or MEMD on the one hand and the stakeholder community on the other. The consultation process should accord the stakeholder community every opportunity to comment on the merits, demerits and any other aspect of the proposed project. The process must be well-planned and coordinated so that participation is convenient and cost-effective for all the parties involved. An effective consultation process should generally ensure that the public has got a clear understanding of the proposed project and that the feedback mechanisms are clearly laid out and known by the parties involved.

33. Consultation Methodology

597. There are numerous techniques and approaches that can be used for seeking the views of the public and consulting various project stakeholders. The following are recommended for energy projects in Uganda.

34. Public Meetings

598. These may be specially convened meetings for people living in or near the project area. In Uganda, these may target LC officials and residents of villages adjacent to the project area. They may also apply to larger urbanized communities. The meetings are generally open, and anybody is free to attend and participate in the proceedings. Public meetings are an ideal technique for a project developer to inform or educate the public about what the proposed development is about in general terms. To a good extent, they also enable the public to express their views and feelings about the project. Though the meetings are not formal, detailed notes of the important points and issues raised during the session should be noted down by the developer. These should be kept on file for reference purposes.

35. Interviews

599. These may be structured or semi-structured. Interviews should be undertaken with key individuals representing the range of the public likely to be interested or affected by the project. For energy projects, these may include LC officials, elders and civic leaders adjacent to the project area. They should also target individuals considered to represent the views of distinct social groups, such as women and the poor. Interviews are very effective in assessing public sentiments about the project.

36. Surveys

600. Surveys are an effective technique for determining public attitudes, values, and perceptions on various issues regarding the proposed project. Surveys can be conducted through individual interviews or small group interviews. The respondents should be carefully selected for this technique to achieve its objective.

37. Operating Field Offices

601. The establishment and operation of special field offices serve as a liaison between the developer and the public. This is quite applicable to projects necessitating close local contact and coordination, an example being a hydropower project where compensation and resettlement for displaced people must be undertaken. For this approach to be effective, the offices must be well publicized so that they are known to the public.

38. Open Houses

602. These are publicized accessible locations where the information on the proposed project and the ESIA can be found. A member of the ESIA team should be present to explain and discuss issues and record the viewpoints and concerns of visitors. An open house is open and accessible to any person and the times of opening should be well publicized.

39. Advising Stakeholder Panels

603. Good experiences have been made with the establishment of official advising panels, which consist of representatives of the different stakeholder groups. These panels are especially useful for negotiations concerning EIS and resettlement plans.

40. Responsibility for Ensuring Public Participation

604. MEMD takes the lead in ensuring that the public fully participates in the ESIA process. As a matter of good practice, developers should also ensure an optimal level of public involvement at different stages of the ESIA process. Where MEMD is the developer, the responsibility for ensuring public participation is taken over by NEMA.

41. Public Consultation within the ESIA Process

605. In practice, public consultation is not a linear but an interactive as well as an ongoing process. Decision-making, monitoring action impacts, impact prediction, impact significance and reviewing different stages of the ESIA process do require different levels of public consultation and involvement. However, public involvement becomes very critical at the following stages: public consultation before the commissioning of the EIS, public consultation during the EIS and public consultation during the EIS review.

42. Public Consultation before Commissioning of the EIS

606. On submission of the project brief to MEMD and NEMA, it might be decided that the views and comments of the public on the project should be sought. NEMA is obliged to publish the developer's notification and other relevant documents in a public notice within four weeks from the date of submission of the project brief and/or notice of intent to develop. For publishing the developer's notification in the public notice, the project brief should be appropriately summarized out, including the following: nature, size, location of the project and the site characteristics. The notification should also clearly specify where the developer's documents can be found. The public and other stakeholders should submit their objections, views and comments to NEMA and MEMD within twenty-one days from the date of publication of the notice.

43. Preparation of Public Consultation Plan

607. It is important that a plan for stakeholder involvement is prepared before the EIS begins. This should be one with input from an anthropologist or rural sociologist with knowledge of the local cultures and different approaches or techniques available for implementing stakeholder involvement. Such a plan should consider: the stakeholders to be involved; matching stakeholders with approaches and techniques of involvement; traditional authority structures and political decision-making processes; programming of the implementation, in time and space, of the different approaches and techniques for stakeholder involvement; mechanisms to collect, synthesize, analyse and, most importantly, present the results to the EIS team and key decision-makers; measures to ensure timely and adequate feedback to the stakeholders and budgetary/time opportunities and constraints.

44. Public Consultations during the EIS

608. During the EIS, the study team should endeavour to consult the public on environmental concerns and any other issues pertaining to the project. Though ESIA Guidelines for the Energy Sector consultations are very critical at the scoping stage, ideally, it should be an ongoing activity throughout the study.

45. Public Consultation during the EIS Review

609. During the EIS review, the public is given additional opportunities to ensure that their views and concerns have been adequately addressed in the EIS. Any earlier omissions or oversight about the project effects can be raised at this stage. To achieve this objective, the EIS and related documents become public documents after submitting them to NEMA. Upon receipt of EIS for an energy project, NEMA should publicize its contents and go further to identify the relevant stakeholders and the concerned area or region, and also, the location of places for inspection of the EIS. Further, NEMA should make copies or appropriate summaries of the statement available for public inspection. This should be accomplished within two weeks from the receipt of the EIS. NEMA, in close consultation with MEMD, will decide on the most suitable locations or places where the EIS content can be accessed conveniently by the public. The public notice should include a concise summary of assessment data indicating the following: size and nature of the project; location; site characteristics; key results of the EIS. The notice should also specify the locations or places where the EIS may be consulted or viewed in addition to a notification to send or copy any comments to NEMA. An official review appointment will be announced, where the reviewing authority has to answer questions and remarks from the public. These questions have to be handed in written form beforehand.

46. Guidelines for Resettlement and Compensation

610. The energy projects for which these guidelines apply are likely to fall into two categories: the old projects that may need rehabilitation or expansion and thus require additional pieces of land and the new projects that may require new land altogether. In both cases, the relocation of populations and disruption of the people's livelihoods might occur. This is most likely, especially in the development of hydropower, exploration of petroleum resources and large renewable energy projects. When relocation of people or communities is inevitable, there is a need to resettle them and ensure that their new places offer similar or better facilities compared to the old environmental and socioeconomic set-up.

611. Resettlement in Uganda is covered under the Land Act, while compensation is covered under the Uganda Constitution. Currently, a resettlement policy is being prepared by the Commissioner for Resettlement in the Office of the Prime Minister. However, in all types of energy projects, every effort must be made to avoid relocation of communities. Involuntary displacement is generally known as an agent for disrupting and impoverishing communities. It should, therefore, be avoided or at least minimized. Where it is unavoidable, the displaced persons should not only be adequately compensated for their losses at replacement cost but also be given opportunity to share in energy development project benefits. Further, they should be assisted in all ways possible in order to improve their livelihood. Compensation is considered an appropriate mitigation measure for unavoidable impacts when actions to minimize such impacts on people are not possible or insufficient. Provisions for compensation are supposed to avail enough resources for the affected communities to purchase replacement properties. The compensation scheme should also ensure that displaced people are not worse off, economically and socially, than they were before their displacement. For energy projects, compensation would have to be paid for land, property and crops, where land is acquired for the purpose of enabling the development project to take place. However, no compensation needs to be paid for any buildings, property or crops that were erected or grown after the cut-off period or in areas designated for energy projects, such as the right of way for transmission lines in a road reserve.

47. Policy Framework for Resettlement

612. The objectives of the policy framework include the following key elements: involuntary resettlement should be avoided or minimized through design efforts. Where involuntary resettlement is inevitable, resettlement activities should be conceived and executed as sustainable development programmes, providing sufficient investment resources to give the persons displaced by the project the opportunity to share in project benefits. Displaced persons should be assisted in their efforts to improve their livelihoods and standard of living or at least to restore them, in real terms, to pre-displacement levels. According to the Uganda government policy as well as the policies of the development partners, the term affected people/communities refers to people who are directly affected socially and economically by the energy development projects. This will usually be caused by the involuntary land-take or use of other assets that may result in relocation or loss of shelter; loss of assets or access to assets; loss of income sources or means of livelihood, whether or not the affected persons must move to another location.

613. The involuntary restriction of access to legally designated parks and protected areas could result in adverse impacts on the livelihood of displaced persons. The resettlement policy applies to all development projects and activities in the energy sector, irrespective of the developer or financier of the project. This policy also covers resettlement and compensation resulting from complementary activities that are not directly part of the immediate energy investment project but are necessary to achieve its objectives as set forth in the energy investment project documents. The policy applies to all displaced persons regardless of the total number affected or the severity of the impact. Particular attention should be paid to the needs of vulnerable groups among those displaced: especially those below the poverty line, the elderly, women and children, the disabled local communities and ethnic minorities.

48. Legal Framework

614. The EIS team should determine the legal requirements for compensation, including the existence of local by-laws, if any. In addition, it should work out a framework for coordination between the different players in compensation. The position of the GoU in relation to resettlement and compensation to be paid if damage is caused to land is clear under the constitution and other Ugandan laws, as well as for most of the development partner policies and guidelines. The relevant laws that provide a framework for resettlement and/or land acquisition exercise for energy projects are: the Uganda Constitution (1995), the Land Act (Cap 227), the

Land Acquisition Act (Cap 226), the Roads Act 2019 and the Guidelines for Compensation Assessment under Land Acquisition 2017.

49. Institutional Framework

615. Overall, there are four main institutions involved in carrying out resettlement for energy projects. These are the Ministry of Water, Ministry of Lands and Ministry of Environment (Compensation), the Prime Minister's office (Resettlement), MEMD and the Local Governments. Although the Prime Minister's office is mandated to handle resettlement, it tends to limit itself to disaster situations. For the purpose of energy projects, MEMD takes responsibility for resettlement, identifying and coordinating all the players in the resettlement programme. In general, the developer liaises with the Ministry of Water, Lands and Environment to harmonize the compensation rates in consultation with the Chief Government Valuer. In addition, the LC officials, the contractor or developer and the affected local communities work closely to ensure a fair resettlement exercise. All districts in Uganda operate under a five-tier system of local government. The highest level is the LC V, headed by a district chairperson, followed by the LC IV, LC III, LC II, and LC I, all headed by the respective LC chairpersons.

616. This hierarchy is the political wing of the district administration, while the district Chief Administrative Officer (CAO) heads the technical wing. Within the district, the Central Government is represented by the Resident District Commissioner (RDC). The district officials who will facilitate the resettlement exercise are the RDC and the LC V Chairman.

617. The technical personnel at the district level are headed by the CAO and will usually include the Community Development Officer (CDO), the District Land Officer, and the District Surveyor. At the energy project development level, the parish chiefs of Counties, as well as LC officials at LC 1, should form part of the resettlement committees. The Parish chief, together with the CDO at the district level, should be involved in the resettlement programme as they should have been involved in the census exercise.

50. Stakeholder Analysis and Census of the Affected Persons

618. Prior to any compensation or relocation of people/communities, it is imperative to identify the stakeholders and carry out a census of the affected persons and communities. The census will take into account all the people affected together with their means of livelihood. The census will, in particular, identify the vulnerable groups which should be protected. These include women, the disabled, orphans, widows and other minorities. During the census exercise of the affected persons, the local leaders, CDO, as well as Parish Chiefs from the project area, should work together with the developer to ensure a smooth exercise. Both immovable and movable properties will be counted and eventually valued. The major stakeholders in the energy projects should include the following: Local Governments (District Administration and the Parish chiefs); The District Resident Commissioners; LC V, III and II Executives and Councillors, as well as the Office of the LC IIIs in the town council, respectively; LC I Chairmen in all the affected settlements; Representatives of the MEMD and Development partners if relevant.

51. Compensation in Energy Projects

619. Compensation is considered when steps to minimize impacts on people are not possible or insufficient. Compensation provisions are supposed to avail enough resources for the affected communities to purchase replacement assets. They should also ensure that displaced people are not worse off economically and socially than before the displacement. Monetary compensation as a means of compensating those directly affected by a development project has not been very effective in Uganda. There have been a significant number of cases where compensation provisions and property acquisition practices did not provide sufficient resources to enable the affected communities to purchase replacement assets. There are several reasons for this, and these include the following: under-valuation of assets by government valuers, changes in the price of the alternative properties, delayed payments leading to loss of value (e.g., because of inflation), unsuitable manner of payment whereby it is not clear whether people should be paid a lump sum or instalments and misappropriation of funds earmarked for compensation.

620. In view of the foregoing, monetary compensation may not be the best mode of compensating local communities. Thus, there is a need to put in place a community-driven development plan to implement compensation. Furthermore, compensation or resettlement for large energy development projects is complicated by the fact that these responsibilities are handled by different institutions altogether. Energy projects for which compensation and resettlement are vital fall under the aegis of the MEMD, while compensation issues are handled by the Ministry of Water, Ministry of Lands and Ministry of Environment. However, resettlement is under the jurisdiction of the Office of the Prime Minister. This creates coordination problems since the different budgets and other forms of logistical support may not be easily synchronized and may lead to unnecessary delays in project implementation.

52. Compensation Guidelines

621. Article 26 of the Constitution of Uganda, 1995, states that compulsory deprivation of one's property is prohibited except when taking possession or acquisition is necessary for public use. If this is proved to be the case, as for an energy project, then acquisition is subject to prompt payment of fair and adequate compensation. Compensation should aim to minimize social disruption and assist those who have lost assets as a result of an energy project to maintain their livelihoods through income restoration. The Guidelines for Compensation Assessment under Land Acquisition 2017 detail the compensation process.

622. Compensation is paid by the GoU through the Ministry of Lands, Housing and Urban. The EIS team must undertake a detailed survey of all losses that will result for each household, enterprise or community affected by the project. The survey should account for land acquisition and loss of physical assets as well as loss of income, either temporary or permanent, resulting from the displacement of household members from employment or income-generating resources (for instance, potters from clay deposits, fishers from fishing grounds, small-scale suppliers or vendors from customers). Assets held collectively, such as water sources, livestock grazing areas, irrigation systems and community structures, should be recorded separately. It is essential for resettlement planners to consult with the affected people during this stage to develop a reasonable consensus on the methods and formulae for assigning value to lost assets and income forgone during resettlement. In some jurisdictions, it may be necessary for local authorities to validate claims to assets. However, inventories of assets are compiled, and heads of households should be required to countersign them to minimize the possibility of subsequent claims or disputes regarding claims. The following are important inventory categories.

53. Land Use/Land Capability

623. All land acquired or otherwise affected by the project, whether on a permanent or temporary basis, must be surveyed, classified by type, and recorded. Civil authorities typically classify and assess the value of land by use (for instance, irrigated agriculture, non-irrigated agriculture, pasture, forest, housing and commercial). However, such classification may overlook the difference between the present and potential land use requirements of affected people. For example, shifting cultivators practice crop rotation over wide areas and long periods of time. In such a case, land that appears unused may, in fact, be in a fallow cycle awaiting cultivation for some years. Such a differentiation typically requires detailed soil maps and an assessment of land capability and carrying capacity. In addition, even in cases where cadastral survey maps demarcating land ownership and classification are available from the local land revenue office, these maps may be outdated and no longer accurate.

624. For this reason, the EIS team should be prepared to undertake independent surveys of land use and assessments of capacity to ensure the accuracy and equitable payment of compensation claims. Additional follow-up studies are usually required to support estimates of the annual revenue derived from different land uses or land types, such as irrigated land, rain-fed land, fish-farming ponds, and woodlots. Resettlement planners must establish the difference between present and potential land use to ensure that replacement land provided to affected people is of value equivalent to the land acquired from them.

54. Houses and Associated Structures

625. Dwellings, separate kitchens, toilets, storerooms, barns, stables, livestock pens, granaries and workshops for cottage industry should be classified by construction materials (timber, wattle, bamboo, reed, brick and mortar, concrete, earth). All structures should be included in the inventory regardless of whether they are permanently inhabited or occupied intermittently by transient populations.

55. Other Private Physical Assets

626. Such assets include non-moveable assets such as standing crops, fruit and fodder trees, firewood and timber woodlots, plantations (rubber, oil palm), fencing, wells, irrigation structures, and graves or tombs.

56. Private Enterprises

627. Shops, workshops, stalls, factories and other business establishments should be surveyed and recorded. These should be classified according to ownership (private business, public enterprise, joint venture, etc.). Individuals losing their enterprises, employees losing jobs or vendors losing customers should be enumerated, and the value of these losses incurred during the resettlement period should be estimated. At the community level, the assets survey should provide an inventory and an assessment of the losses of public resources, including common property resources: such resources include forest and woodlands (sources of building and craft materials, biomass for domestic energy) and pasture. Public structures include schools, clinics, meeting halls, places of worship, wells/community water points, livestock watering points, bathing and washing platforms, bus shelters, and monuments and cultural property. Cultural property includes archaeological sites, burial grounds, monuments, shrines, places of worship, artefacts, and sites of religious or historical significance.

57. Infrastructure

628. All infrastructure that will be destroyed or disrupted by the construction of the project should be enumerated, including roads and bridges, irrigation and drainage channels, water and sewage lines, power lines, and communication lines. The inventory of assets should be cross-referenced with the census and linked with the census in a single database. It is advisable for resettlement planners to photograph, document and register all assets described above by household, enterprise, or community organization. Digitized photographs can be used to record assets for storage in computerized census and socioeconomic databases.

58. Valuation for Lost Assets and Payments

629. The EIS team should establish transparent methods for the valuation of all assets affected by the project. These methods should include consultation with representatives of the affected communities to assess the adequacy and acceptability of the proposed compensation. Such consultation is especially important where market values for assets are not well established or are intangible (social or cultural values that are not readily monetized). The study should also take note of changes in the price and values of assets between evaluation and compensation. After acceptable compensation rates are established, they are applied to the inventory of losses for all households and enterprises affected by the project. A simple software application can be used to create a database that combines census data, inventory of losses data and compensation formulae. This database can then be used to budget compensation payments and to track progress in settling compensation claims.

630. The EIS team should draw up a payment plan, which will streamline procedures so as to avoid delayed payments. The team should establish the best criteria for effective payments. The latter may include instalments, pre-season or lump sum, depending on the socioeconomic characteristics of the society in question. Payments should be made at the people's place of residence or other places that are easily accessible. Peasant communities are often unable to properly manage large sums of money following compensation. Special attention should be paid to this point in order to guarantee that compensated people are economically not worse off than before the displacement.

59. Resettlement in Energy Projects Resettlement Policy Framework

631. In Uganda, the resettlement policy is currently under development by the Commissioner for Resettlement in the Office of the Prime Minister. A white paper is currently being prepared. It would appear that the resettlement policy is designed to meet the needs of people who have been affected by disasters that are man-made (e.g., wars) or natural (floods). In this case, people to be resettled are given basic tools and necessities to start a new life. In many cases, resettlement has been on a case-by-case policy and is often donor-dependent. This has often resulted in serious negative effects on displaced people. Nevertheless, examples of projects that have necessitated resettlement in Uganda include national parks, housing projects, refugees and the Owen Falls Dam Construction. However, the GoU's fundamental policy goal is to improve living standards and earning capacities of displaced persons. In this way, involuntary resettlement of people is transformed into an opportunity for development and self-improvement as they are enabled to share the benefits of development projects that cause their displacement. The concern is that displaced groups are further economically disadvantaged. There is the possibility that they will engage in appropriate income-generation activities that will result in environmental degradation. The GoU's policy is to avoid involuntary resettlement of indigenous or ethnic minority groups.

632. The main objective of resettlement is to ensure that the displaced population receives benefits from the displacing project. Involuntary resettlement, therefore, should be an integral part of the energy development project and should be handled at the onset of the project, that is, at the planning and feasibility stages. When communities or individuals are forcibly moved, it is likely that production systems are dismantled, kinship groups may be scattered, jobs may be lost, and social networks may collapse, leading to a host of other socioeconomic ills. This is why involuntary resettlement should take into account all the socioeconomic characteristics of the affected people. There are at least four basic requirements for energy development projects where resettlement will occur. These are as follows.

60. Resettlement Timetables

633. It is essential that a resettlement timetable, which is well-coordinated with proposed energy development activities, be put in place so that the resettlement exercise is not left to be implemented towards the end of the energy project. Resettlement timetables should provide for phased resettlement to allow construction/ improvement works and resettlement to take place at a minimal cost.

61. Restoration of Lost Incomes

634. Resettlement plans should target restoration of lost income due to energy development projects. The desirable plan to restore lost incomes should include compensation costs, resettlement costs, administrative costs, rehabilitation costs and costs of lost local government or Central Government public assets. To minimize losses to the community, it is essential that compensation is paid upfront and a compensation timetable/programme is put in place.

62. Resettlement Budget

635. Inadequate financial resources for a resettlement programme may lead to its failure. Therefore, it is necessary to prepare an adequate budget to meet the costs of resettlement. There are two aspects to preparing the resettlement budget. These are as follows: if the budget is too low, then the funds will be inadequate, and this will lead to delays in implementing the energy project; and if the budget is excessive, it may discourage the Developer/Development partners from investing in that particular project.

63. Contents of a Compensation and Resettlement Plan

636. Where the energy project will displace people involuntarily, severe socioeconomic problems are likely to arise. It is necessary, therefore, that the Developer ensures that the displaced population receives benefits from the project. This can only be possible if a people-oriented resettlement plan is evolved and implemented. Resettlement plans should include the following key components. First, the objective of the plan should be well considered to the effect that the displaced people should benefit from the proposed energy project through compensation assistance in moving, assistance to improve their former living standards and any other considerations relevant to the development area. Second, the current government policy on resettlement should be stated, as well as other regulations, particularly with respect to land tenure, local governance and environment. The project development partners' policy on resettlement should also be included. It should also show community participation. All the identified key stakeholders should be actively involved in community participation, baseline survey legal framework, alternative sites, valuation of and compensation for loss of assets and land tenure, acquisition and transfer, access to training and credit shelter, infrastructure and social services. It is essential that a sound schedule for executing the resettlement operation evenly over the duration of energy development projects requiring resettlement is put in place so as to avoid 'end-bunching'. The resettlement plan should include an implementation schedule for each activity covering the initial baseline and preparation, actual relocation and post-relocation economic and social activities.

64. Grievance Redress Mechanism

637. The affected community should be given an opportunity to review the survey results. In case any complaints arise from the affected communities, a grievance committee must be put in place to quicken the process of conflict resolution. This is to avoid the tedious process of courts of law, which are often not appreciated and out of reach by local communities. The grievance committee should be formed at the lowest level of activity (e.g., village level) and should include some of the following: a village elder, woman leader and a person from the Land Committee, representative of MEMD or developer. The procedure should be such that if the complainant still does not agree with the decision of the grievance committee, she or he should be encouraged to appeal to the Probation Officer of the Local Government based in every district. If he or she still does not agree with the decision, he or she may be encouraged to go to court as a last option. It is important that the grievance committee is acceptable to all the stakeholders. This can be achieved by circulating its membership to the community for acceptance.

65. Resettlement Monitoring and Evaluation Arrangement

638. It is important that a resettlement implementation plan is formulated so that it can serve as a basis for resettlement monitoring and evaluation. The plan will ensure that the contractor is aware of his or her responsibilities. The plan needs to define criteria and indicators against which to measure the success of the resettlement. To implement this plan, it is imperative that a social monitoring team is instituted. This will be responsible for monitoring the resettlement/compensation activities and implementing the social mitigation measures proposed in the resettlement/compensation plan. The monitoring team should closely liaise with local implementation committee, which would have been put in place for that purpose. The monitor should report to the MEMD/developer, and his or her reports should be availed to the district authorities who may wish to make comments or adjustments in accordance with emerging local by-laws or concerns. Depending on the project-specific situation, the monitoring team should include sociologists, urban physical planners, psychologists, doctors, public health specialists, anthropologists, economists and agricultural experts.

639. The Resettlement monitoring team's main activities should include: overviewing and reviewing compensation and/or lease agreements for land-take (both temporary for the use of the contractor and permanent for the energy development works); checking that no land has been taken unnecessarily; no crops destroyed unnecessarily, and no buildings or trees destroyed unnecessarily and reviewing reinstatement and/or future management plans of construction facilities such as camps.

Part V. Interaction Between Energy Law and Tax Law

640. Uganda has a well-developed taxation regime consisting of taxes of general application under the Income Tax Act. It does not contain specific taxes applicable to the energy sector only. However, there is growing awareness that a taxation provision concerning a particular industry may be gathered and compiled so that investors can understand and appreciate the risk and reward scenario. The Petroleum (Exploration, Development and Production) Act of 2013, whose main objective is to restrict and regulate the import, transport and storage of petroleum, governs all transactions to do with petroleum. It, however, lacks clear and pointed provisions on the aspect of taxation.

§1. Public Finance Management Act 2015

641. Petroleum Taxation was incorporated in the Public Finance Management Act 2015. The Public Finance Management Act 2015 contains detailed provisions on petroleum revenue management;[123] it provides for the collection, deposit, management, investment and expenditure of petroleum revenues. It also establishes the Petroleum Fund to be managed by the Minister of Finance, who shall oversee the transfer into and disbursements from the Fund. Parliament shall, for every financial year, appropriate money to be paid from the Petroleum Fund to the Petroleum Revenue Investment Reserve. The BoU shall be responsible for the operational management of the Petroleum Revenue Investment Reserve.[124]

§2. Companies Act 2012

642. The corporate structure of a company in Uganda is determined and regulated by the Companies Act 2012. The Registrar General administers the provisions of this Act. The promoters of a company are required to submit a Memorandum of Association and Articles of Association for incorporation to the Registrar of Companies. Section 19, in this context, is to the effect that the memorandum and articles, if any, shall be delivered to the registrar, and he or she shall retain and register them.

123. Public Finance Management Act 2015, Part VIII.
124. *Ibid.*, s. 64.

After incorporation, a certificate of incorporation is issued, and the company assumes legal personality with the capacity to sue or be sued, with perpetual succession and power to hold land and any property. The companies incorporated under the Act can be either a public or a private company with limited or unlimited liability.

643. The limited liability structure can be achieved through limitation by shares or by guarantee. Under section 4(2), the memorandum of a company limited by shares or by guarantee must also state that the liability of its members is limited. Under the same subsection, there is a requirement that the memorandum of a company limited by guarantee must also state that each member undertakes to contribute to the assets of the company in the event of its being wound up while he or she is still a member or within one year after he or she ceases to be a member, for payment of the debts and liabilities of the company contracted before he or she ceases to be a member and of the costs, charges and expenses of winding up, and for adjustment of the rights of contributors among themselves, such amount as may be required, not exceeding a specified amount.

644. An unlimited company can also be incorporated under the Companies Act, which like a partnership, exposes promoters to unlimited liability. According to section 12 of the Companies Act, in the case of an unlimited company, the articles must state the number of members with which the company proposes to be registered and if the company has a share capital, the amount of the share capital with which the company proposes to be registered. The finance may be raised either by means of equity or debt. Ordinary or equity shares are the basic element of ownership of a company and carry voting rights and, therefore, are the ultimate means of exercising control over a company, as well as rights to dividends and return of capital upon winding up.

§3. Income Tax Act

645. The Income Tax Act contains the law relating to income tax. Amendments to the Act are made through the annual Finance Act or Special Amendment Acts. The companies incorporated in Uganda are taxable in Uganda on their worldwide income, irrespective of source and origin. Foreign companies are taxed only on income which arises from operations carried out in Uganda; however, in certain cases, foreign companies are taxed on income that is deemed to have arisen in Uganda. The deemed income includes royalty, fees for technical services, interest, gains from the sale of capital assets situated in Uganda, including gains from the sale of shares in a Ugandan company and dividends from Ugandan companies. In arriving at the taxable income, outlays incurred wholly and exclusively for business purposes are deductible. Certain expenses are specifically disallowed for the purpose of deduction, or their quantum of deduction is restricted.

646. The Corporate tax levied on companies other than mining companies is 30%. The income tax rate applicable to mining companies is calculated according to the following formula (70 – 1500/X), where X is the number of percentage points represented by the ratio of the chargeable income of the mining company for the year of income to the gross revenue of the company for that year. If the rate of tax exceeds 45%, then the rate of tax is 45%. If the rate of tax calculated is less than 25%, then the rate of tax becomes 25%. The Income Tax Act defines a mining company to mean a company carrying on any mining operations in Uganda.

§4. ELECTRICITY ACT CAP 145

647. Under section 59 of the Electricity Act, a provision is made for a sales license. A licence holder is allowed to collect charges for electricity consumed by a consumer and, in case of neglect to pay and may resort to disconnection and discontinuance of supply. Section 58 entitles a licensee to fees and other fees and other charges for services as may be approved by the authority, having regard to circumstances. Under section 57, no person shall distribute electricity without a distribution licence granted by the authority. The terms, conditions and tariffs for the sale of electricity by a generating company are dealt with in section 75 of the Act. Accordingly, the tariff structure and terms of supply shall be in accordance with the principles of tariff calculation and terms of supply prescribed by the authority taking into account the licensee's total revenues from tariffs covering all reasonable costs and a reasonable rate of return. The contents of an application for a licence, *inter alia*, include a proposal for terms of supply and for fixing the tariffs, including total tariff revenues. A generating company may enter into a contract for the sale of electricity generated by it.

§5. INTERNATIONAL CONVENTIONS AND TREATIES

648. In addition to domestic law on taxation, there are international conventions and treaties signed by Uganda with various countries for the avoidance of double taxation. These treaties provide an alternative mode for taxing business profits in lieu of the domestic tax law. The treaties also deal with the mode of taxability of income in the nature of dividends, interest, royalty and fees for technical services.

Selected Bibliography

African Development Bank (ADB). 'African Development Report 2001'. Abidjan: Cote d'Ivoire, 2001

Bibangambah, J. Foreign Aid and Africa's Search for Improved Socio-Economic Performance. Discussion Paper No. 2. (Kampala, Uganda: Uganda Debt Network, 2000)

Holmgren, T. and Kasekende, L. Aid and Reform in Uganda: Country Study. Unpublished Report (Kampala, Uganda, 1999)

Little I.M.D, *Aid to Africa: An Appraisal of U.K. Policy for Aid to Africa South of the Sahara* (Overseas Development Institute, 1964)

Mbuza, F. *Current Status of Uganda's Domestic Animal Diversity: Contribution to the Biodiversity Strategy and Action Plan for Uganda* (Kampala: National Environment Management Authority, 1998)

Ministry of Energy and Mineral Development. Energy Policy. 2002

Ministry of Energy and Mineral Development, Power Sector Restructuring Strategy and Plan. 1997

Ministry of Energy and Mineral Development. The Rural Electrification Strategy and Plan. 2001

Ministry of Finance Planning and Economic Development. Plan for Modernization of Agriculture. 2001

Ministry of Finance Planning and Economic Development. Revised Poverty Eradication Action Plan. 2004

Ministry of Finance, Planning and Economic Development. The Poverty Eradication Action Plan (PEAP II) (Kampala, Uganda, 2001)

Ministry of Finance, Planning and Economic Development. Uganda Poverty Status Report, 2001 – Milestones in the Quest for Poverty Eradication (Kampala, Uganda, 2001)

Muhereza, F. 'The Participatory Poverty and the Environment Case Study: A Review of Linkages between Sustainable Development and Natural Resources' *Journal of Environmental Science and Policy* 125 (November 2021): 96–104

National Biodiversity Unit. 'Department of Environment Protection, Ministry of Natural Resources. Uganda Country Study on Costs, Benefits and Unmet Needs of Biological Diversity'. (Kampala, Uganda, 1992)

Quraishy, B. 'Foreign Aid and the Development of Agriculture in Ghana'. In *Rural Development Economics: Lessons for Developing Nations*, edited by A. Paris (Nairobi, Kenya: EALB, 1977)

Selected Bibliography

The Republic of Uganda. Energy Sector Investment Guide. Ministry of Energy and Mineral Development. 2004

Uganda Bureau of Statistics. Statistical Abstract 2001 (Entebbe, Uganda, 2001)

Uganda Bureau of Statistics. Statistical Abstract 2014 (Kampala, Uganda, 2014)

United Nations. World Summit on Sustainable Development – Plan of Implementation (Johannesburg, South Africa, 2002)

Wabunoha, R. Review of Development Policies, Legislation, and Regional Processes and Frameworks That Affect the Conservation of the Great Apes in the Democratic Republic of Congo, Uganda and Rwanda, A Consultancy Report for the International Gorilla Conservation Programme, April 2004

Wagaba, F.X. The Decentralization System: Uganda's Experience. Decentralization Secretariat. 2002 *German Institute for Global Area Studies* 31(2006)

World Bank. *Uganda Agricultural Sector Memorandum*. Vol. II. (Washington, DC, 1993)

Index

The numbers here refer to paragraph numbers.

Index

www.ingramcontent.com/pod-product-compliance
Lightning Source LLC
Chambersburg PA
CBHW071435230926
51846CB00001B/239
* 9 7 8 9 4 0 3 5 3 4 6 6 4 *